Personality in the Workplace

David Fontana

Distinguished Visiting Fellow
Cardiff University
Visiting Professor
Liverpool John Moores University

First published 1977 by
Open Books Publishing Ltd as
Personality and Education
Second edition published 1986 by
Basil Blackwell Ltd as
Teaching and Personality

Third edition published 2000 by
MACMILLAN PRESS LTD
Houndmills, Basingstoke, Hampshire RG21 6XS
and London
Companies and representatives
throughout the world

ISBN 0–333–73546–3 hardcover
ISBN 0–333–73547–1 paperback

A catalogue record for this book is available
from the British Library.

This book is printed on paper suitable for recycling and made from fully managed and sustained forest sources.

10   9   8   7   6   5   4   3   2   1
09   08   07   06   05   04   03   02   01   00

Copy-edited and typeset by Povey–Edmondson
Tavistock and Rochdale, England

Printed in China

Contents

Preface to the Third Edition

In the years since the first and second editions of this book (under their then titles), there have continued to be exciting developments in the study of personality. Some well-established viewpoints have come under forceful attack, while certain newer approaches have gained steadily in popularity. Yet other work, while remaining potentially valuable, has marked time, and appears to be increasingly in need of new research initiatives.

Perhaps the most important development, however, continues to be in the state-based approach to personality – that is, in the approach which sees personality as a fluid, ever-changing process rather than as a set of relatively enduring traits. Much of the debate in personality studies in recent years has been between the respective advocates of state-based and trait-based theories, and this debate is likely to remain an intense and interesting one. In view of the importance and implications of this controversy and of the many other new developments in personality study, it has been necessary to incorporate much fresh material in this new edition. But, most importantly, the book has been greatly expanded in scope, so that it now covers all major aspects of personality in the workplace, rather than focusing primarily upon personality within the educational context. Existing chapters have been recast, topics that were attracting attention when the first two editions were written but which have since dropped out of the limelight have been discarded, and new ideas that are becoming prominent have been incorporated. References and reports of research findings have been updated, and new terminology introduced where appropriate.

The aim of the book is now to give students of personality, organisational psychology/organisational counselling and education, as well as teachers, managers and all those responsible for the work and development of others an introduction to the whole field of personality, emphasising throughout the practical lessons that can be drawn from psychological research. The approach is intended to be a balanced one, presenting all relevant shades of opinion rather than focusing exclusively on any one set of views.

Where possible, the intention is to show that, far from conflicting with one another, each of these shades of opinion has its own particular contribution to make to the practical tasks of the workplace. Each advances in its own way our understanding of others and ourselves, and the methods by which we can assist those for whom we carry responsibility to make the most of themselves. Throughout the book the emphasis is not upon personality theories and models for their own sake, but on the theories and models that can improve the professional skills and confidence of managers, teachers and other relevant personnel.

Those who work exclusively with adults may question whether the chapters on childhood and early personality development have relevance for them. The answer is that, if we wish to understand other men and women – and indeed ourselves – we must know something of how individuals have come to be as they are. No architect would concern him or herself exclusively with the upper storeys of a house, ignoring the foundations and the basement. We each of us carry our childhood with us throughout life. Time spent reading about the early years pays enormous dividends in helping us to recognise why others have the strengths and weaknesses of personality that they have, and in helping us to decide what we can do to assist them in the process of adapting to the demands the environment makes on them. The more we read about and study childhood, the more obvious does this become for us.

DAVID FONTANA

Introduction

The aim of this book is to discuss those psychological insights into personality that are of most relevance in the workplace, whether this be school, office or shop floor. By the end of the book, the reader should know something of the origins, development and functioning of personality; something of those theories of personality that are of most relevance in this context; something of the most popular devices for measuring personality; and should also understand the implications of these topics for the work of managers, teachers, and all those responsible for the work of others. Because it is an introductory text the purpose will be to draw the reader's attention to what is important rather than to go into topics in great detail. Personality is such a vast field within psychology that we cannot hope to do more.

Perhaps this is as good a place as any to make one important reservation. This is that while psychologists have spent a great deal of time and effort researching into personality over the last half-century or so, they are still very far from knowing the whole truth about it. Psychologists like to construct theories and to measure things, but theories and measurements can only take us so far. A psychologist may, for example, construct a theory on the meaning of happiness, devise a test to measure its presence in people, and then find that two individuals obtain identical scores. But this does not mean that their relative degrees of happiness can really be reduced to equal marks on a paper-and-pencil test. Even if the test is a good one it still does not tell us whether the two people will be made *equally* happy by the same events. Nor does it tell us how happiness *feels* to them, the extent to which in each case it can stand up to the blows of fate, the extent to which it will change with time and so on. Each individual is unique. The only way to know someone is, obviously enough, to get to know them. Psychology books are aids towards, and not substitutes for, this process of 'getting to know'.

What is personality?

There are two particularly important reasons why those who manage or teach others should be interested in personality. First, because managing or teaching others effectively demands that we know something of how they relate to others and to themselves; how they conceptualise their goals and ambitions in life; how they acquire, maintain or change codes of conduct and styles of behaviour; and how they adjust to the inevitable problems and challenges that are part of being human. All these things are intimately associated with personality and personality development. Second, because to manage or teach effectively we need to know how these things influence performance on the various learning, administrative and other tasks on which those for whom we are responsible are engaged. We know that performance is dependent not just upon such things as intelligence, but upon the whole range of personal functioning that is brought to bear upon what is being done.

Knowing something about personality thus helps us to relate more successfully to others, and to understand their strengths and difficulties, their anxieties and enthusiasms, their preferred ways of interacting with the world both socially and cognitively, and their general moods and dispositions. In short, it helps us to get the best out of people, and thus indirectly out of ourselves. Mention of ourselves suggests a third reason why it is valuable for us to know something about personality – namely as a way towards greater self-understanding. In the workplace, our own personalities are as important as those of the men, women and children with whom we work. The more we know about ourselves, the better able are we to develop our strengths and to cope with the weaknesses that, like it or not, we all possess.

A problem arises, however, when we come to define personality. Personality is one of those tantalising terms that seems to retreat further from us the more we try to grasp it. We all think we know what the word means, but the effort of expressing this meaning in any generally acceptable form is often beyond us. Psychologists are no exception to this. As long ago as 1937, Gordon Allport (1961) listed no fewer than fifty attempts by psychologists at a definition, and commented that some of them were so all-embracing that they included practically everything that interests the psychologist about people - for example, 'personality is the entire mental organisation of a human being at any stage in his development'.

More recently, psychologists have tried to be more precise by taking personality to include only such things as sentiments, attitudes, complexes and unconscious mechanisms, interests and ideals (Vernon, 1975), and have excluded from it cognitive and physical attributes such as intelligence and motor skills. The term 'affective' is sometimes used to distinguish personality variables from cognitive or physical ones, but strictly speaking this term relates only to those aspects of personality that have to do directly with the emotions.

Having made this distinction between personality and cognitive and physical variables, we next have to admit that the three influence each other so closely that the layman may feel this distinction has more to do with the psychologist's convenience than with anything else. Psychology is such a vast subject that it has to be parcelled up into more manageable units, even if the parcelling is somewhat arbitrary. But separating personality from cognitive factors in this way helps us at least to focus attention on men and women as creatures of feelings and moods as well as creatures of intelligence. It helps us to emphasise that we are social human beings, with characteristic ways of reacting to others and towards ourselves, human beings with beliefs, aspirations and dreams, ruled, as the ancients had it, by the heart as well as by the head.

One of the most satisfactory attempts to define personality is still that of Eysenck, Arnold and Meili (1975):

> Personality is the relatively stable organization of a person's motivational dispositions, arising from the interaction between biological drives and the social and physical environment. The term . . . usually refers chiefly to the affective-conative traits, sentiments, attitudes, complexes and unconscious mechanisms, interests and ideals, which determine man's characteristic or distinctive behaviour and thought. (Page 779)

This definition stresses not only the content of personality, but also that personality is *stable* (that is, we do not change into fundamentally different people from day to day); that it is *organised* (that is, its attributes are interrelated); that it is formed as a result of *interaction* between innate biological mechanisms and the environment; and that it is *distinctive* (that is, each personality is unique).

I shall adopt this as my basic definition, but it is necessary to make three further points. First, the psychologist never uses 'personality' in the value-loaded sense often employed by the layperson. Popularly, to have or to be full of 'personality' means to be outgoing, lively and interesting; and to be lacking in it implies the opposite. But to the psychologist, everyone has personality. The emphasis is on understanding people, not on passing social judgements upon them. Second, the word 'character' is sometimes used synonymously with 'personality' in ordinary conversation. The former comes from a Greek word meaning 'engraving', while the latter is from a Latin word meaning 'mask'. The former would thus seem to be something deep and fixed (that is, innate), and the latter something superficial (that is, acquired). Paradoxically, some psychologists take the former to mean acquired attributes and the latter to mean innate characteristics. This is confusing, and I shall in consequence avoid the term 'character', and stick to 'personality', taking it to refer to both innate and acquired factors.

The third point is that, since the aim of this book is to draw attention to all those areas of personality that are of practical relevance in the workplace, we shall have to cover a great deal of ground. Inevitably, in a subject as rich and complex as human psychology, this will mean introducing the reader sometimes to the work of psychologists who appear to stand in disagreement with each other. Nevertheless, much of this disagreement is more apparent than real. It is rather as though the psychologists concerned are simply looking at the same scenery from different vantage points. If we want to build up an accurate description of the scenery, we therefore have to fit their various descriptions together, and wherever possible this is what I shall attempt to do.

Chapter 1

Personality Determinants

Only by knowing where personality comes from can we decide the extent to which it can be influenced – particularly in the young – by environmental factors. If personality is fixed by inheritance, there isn't very much we can do to change things. On the other hand, if it depends in part upon environment, there may be a very great deal that we can do.

The definition of personality quoted in the Introduction in fact made it clear that personality is the result of interaction between inherited and environmental factors, and we need to look at some of the evidence for this.

The influence of heredity on personality

Common observation has always led people to believe that we all inherit something of our personalities. We say that one person has her father's cool head, that another has his mother's determination, even that another has her grandfather's love of music. We describe people as born optimists or pessimists, born teachers or nurses, or comedians or entrepreneurs. But common observation could be wrong in ascribing these things to inheritance. They could just as readily be explained as being a result of the close contact children have with their parents and other adults during the early formative years of their lives. So the value of a cool head may have been learnt from the calm behaviour of a father, and determination from the behaviour of a mother, while the 'born' comedian may simply have found that making people laugh was a sure way to win popularity.

The difficulty of separating the relative influence of heredity and environment in any area of psychological development is considerable. From the moment of birth – indeed, from the moment of conception, since the interuterine environment itself is important – heredity and environment interact with each other in a highly complex way. Many of the experiments that might help the

---

Father to the Man and Mother to the Woman

Any building is only as strong as its foundations. While faulty foundations can to some extent be put to rights in later years, the task is a difficult and often very expensive one. It is useful to think of childhood as laying the foundations of personality. However, although the analogy is appropriate, it provides us with only part of the story, because the foundations of a building are hidden from view whereas the foundations of our personalities are apparent in the way we think and behave every moment of our lives.

Whatever our role in the workplace, we cannot properly understand personality without some knowledge of what happens in childhood. In acquiring this knowledge, people sometimes ask which is the greater influence upon personality – heredity or environment. Children come into the world having inherited the raw materials of their various physical and psychological endowments, but the environment plays a vital part in determining how these develop. Which contributes the most? The answer is – to use another analogy – that heredity and environment interact much as length and breadth interact in order to give us the area of a field. Without the one, the other is meaningless.

---

psychologist to distinguish their respective levels of importance, such as keeping individuals in a strictly controlled environment from birth and denying them certain kinds of potentially valuable stimuli, are for obvious reasons ethically unacceptable, and those that *can* be carried out sometimes produce limited or conflicting results.

The role of heredity

Some of our strongest evidence for the role of heredity in personality comes, therefore, not from psychology but from our knowledge of the biological mechanisms of inheritance. At conception, each child, with the exception of identical twins, receives a unique complement of forty-six chromosomes – twenty-three from each parent. These chromosomes contain the genes responsible for the transmission of attributes from the parents to the child, and work is currently being done on the colossal task of mapping which genes transmit which biological attributes. It has long been known that all major physical characteristics such as height, colour of hair and eyes, size of feet and hands and so on, are all genetically determined (although extreme malnutrition can influence them), and there is also evidence that genes play a part in determining many individual differences in behaviour such as those associated with some intellectual abilities.

One line of research has been to look at those children who inherit identical chromosomes at conception (that is, identical twins), and see if their personalities are any more alike than are those of fraternal twins. Identical or monozygotic, twins (M2 for short) are formed from a single ovum and a single sperm which, in the course of normal cell division, split completely into two separate embryos; while fraternal, or dizygotic (D2) twins are formed from two separate ova and two separate sperm, and are therefore no more alike genetically than are any other siblings. Assuming that the twins in each M2 and D2 pair are brought up in similar environments, any tendency by M2 twins to show more resemblance to each other than D2 twins do to each other could be seen as evidence for the effects of heredity.

Research has, in fact, shown the existence of such greater resemblance. Hans Eysenck (for example, 1983) reported evidence for closer similarities between M2 than between D2 twins on a range of personality measures (see Chapter 5 of this volume). In a comparison between ordinary siblings as well as twins, R. B. Cattell and his colleagues (see Scheinfeld, 1973) concluded that heredity weighs more heavily than environment on such personality traits as warm-heartedness and sociability. So far so good, but the problem has further complications. M2 and D2 twins may not enjoy similar environments. M2 twins, who are always of the same sex, and who resemble each other closely physically, are often consciously treated much more alike by parents and other adults than are D2 twins. They are also treated more alike by school friends, many of whom cannot tell them apart. The only way to avoid this problem is to look at instances where M2 and D2 twins have been separated at birth and brought up in a different homes.

A very early study by Newman et al. (1937) concluded that even here M2 twins resembled each other on personality measures more closely than did D2 twins, while subsequently Shields (1962) found that, on Eysenck's measures of extraversion and neuroticism, the resemblance between M2 twins was so much greater than that between D2s, that even M2s reared apart were more alike than D2s reared together. Bouchard et al. (1990) produced similar findings, noting that personality variables, abilities, attitudes, interests and fears in sixty-nine pairs of identical twins reared apart showed significant similarities.

Fortunately – from a humane point of view, even if not from that of the researcher – instances of M2 twins reared apart are rare, and we cannot regard the samples in the above studies as being large enough to put the matter beyond dispute. Taking the whole range of twin-studies, however, and applying statistical techniques, Eysenck attempted to answer the question of how much of the measurable personality differences between people is caused by heredity and how much by environment, and concluded that, for his own measures of neuroticism and extraversion at least, 65 per cent may be caused by heredity (Eysenck, 1978). In the light of more recent evidence (for example, Lykken *et al.* 1992), twin and adoption studies would seem to show that around 50 per cent of personality traits such at outgoingness and emotional stability appear to be accounted for by genetic influences.

More evidence for the role of heredity comes from studies which seek a relationship between physique and personality. We know that the former is genetically strongly influenced, and if it can be established that certain kinds of physique usually accompany certain kind of personality, this might argue a genetic basis for the latter as well. If we go back to common observation once more, we find that people have long claimed the physique–personality relationship to exist. The ancient Greeks, who studied men and women almost as keenly as does the modern psychologist, held that people resembled in temperament those animals they most closely resembled in appearance (perhaps there are still echoes of this when we describe people as sheepish, or bovine, or wolfish, or owl-like), while Shakepeare's reference to men with a 'lean and hungry look' being more thoughtful and dangerous than those who are fat has passed into popular usage, along with many other examples of his acutre observations about his fellow men and women.

Whether the modern psychologist can improve very much upon the Greeks or Shakespeare in this field is open to question, but extensive work was carried out more than a quarter of a century ago by the American, William Sheldon. On the basis of studies with large sample of people, Sheldon postulated the existence of three basic types of body-build: the *endomorph*, who is round and fat; the *mesomorph*, who is hard and muscular; and the *ectomorph*, who is lean and linear. Personality tests with the same samples revealed that each body build tends to be associated with a corresponding set of personality characteristics: thus the endomorph is inclined to be tolerant, complacent, sociable, easy-going, affectionate and dependent; the mesomorph to be aggressive, tough-minded, competitive, energetic and dominating; and the ectomorph to be restrained, withdrawn, intellectual and anxious.

Nobody belongs to only one of these physical types, however. We each have elements of all three in us, and in measuring a person's physique Sheldon assigned a score from 1 to 7 for each type. Thus an extreme endomorph would score 7 for endomorphy, and 1 each for mesomorphy and ectomorphy, giving a combined score – known as a *somatotype* – of 7–1–1. An extreme mesomorph would score 1–7–1 on the same scale, and an extreme ectomorph 1–1–7. In practice, such extremes are rare, though in most people one of these scores will predominate over the other two.

The work of Sheldon and his associates indicated that these three physical types are found in both sexes (though the distribution of the three types is rather different); that the somatotype can apparently be assessed with some reliability from the age of six onwards; and that it remains relatively constant throughout life (see for example, Sheldon, 1954). Certainly, many people put on weight or get more muscular as they grow older, but it seems that these gains can be fairly accurately predicted from a knowledge of their somatotype at the end of adolescence (Parnell, 1958). Unfortunately, Sheldon's findings were not fully confirmed by other investigators. Some claimed not to find the same three physical types, while others doubted the relationship between them and personality.

However, further work by Sheldon (Sheldon *et al.*, 1969) uncovered additional corroborative evidence, and his assertions seem, partially at least, to be well-founded. We cannot conclude from Sheldon's findings that the link between heredity and personality is conclusively proved, however. Muscular people may be more aggressive and competitive simply because life has taught them that with their physical strength aggression and competitiveness pay off, while thin people, who find the reverse to be true, retire to their books. Child-rearing practices may also play some part, with the fat person developing an expansive waistline and a love of comfort in response to over-indulgent parents. The most reasonable conclusion is probably that both heredity and environment lie behind the physique–personality relationship.

From an educational point of view, Sheldon's work attracted particular interest because correlations were found between the somatotype and, respectively, personality disorders and educational achievement. For example, samples of delinquent youths were shown to contain a significantly large percentage of mesomorphs (Glueck and Glueck, 1956), while samples of good honours degree holders were found to show a significant tendency towards ecto-morphy (Parnell, 1958). On the strength of this, it was suggested that, if the somatotype does give us an insight into inherited personality characteristics, it would be useful to take measurement of children's height–weight ratio and chest girth, thus giving us a simplified somatotype and an early clue to the trend of a child's future personality development. There is the danger that such clues might develop into self-fulfilling prophecies, but the idea is an intriguing one nevertheless.

Unfortunately, no major research into somatotyping has been carried out in recent years, which, in view of its implications for personality, must be seen as a disappointment. Such disappoint-ments are not ·uncommon in psychology. Researchers follow a particular line of enquiry, establish interesting findings, attract well-deserved attention from their colleagues, then find that interests move on elsewhere, and their work becomes virtually forgotten. Thus we are still unable to draw firm conclusions from Sheldon's work, though Wells (1983) reaffirmed its importance, and there is no doubt that it represent a fascinating area of research that could repay new research initiatives.

Longitudinal studies

An alternative approach to the relationship between heredity and personality is the longitudinal study, in which researchers look for evidence of temperamental differences between babies in the early weeks of life, when environment has had little chance to exert its influence, and then follow them through into later life to see if these differences remain apparent. One of the most revealing longitudinal studies was that of American paediatricians Thomas, Chess and Birch (1970). Taking a sample of 141 children, at eight to twelve weeks old, the researchers obtained ratings for them from parents and social workers on such items of behaviour as activity levels, regularity of bodily functions (feeding, sleeping and so on), adaptability, sensitivity to stimuli and environmental changes, and disposition (cheerful, irritable and so on).

Results showed that 65 per cent of the children could be assigned unequivocally to one of three groups: the *easy* group characterised by regular bodily functions, adaptability, a positive approach to new people and situations, and cheerfulness of mood (40 per cent of sample); the *difficult* group characterised by irregular body-functions, low adaptability, a negative approach to new people and situations, overreaction to stimuli, and negativity of mood (10 per cent of sample); and the *slow-to-warm-up* group characterised by low activity levels, low adaptability, some withdrawal in the face of new people and situations, mild reaction levels, and slight negativity of mood (15 per cent of the sample). The sample was then followed through childhood and into adult life (Chess and Thomas, 1987), and membership of the three groups was found to remain reasonably consistent. Not surprisingly, the easy group presented fewer behavioural problems than did either of the other groups. When starting school they proved readily adaptable, joined in activities, and learnt rules quickly. Only 18 per cent of them developed what might be termed personality problems during childhood, as opposed to 70 per cent of the difficult group.

Other longitudinal studies support these findings. Although starting their studies with rather older children, Newman *et al.* (1997) found that emotionally reactive and impulsive three-year-old boys developed into somewhat more impulsive, aggressive and conflict-prone 21-year-olds, while inhibited three-year-olds still tended to be more cautious and unassertive eighteen years later. Obviously, environmental factors played an important role in heightening or diminishing these early temperamental characteristics, but in the Thomas and Chess study parental behaviour styles were evenly distributed across the three groups of children, suggesting that environment was not the key variable. Parental styles *were* important, however, in helping to determine the success with which each group of children came to terms with their temperaments. The easy children flourished under most parental styles (this would probably not have been the case had there been any really unsatisfactory parents in the sample), but the difficult children became increasingly awkward and negative if reared by parents who tended to be inconsistent, impatient or over-punitive. Difficult children, it seemed, needed extra skilful, objective and careful handling. And the same appeared to be true for those in the slow-to-warm-up group. Such children showed a particular need for encouragement and parental support. Without it, or in the face of abrupt precipitation into new experiences, they tended to withdraw even further into themselves. The key seemed to be to present them with plenty of new and interesting stimuli, but to allow them to tackle these at their own pace, providing them meanwhile with plentiful praise and guidance, and urging them not to give up in the face of difficulties.

Temperament

Findings that early characteristics seem linked to future personality development allow us to agree with Gordon Allport, an early pioneer of personality research, who considered that we inherit the raw material of our personality (usually called temperament), and that environment then moulds this into its mature form (Allport, 1961). Temperament affects a great deal of what children do in school, from the way they relate to teachers and other children to the way they tackle learning tasks. Children with high activity levels are likely to become frustrated and fidgety if made to sit still for too long; children with a short attention span may respond best in an environment with plenty of variety; fearful or apathetic children may need repeated and patient exposure to a learning task before they become confident or engaged enough to be able to tackle it; and children with negative dispositions may become worse if their own moods are matched with similar ones in adults, and with consequent battles of wills.

This has relevance to teaching styles. An over-permissive style may be unsuitable for the nervous child, who may do better with clear and patient guidance from the teacher in a more formal structured classroom; while the confident, outgoing child may do better in an environment which gives ample scope for initiative and social interaction. This suggests that there is no single set of teaching methods likely to prove of optimum benefit for all children. So whatever methods are used, teachers must always be alert to children as individuals, a point to which we shall be returning at greater length in the next section.

The role of environment

The obvious place in which to start an examination of the role of the environment is the home, where children spend their early years and a large proportion of their later ones. Within the home, most research interest has focused on the mother–child relationship, as the mother has, at least in the past, been the primary care-giver. This is not to minimise the role of the father, or to ignore the fact that in many households some of the primary parental role has always been taken over by the father or by other adults. But for the majority of children, the mother has typically provided the main human contact in the early years.

A traditional way of assessing the importance of this contact for the child's personality development has been to look at those instances where the child is deprived of adequate care through maternal absence or neglect. The evidence here is not as clear-cut as it might be, partly because so many other factors (the quality of substitute care, the reasons for maternal absence, life-events following this absence, socioeconomic factors, age and sex of the child, to name only a few) enter the equation. Classic studies such as that by Goldfarb (1955), back in the bad old days when children were sometimes kept for long periods in institutions, showed that children placed for adoption early in life were much more likely to show satisfactory subsequent personality development than children institutionalised for much of their first three years, and only placed for adoption later on. More recent studies, such as that of Benson *et al.* (1994) show that most adopted children do, in fact, thrive, particularly when adopted early. They also score higher than their biological parents in intelligence tests; show strong attachment to one or both of the adoptive parents, sharing their values, beliefs and social attitudes; and may be less likely to divorce in adult life (perhaps because adoptive parents, who are carefully screened before acceptance, are likely to have more stable marriages than the rest of the population).

In an extensive and still influential study, Rutter (1972) concluded that while single brief instances of parental separation or neglect in early life rarely appear to have long-term effects upon the child, recurrent instances are likely to do so, particularly if other forms of disadvantage are also present. In addition, many children who suffer deprivation in early life go on suffering it in the years that follow. Thus, whether or not we regard the first few years of life as being any more crucial for personality development than the years that follow, Rutter's evidence, together with that of more recent studies such as the work of Malinosky-Rummell and Hansen (1993) leaves us in little doubt that children who are denied appropriate care by a mother or mother-substitute for significant periods of childhood run grave risks of long-term personality damage.

The exact nature of this damage may vary from child to child, but it appears to be much more marked in instances where ill-treatment or domestic strife are present, and in instances of parental death or prolonged absence. As Rutter (1975) showed, children from homes in which there is both a high degree of parental discord and a low level of warmth in the parent–child relationship show a much greater incidence of disturbed and antisocial behaviour, and of attendance at child guidance clinics, than do children from more fortunate homes. It seems that children require emotional warmth and affection, and a reasonably stable and secure home life, if they are to stand the best chance of developing the mature, well-adjusted personalities we shall discuss in Chapter 2.

Even where parental care appears on the surface to be adequate. but where there is a generally cold, strict and censorious attitude on the part of parents, there is likely to be a greater than usual level of feeding problems, overdependency, poor socialisation and fearfulness among children. Something of the more extreme effects that bad or absent parental care can have upon the young are observable from experiments with animals, and in particular from controversial work carried out some years ago by Harold Harlow at the University of Wisconsin (see for example, Harlow *et al.*, 1971; Suomi, 1987). Quite apart from the ethical reasons for not using animals in experiments, such studies are not entirely relevant for humans, who have linguistic skills and higher order cognitive functioning, and are now rarely used. However, Harlow's experiments are still considered to throw valuable light on the subject of maternal deprivation.

Briefly, Harlow raised several generations of rhesus monkeys under conditions of maternal deprivation, and studied the results. Those raised in social isolation and with only a simple wire model equipped with nothing but a feeding-bottle and a teat at breast level for a surrogate mother fared worst, showing every sign from infancy onwards of emotional disturbance and withdrawal, rocking quietly to themselves and cowering in terror if a potentially frightening stimulus (such as a small but noisy clockwork toy) was near. They spent little time with the wire surrogate mother, showed no confidence in exploring their environment, and manifested many of the symptoms we classify in humans as autism. Studies with human infants, such as that of Kagan (1995), show that those with what is called insecure attachment to their mothers show similar anxiety levels, and a similar reluctance to explore their surroundings.

Harlow found that monkeys reared with a wire model covered with terry-towelling as a surrogate mother fared much better than their wire-model-only peers. They appeared to enjoy contact with the soft material and used it as a secure base from which to explore their surroundings. However, by the time they reached the age of three, they showed extreme behaviour problems, and when they were allowed eventually to mix with other monkeys were unable to relate to them satisfactorily, either socially or sexually. Those females who did eventually become mothers proved themselves to be, in Harlow's words, 'hopeless, helpless and heartless', either ignoring their offspring altogether or abusing them cruelly.

Harlow (Suomi, 1987) showed that the behavioural problems of these maternally deprived monkeys could be rectified to some degree by placing them with younger female monkeys for a therapeutic period of twenty-six weeks, but this hardly lessens the impact of his findings. As indicated earlier, children disadvantaged in the early years of life rarely have the opportunity of subsequent intensive remedial care. Early personality damage may indeed be reversible granted the right conditions, but in the absence of these conditions such damage may have little to prevent it from becoming long-term. Harlow suggested that, in monkeys, the major damage is done if the deprivation takes place for the first six months of life, which is roughly equivalent to the first two or three years of human life. Deprivation in the first sixty days of a monkey's life – equivalent to the first six months or so of human life – appeared to him to be reversible, but the longer the period extended beyond this, the greater the chance of enduring emotional scars.

For ethical reasons, work such as that attempted by Harlow is no longer regarded as being acceptable, but the lessons derived from it nevertheless hold good. Satisfactory personality development in children requires that they be cherished and stimulated. Satisfactory personality development and good parenting in the early years of life go together. The effects of early deprivation may perhaps be reversed later, but only given a particularly supportive environment.

Socioeconomic circumstances

Studies of children who grow up in economically underprivileged homes, where parents may find it difficult to give them the attention and care they need and deserve, also point to the enduring importance of early experience. McCandless (1969) argued that economically favourable circumstances also tend to go with value systems that lead children to espouse hard work, ambition, cleanliness and self-control (particularly in relation to aggression and to sex). The greater incidence of aggressive, violent and delinquent behaviour among children from economically deprived backgrounds is still thought to be attributable in large measure to the poorer training in social control, and to the social deprivation and frustration that such children often suffer (see Mussen, *et al.*, 1984 for a review of the relevant literature).

Sociological studies show that some economically deprived environments develop their own subcultures which espouse forms of behaviour that are at variance with what is taught at school and upheld by the law of the land. Often these subgroups lay positive emphasis on toughness, quick wits, excitement and the desirability of resisting restraint, and until such time as children start school and come into contact with a different order of things, they are led to believe that such behaviour is the norm. Subcultures also arise as a result of ethnic differences. Studies by Morelli *et al.* (1992), Triandis (1994) and others show the extent to which the values of these subcultures influence child-rearing practices, with Japanese and Chinese groups, for example, placing particular emphasis on social harmony, loyalty, and concern for parental approval. Gender-typing, with boys allowed more independence and girls more freedom of emotional expression, also appears learned in part from cultural and subcultural values (Lytton and Romney, 1991), a point to which we return when discussing social learning in Chapter 5.

Personality development in adult life

The particular importance of the findings quoted in the present chapter is that the child – and later the adult – who appears to be awkward or difficult, violent or aggressive, withdrawn or sullen, should not automatically be held fully to blame: personality is not a person's own wilful creation. While stressing the importance of clear and consistent standards in the education of the young, we must take the trouble to understand why youngsters are as they are. Only then are the methods we use to foster their development likely to be well-chosen, and to prove beneficial to them now and in the years to come.

However, those who work with adults often ask whether, if the early years lay the foundation of personality, personality goes on changing and growing in adult life. The answer is, yes it does, just as we can go on adding to a building long after the foundations are in

Working on Ourselves

The Temple of Apollo at Delphi in Greece, one of the major spiritual sites of the ancient world, had the words 'Know Thyself' engraved above the portal. Personality growth and development throughout life, whether in the workplace or in private life, depends to a large extent on the degree to which we follow this injunction.

Knowing ourselves means understanding our own strengths, weaknesses and potentialities, but there is more to it than this. It means understanding the emotional side of our nature – an understanding to which we return at several points in the book – that is, knowing what motivates us, what disturbs and angers us, what makes us happy, and what makes us fulfilled. The more we understand these things, the more power we give ourselves over our own lives. But there is more to it even than this. Understanding ourselves means identifying realistic and satisfying long-term goals, predicting accurately how we will react in given situations and how we will relate to others, and developing the harmony that goes with an absence of self-doubt and inner conflict.

Self-knowledge is rightly said to be the beginning of all wisdom.

place. Learning about ourselves as well as about the world goes on throughout life, and this learning can be put to use in the service of personal growth. Of course, we may find it hard to change our basic temperaments. A person who is temperamentally more likely to experience anxiety, or who is very socially-orientated, may not be able to change such genetically determined variables. But the way in which he or she handles these temperamental predispositions can certainly mature and change as a result of experience. Chess and Thomas (1987) found in their longitudinal study that although temperamental factors showed significant consistency, troubled children could become stable adults. In other words, they could learn to cope satisfactorily with themselves.

Similarly, the way in which we handle relationships can change, as can our attitudes, values and opinions. Our self-concepts and self-esteem can grow as a result of success in areas important to us. Our motivation towards work can develop, our interests and enthusiasms can vary, and our philosophy of life can alter; and all of these can profoundly influence aspects of our personality. There is indeed a basic stability to our social and emotional style (Block, 1981), but individuals often turn out much better than had been predicted when they were children.

However, people generally change rather less from early to late adult life than they do from childhood to adulthood. Variables such as outgoingness, emotional stability, openness, agreeableness and conscientiousness tend to remain relatively consistent from around the age of 30 onwards (see for example, Costa and McCrae, 1993). The capacity to change during adult life seems to depend a great deal on the conscious effort we make to work on ourselves and deal with our perceived shortcomings.

The great Swiss psychologist Carl Jung (1933) in fact argued that the later years of life can be as important – and perhaps more important – than the early years in determining the person we are, but much depends upon the work we put into ourselves. Our ability to meet life's challenges and struggles, our sensitivity towards the needs of others, our conviction that life has a meaning and a purpose beyond the material, and our feelings about the importance of life and our attitudes towards death can, if we choose, change to such an extent that we feel ourselves to be different (and, one hopes, kinder and wiser) people than we were when we were young. Our lives are in a sense our own experiment, from the cradle to the grave, and the more we study and respect them and the lives of others, the better are we able to understand them and do our best to put them to good and worthwhile use.

Chapter 2

Personality Development

The first three years of life, during which, as we have seen, the effects of early deprivation seem particularly hard to reverse, are an example of what the psychologist calls a *critical period* in human development. A critical period is, in fact, any stage in life during which the individual is most likely to benefit from certain kinds of learning experiences. If we are denied these experiences at the appropriate time, the learning concerned may be more difficult to achieve later on. In some instances, there may be a considerable gap in time between the critical period and the age at which the learning manifests itself. Thus children deprived of a warm and loving relationship with their care-givers in early life may find it more difficult to provide such a relationship for their own children in the future, as any veteran social worker who has watched the depressing cycle of aggressive and violent parenting styles pass from one generation to the next will readily confirm.

The whole of childhood can, in fact, be regarded as a critical period, with some variation between children as to which years are critical for which particular kinds of development, and some variation, as we saw in the last chapter, between them in their ability to compensate later on for early deprivation. The experiences of childhood are not directly analogous to those of adult life, since the adult views existence in the context of an extensive life history and against the background of a wide knowledge of the world and how it operates. The child's immature emotions and thought processes mean that events are assimilated at a much more funda-mental level, thus often imprinting indelible lessons, for good or ill, on how relationships function, and on such things as values, social skills, and personal worth and identity. A child brought up by rejecting parents will come to see the world as a much more hostile place than the child raised in happier circumstances. The child who has to beg or pester before receiving adult attention will have a different idea of social living from the child whose needs are respected and satisfied. The child who is brought up in the shadow of his or her parents' unhappy marriage, or who is the victim of constant demands that are difficult or distressing to meet will see the world as a more threatening place than the child who is treated sensibly and realistically.

An unstimulating background may handicap a child cognitively as well as emotionally. Though we cannot be sure that such results hold good for humans, there is evidence that animals brought up in environmental impoverishment may even suffer retarded brain development. In the days when such experiments were deemed ethically acceptable, Teyler (1975) reported evidence that rats raised in social isolation and in bare cages had a thinner cerebral cortex, less developed neural connections, and secreted fewer brain chemicals than rats raised in a stimulating and enriched environment. Not surprisingly, the unfortunate creatures also performed less well on the kinds of discrimination problems that in humans are normally regarded as signs of intelligence. Such physiological impairment seemed to persist into maturity. Because of their social isolation and impoverished surroundings during critical periods of growth, the rats appeared in fact to have been unable to fulfil their physiological potential.

We do not know whether the same findings would hold good for humans because, quite apart from other differences, our cerebral cortex is some 400 times larger than that of a rat. In addition, as we seem to use only a small percentage of our brain's potential, it may be that small retardations in development caused by an unstimulating environment may have no measurable effect on later performance. However, we do know that in an area such as language, early deprivation can have a permanent effect. From around the age of one year onwards, we begin to lose the ability to discriminate between sounds we haven't previously heard (Werker, 1989). Thus adults who speak only English cannot discriminate between certain sounds in Japanese, while those who speak only Japanese cannot discriminate between some English sounds. Something similar may be true for spatial awareness, at which Native Americans appear to surpass their countrymen, and also for tactile and visual awareness.

The stages of personality development

One approach to the subject of personality development is to see it as being composed of a number of stages, each of them dominated

---

A Stimulating Environment

A stimulating environment is conducive not only to all aspects of psychological development in the early years, but also to optimum performance in the workplace throughout life, no matter what the context. Such an environment depends particularly upon:

- *Interest*   A difficult word to define psychologically, but generally we are interested in things which arouse our curiosity (we want to know more about them; they present us with puzzles; they have a novelty value).
- *Variety*   Attention spans vary, but even those with a long span require changes in activity from time to time.
- *Relevance*   Another difficult word to define psychologically, but things are relevant to us if in some way they help us to understand or control our lives better.
- *Aesthetic attraction*   Certain colours, shapes and sounds have an intrinsic appeal, and thus capture our attention and produce a positive emotional response.
- *Positive feedback*   Success feeds success. A stimulating environment provides tasks and opportunities which are within our competence, which reinforce our sense of personal power, and which encourage us to go on to the next level of challenge.

Even the most unpromising working environments can be made to include some or all of these essentials.

---

by certain learning tasks which must be completed properly if the individual is to move satisfactorily on to the next stage. One of the main proponents of this theory in the field of personality was Erik Erikson (for example, 1987), whose work remains very influential. Erikson held that, in personality, there are eight critical developmental periods, or stages, spread out over the whole of the lifespan. These stages can be defined in terms of the positive learning that takes place if they are negotiated successfully, and the negative learning that takes place if they are not. The eight stages are given in Table 2.1. It would be a mistake to see them as concrete and invariable, but they are useful to us in that they help us to understand something not only of the influence of environment on personality development, but also of the way in which this influence changes as we go through life. In the following sections, Erikson's stages will be used as a convenient framework for discussing

TABLE 2.1   Erikson's developmental stages

		Positive	Negative
1	Early infancy	trust	mistrust
2	Late infancy	autonomy	shame and doubt
3	Early childhood	initiative	guilt
4	Middle childhood	competence	inferiority
5	Adolescence	identity	role confusion
6	Early adulthood	intimacy	isolation
7	Middle adulthood	generativity	stagnation
8	Late adulthood	self-acceptance	despair

development, though this discussion will range more widely than Erikson's own work.

Erikson isolated the eight stages as a result of his experiences in clinical psychology in both Europe and America. However, he did not propose that these stages represent all the major learning tasks that an individual has to face if the personality is to develop successfully. What he suggested is that they are a useful way of identifying some of the points at which the development of a child or adult may go astray. However, he made it clear that even though the individual might apparently come through each of the stages satisfactorily, some negative learning will almost certainly take place, and may remain within the personality as a potential source of insecurity.

Let us take each of the stages listed in the table in turn.

Trust versus mistrust   Erikson accepted the great importance of the child–mother (or mother-substitute) relationship in the first three years of life, and divided these years into his first two developmental stages: *Stage one* covering the first year, and *Stage two*, years two and three. In year one, Erikson saw all the aspects of good care-giving combining to produce in the child a sense of trust. From the love and care given by the mother or mother-substitute, and from this person's presence as the prime satisfier of physical and emotional needs, the child learns that life can be trusted, and that one's safety and well-being can be left in the secure hands of others. In consequence, he or she becomes free to turn attention outwards, and to explore the wealth of interesting things that life has to offer.

Denied this sense of trust, the child may become fearful and anxious and, depending on temperament, either have little energy or confidence to relate to the outside world, or feel that needs are best satisfied by aggression and hostility. Results by Sroufe (Sroufe *et al.*, 1983) demonstrated the importance of trust. Babies who were securely attached to their mothers and used them as a safe haven from which they could explore the world functioned more confidently by ages two and three, and were more enthusiastic and persistent when dealing with challenging tasks. Erikson would doubtless have predicted the more recent findings of several investigators (for example, Shaver and Hazan, 1993) that adults in romantic relationships exhibit either secure trusting attachment, insecure anxious attachment, or the avoidance of attachment of any kind, and would have related such results back to early childhood experiences.

Autonomy versus shame and doubt   If the child comes through this first stage successfully, the growing urge to reach out and explore the world is aided from the second year of life onwards by increasing physical competence. From the secure base provided by a trust in parents and care-givers, the child is free to set out on a voyage of discovery. Inevitably, this voyage involves experimenting to find out the extent of his or her power over the people and objects in the immediate world and, just as inevitably, the increasing exercise of self-will. This sudden expression of self-will often gives rise to particularly negative behaviour during the third year of life (the so-called 'terrible twos'), with children appearing deliberately to defy those around them. If thwarted, they may indulge in temper tantrums and become aggressive and destructive. This phase seems to be part of the growth of self-awareness, and a necessary sign that children are beginning to see themselves as distinct, autonomous individuals, differentiated from those around them. Fadiman and Frager (1994) see autonomy as being linked particularly to the child's ability to choose between alternative courses of action. Previously behaviour had been dictated primarily by the need to satisfy physical needs such as hunger, thirst, tiredness, the need for warm and loving physical contact, but now there is a growing sense of the mind interacting with the outside world, and capable of making decisions as to how to relate to it and what to do with it.

The long-term consequences of adult reactions to children during this phase are likely to be considerable. If the adult meets the child's growing wish for self-assertion with a clash of wills then, dependent upon temperament, the child will tend either to become increasingly difficult, determined to prevail even at the cost of conflict and unhappiness, or to abandon attempts at self-assertion, and become inhibited and prone to self-doubt and uncertainty – that is, to what Erikson calls shame, and which seems to be particularly prompted by feelings of self-exposure, of a recognition that deficiencies are observed, identified and censured by others (Fadiman and Frager, 1994).

Often it is difficult for adults to avoid this conflict of wills. The child seems to be threatening adult authority, which may be difficult to accept from a two-year-old; but the role of the adult should ideally be one of patience and understanding, a role in which the child's autonomy is respected and encouraged where practicable, and limited consistently and with gentle firmness where it is not. Thus the child will learn that the world is a place in which certain laws and standards obtain, within the limits of which one can be independent and take decisions for oneself. By learning that control is not always exerted from outside, children also begin to under-stand they have responsibilities for self-control. Just as they can influence the behaviour of people and things in the world around them, so they can influence their own behaviour, and gain in consequence the rewards of adult approval which such self-control brings.

Erikson sums up the stage of autonomy *versus* shame and doubt by saying that it is decisive for the balance within the child's future behaviour of 'co-operation and wilfulness, self-expression and its suppression. From a sense of self-control comes a lasting sense of good will and pride; from a sense of loss of self-control and of foreign overcontrol comes a lasting propensity for doubt and shame.'

Initiative versus guilt This stage, which begins at the age of about three or four, is the first one in which the workplace – in this case the nursery school or playgroup – is directly involved. If children have successfully consolidated autonomy within the home, they are now free to explore the extent to which they are allowed to exercise this autonomy in the wider world, and to explore its effectiveness. Increasing physical agility on the one hand, and increasing linguistic skills on the other, allow them to communicate more fully with the people and things around them, and to give more scope to their powers of initiative.

As this period of development also marks the growth of moral behaviour and of the conscience (Kohlberg and Candee 1984), an over-restrictive and censorious environment may lead children to develop feelings of worthlessness and guilt for being as they are, and for wanting to assert their own preferences. They are also likely to be increasingly influenced by the behaviour of those around them, in particular of those who are older. Parents still remain the most important models of behaviour (*role models*), and from them children also begin at this time to learn their sex roles, but these are also acquired from peers and from cultural stereotypes (Lytton and Romney, 1991). In western society, violent activity is still more readily countenanced in boys than it is in girls. Certain pastimes are still regarded as boyish; others as girlish. Books, toys, games, even colours, are still chosen for a child with his or her sex in mind.

What this means is that boys and girls have different kinds of limits placed on their initiative. A boy who engages in girlish pursuits is made to feel uncomfortable and guilty about it, as is the girl who engages in boyish ones. Perhaps because of their traditional role in the home, girls have their initiative further curbed in that they are encouraged to be more dependent than boys. Lewis (1972) showed that this dependency training in girls is often evident from the second year of life, and appears to continue right through into adolescence, and Davie *et al.* (1972), in one of the most extensive longitudinal studies ever carried out in the UK, showed that girls are more anxious for parental approval than boys, while boys are more concerned with the approval of other children. Older siblings also help the child to learn a sex role, and boys with older sisters tend, not surprisingly, to take more interest in girlish activities than do boys with only older brothers, while girls with older brothers show a correspondingly greater interest in boyish things.

It is important that as far as possible all suitable activities are available equally to both sexes, and that different standards of behaviour are not demanded of girls and boys. However, it is wrong to impose a form of unisexualism on individuals that will expose them to rejection or hostility from their peers. It is also important to remember that part of the child's sex role is also biologically determined. In primates other than man the male is more prone to engage in aggressive and boisterous physical activity from infancy onwards than is the female, and this difference largely disappears if the female's mother is injected with male hormones during the pregnancy (Smith, 1974).

The growth of initiative has obvious implications both for the home and for formal education. Assuming that we want to encourage in children such things as initiative, independence, responsibility and the ability to take decisions and to use imagination, we must give them opportunities to practise these things. This means not only providing children with an appropriately stimulating environment, but also having the right kind of relationship with them. As mentioned earlier, the restrictions that are laid upon children, and the language we use towards them, may engender feelings of guilt and self-rejection. Obviously, there are many things that children must be prevented from doing, but it is important that children should not be made to feel at odds with themselves simply for wanting to do them. We shall be returning to this point of guilt and self-rejection when we come to discuss personality theories, particularly those of Carl Rogers, in Chapter 4. But it cannot be stressed too strongly that it is very damaging for small children to be made to feel wicked or bad *as people*. Their wants may stem from deep biological drives over which they have little direct control. Labels such as 'good' or 'bad' are inappropriate for these drives; what is important is the way in which the child learns to control them and to channel them into socially acceptable forms.

This teaches us that attention should be focused on the child's actions, rather than on passing moral judgements upon him or her. It is the action that is unacceptable, not the child. Young children's self-concepts are immature, fragile things. They gain their ideas on who they are by listening to what adults tell them about themselves. In the face of constant adult censure, the child's self-image may become negative, leading not only to guilt and unhappiness, but sometimes prompting the very antisocial behaviour that he or she feels adults have now come to expect.

In general, the warmer the relationship between an adult and a young child, the more effective a role model the adult will be. Discipline that relies primarily on harshness, or on the constant withdrawal of love or of privileges, is likely to alienate children, and diminish the adult's role as an agent in their socialisation. The most satisfactory deterrent for unwanted child behaviour is to withdraw approval from the behaviour itself, while at the same time suggesting an alternative, more acceptable activity.

Competence versus inferiority   Having learnt initiative, which frees children to take decisions on how to do things, they now face the task of learning competence (alternatively referred to as industry), which frees them to do things *well*. This stage, which lasts approximately through to the age of eleven, is marked by further major advances in physical and linguistic skills. In a few short years they move from the world of infancy to something approaching an adult's physical co-ordination and verbal fluency. As they do so, they vastly increase their capacity for experience. As developmental psychologists have shown us, they also build up their cognitive skills, which they use to comprehend and manipulate this experience.

These maturing skills profoundly influence the picture children build up of their environment. They ask questions, interpret the answers, watch how things behave, tackle problems, and do things in their own unique way. Not only is there a wide variation in performance between individual children, but each child also develops a broad repertoire of responses. However well we may think we know them, we are often hard put to predict how a particular child will react from day to day. At times, it seems as if different responses to the same situation are being tried out, simply to see which one works best, and to determine the efficacy of existing skills and the need for new ones.

Sadly, on entering the competency stage, many children already show signs of slipping behind their peers in the business of skills acquisition, and in the ability to ask the right questions and comprehend the answers. They may appear to have missed some of the experiences needed in the earlier years, and having failed to learn trust or autonomy or initiative – or sometimes all three – they are already significantly handicapped in their attempts to make use of their innate potential. The older they become, the worse things often are. Their failure to master early skills renders them less able to master later ones. Failure, like success, feeds on itself. With each experience of failure, they become less and less sure of themselves, less and less ready to tackle new things, less and less confident of their own abilities. By contrast, children who are able to develop competence have the constant reassurance that their skills are an effective way of dealing with the world, and of keeping a balance between its demands and their own needs. And with competence comes an increasing conviction of the world's consistency and predictability, and of their own status and prestige within it. They develop defined personalities, within an environment that they comprehend. And, as they watch and identify with parents and teachers, so they recognise that their own skills are a successful version of the way in which adults go about the business of living.

The other role models that children discover during these years make them even more conscious of their developing competence or lack of it. From now on they begin increasingly to discover these models among other children, and become aware of comparisons and differences between relative levels of competence. Other children do things better or worse than they do, get better or worse marks, receive more or receive less praise from the teacher, enjoy more or enjoy less popularity, land themselves in more or less trouble. Parents and teachers reinforce these comparisons even more – for example, by drawing favourable attention to one piece of work, by withholding approval from another, by assigning coveted classroom jobs to some children and not to others, and by giving or not giving extra help. The very uniqueness of children makes it well-nigh impossible, in fact, for adults to treat each according to his or her individual needs.

Significant evidence of the role parents play in this process comes from the outstanding work of Stanley Coopersmith in the USA over thirty years ago. Coopersmith (for example, 1968) followed a group of boys from the age of 10 to early adult life, and found that, on the basis of psychological tests and of self and teacher ratings, they could be divided consistently throughout these years into three groups, which he labelled, respectively, high, medium and low self-esteem. High self-esteem boys were from the beginning active and expressive; they enjoyed joining in, and were generally successful academically and socially. They were confident, not unduly worried by criticism, and had an accurate picture of their own abilities. Medium self-esteem boys shared many of these qualities, but were more conformist, more anxious for social acceptance, and less sure of their own worth. The low self-esteem boys were, by contrast, what Coopersmith calls a sad little group – isolated, fearful, self-conscious, reluctant to participate, and very sensitive to criticism. They were prone to underrate themselves, and were preoccupied with their own problems.

What was of particular interest was that group membership did not appear to be particularly correlated with physical attractiveness, intelligence or affluence (all came from middle-class homes). But on examining their backgrounds, Coopersmith found that the high self-esteem boys came from homes in which they were regarded as significant and interesting people, and in which their views on family decisions were invited and respected. Parental expectations were more consistent and were higher than in the other two groups, and although discipline was sometimes less permissive, it depended more on rewards than on withdrawal of love or on corporal punishment. The boys praised their parents' fairness. The low self-esteem boys, on the other hand, often rated their parents as unfair. There was little sign that their parents were interested in them or gave them clear guidance, and standards of discipline were inconsistent, veering unpredictably from extreme permissiveness to extreme strictness.

Other studies such as those by Buri (Buri *et al*.1988) and Baumrind (for example, 1991) broadly bear out Coopersmith's findings. In particular, they identify four particular parental styles: *authoritarian* (which imposes the parental will upon children and leaves little room for discussion and independence); *authoritative* (which exerts control not by setting rigid rules but by explanation, democratic debate, and realistic appraisals); *permissive* (which allows children to have very much their own way); and *rejecting-neglecting* (which expects little from children and invests little in them). Like Coopersmith, these more recent studies reveal that children with the highest self-esteem, self-reliance and social competence usually have warm, concerned, *authoritative* parents, who both control and communicate, who have clear and consistent standards but who respect children's views and wherever possible include them in decision-making. Baumrind (1991) and Rohner (1994) have also established that these findings hold good across a wide range of cultures worldwide.

Such findings point clearly to the link between the development of competence and children's freedom to feel that they are listened to, have been given some valid control over their own lives, deserve credit for their own successful behaviour, have opinions and ideas worth hearing, and are important enough as human beings to be guided and advised, consulted, loved and encouraged, and to have parents who enjoy spending time with them and drawing them into worthwhile and interesting experiences.

These findings are of interest not only for the light they throw on children's home backgrounds, but also because they have obvious relevance to the classroom. The reason that high self-esteem children are generally more successful socially and often academically, and set themselves higher goals and work more nearly to their potential, is because they are not over-inhibited by fear of failure, or by uncertainties as to their worth. If children or adults have a realistic knowledge of, and confidence in, their own skills, they are less wounded by the occasional failure, less deflated by criticism, less anxious to have the unqualified approval of all and sundry. They are readier to participate, less overawed by challenges, and less daunted by possible setbacks and pressures. High self-esteem children know they count as people because their parents, directly and indirectly, tell them so. By the same token, teachers can also show children that they count. They can be encouraged to use their abilities, and be helped to persevere in the face of difficulties and initial failure rather than be discouraged. A close interest can be taken in their day-to-day progress, and their pleasure in success can be shared. It is one of the golden rules of good teaching that each child should be enabled consistently to experience this success, no matter how low the initial level of performance may be.

The importance of consistency when dealing with children has already been mentioned, and must be stressed again. It is through an experience of consistency in others that children learn that the social world is a predictable place, and that the interpersonal skills acquired today will continue to be of value tomorrow. The infant's sense of trust, and the older child's sense of self-esteem, are both based on the security of knowing that there is pattern and predictability in their relationships with others. The same person isn't kind one minute and arbitrarily unkind the next, involved with them one minute and bored with them the next. Adults who turn away from the social world, and from the business of making and keeping close relationships with others, and who find interest and security only in the inanimate world, often have not had the opportunity to experience social consistency of this kind in childhood. For them, the early lesson was that consistency and predictability is found only in things and not in people.

It is significant that Coopersmith's high self-esteem boys came from homes in which they praised their parents' fairness, a sure sign that they enjoyed consistency in their home lives. In a child's eyes, unfairness is one of the adult's worst shortcomings. Often such unfairness goes with parents who discipline their children through withdrawing or threatening to withdraw love. The withdrawal of love, or, in the teacher's case, the withdrawal of concern and of interest, are particularly damaging to children's self-esteem. Children need to feel they matter enough for such benefits to be no more subject to change or withdrawal than are the natural laws that make the world a reliable place in which to live.

The evidence suggests (for example, Mussen *et al.*, 1984) that children from more socioeconomically deprived backgrounds, especially if they are boys, are generally lower in self-esteem than are those from more privileged homes. And both girls and boys from under-privileged backgrounds show more of the personality characteristics normally associated with low self-esteem such as aggression, withdrawal, depression, and hostility to adults. In the longitudinal study mentioned earlier, Davie and his colleagues (1972) showed that, for all the areas of competence in school that they tested (oral skills, creativity, reading and number work), children from under-privileged backgrounds trailed significantly behind their more socially favoured peers. The inescapable conclusion is that such children are often handicapped in their search for at least the kind of competence that goes with academic success by the poorer amenities and facilities, and the less academically-orientated standards and values that tend to go with their background.

Another factor bearing upon competence, to which brief reference must be made, is family size. Back in the 1930s, Alfred Adler put forward the theory that family size and birth order within the family have a significant influence on personality. Adler's theory was a somewhat elaborate one, but part of it at least has been supported by subsequent research. For example, Davie's extensive study showed an inverse relationship between family size and both school attainment and personality adjustment. Since this relationship appeared to hold good irrespective of social class, it looks as if the unavoidably reduced amount of parental attention, guidance and verbal communication which the individual often receives in a large family has a deleterious effect on a wide range of behaviour. This effect becomes increasingly noticeable as family size increases beyond two children. Davie also noticed that in these larger families it seems to be the oldest child's school attainment and social adjustment that are the most heavily penalised, perhaps because the oldest child may have to take responsibility for younger ones, or may be rather neglected while parents attend to the more pressing demands of younger siblings.

However, other findings on birth order suggest a rather more complex picture. Falbo and Poston (1993) showed that, in the USA, first-born and only children do rather better at school and on intelligence tests than later siblings, and achieve admission to more prestigious colleges. It also appears that over 60 per cent of eminent people in a number of walks of life are first-born. On the other hand, later-born children tend to be more socially relaxed and popular, and are more likely to embrace new scientific and religious ideas, and to be generally more free-wheeling than their more tradition-respecting older siblings. It takes no great stretch of the imagination to conclude that these differences between siblings is occasioned in part by greater parental pressures on the first-born to be conformist, and the greater amount of time that parents typically spend with him or her.

Before leaving the question of competence and personality development, we must address the high level of *hostility to adults* that is a characteristic of some children low in self-esteem. The reason for this hostility is that if children are subjected to the neglect and unfavourable comparison with others that lead to low self-esteem, they can either blame themselves for their negative self-image, and become one of the sad little children to whom Coopersmith referred, or they can try to protect self-esteem by fighting back. If, for example, children experience repeated failure at school, they can either accept this is being caused by their own lack of ability, or they can blame their teachers and the curriculum, and signal, with hostility or with bravado, that they could succeed if things were worth doing. They are thus, in effect, saying that it is not they but the school that is at fault.

Identity versus role confusion Erikson sees all the stages through which the personality passes in its development as being in reality stages in self-discovery. By finding their place in the world, by listening to what other people have to say about them, by identifying with adults and with other children, and by comparing themselves with peers, children gradually build up a picture of who they are. They develop an *identity*. This process comes to a head in adolescence, and while the personality is capable of developing throughout adult life, the more successfully individuals weather the crisis of adolescence, the more sure and realistic they are likely to be as young adults, and the clearer and better defined their identities. Baumgardner (1990) shows that as identity develops during these years, so it tends to become more self-affirming and more positive, particularly among boys and those with satisfying peer group relationships, findings that support those of Waterman (1988).

However, for those adolescents and young adults who fail in self-discovery tasks, there is a danger of suffering from what Erikson calls *role confusion*. This means that they still have no clear idea of who they are, and may become prey to the many diverse and conflicting pressures of adult life, perhaps clinging for security to a rigid and artificial picture of themselves that impedes further development.

The most important biological feature of adolescence is the arrival of physical and sexual maturity. This abrupt transition from childhood to adulthood can cause a range of difficulties. It takes girls approximately four years, from the onset of the adolescent growth spurt at about the age of twelve and a half, to reach adult stature, with boys starting and finishing about eighteen months later. The adolescent may have learned to cope with the business of being a child, but is now faced with the business of learning how to be an adult, and to deal with this learning in a complex technological society which, partly because of the lateness of the school-leaving age, has no recognised way of awarding adult status to those who are leaving childhood behind.

More primitive societies than that of the West, where the child is automatically granted the rights and responsibilities of adulthood at puberty, appear to experience fewer problems with this age group than people in the West do. Sociologists have suggested that these problems are therefore more a product of our 'artificial' culture than of the biological changes of adolescence itself. Be that as it may, there is no denying that these problems exist. Obviously, they vary in intensity from individual to individual, but many adolescents find that some of the concepts they have built up during childhood become suddenly outdated, including the concepts they have about themselves. To make matters worse, partly because of changes in hormonal balance, many adolescents are prone to wildly fluctuating moods. Love and affection towards those around them may suddenly change to irritation, and even active dislike. Not surprisingly, this may cause the adolescent great perplexity. Who, in the midst of all these abrupt changes, is the real person?

To complicate things further, adolescents often find themselves taking on the colour of their surroundings, and behaving one way with friends, another with parents, and yet another with teachers. Each of these ways involves a different set of values, and imposes different demands. If adolescents belong to minority groups, whether ethnic or social, these conflicting demands may be even more confusing. In addition, there is often the need to take important decisions about career and relationships without clear guidance, because there appears to be no experienced person available to give the necessary advice.

Intellectually, the majority of adolescents manifest what Jean Piaget called the stage of *formal operations,* a stage in cognitive development characterised by an increased use of abstract and deductive reasoning, and it is this, together with frustration at the adult world, that often makes the adolescent so liable to question things. Abstract concepts such as freedom, justice and equality take on a deeper meaning, and before the realities of adult life catch up with them, adolescents often go through a phase of intense idealism during which they want to set the world to rights. It is partly this that can prompt them to espouse political and social causes, but there is another reason: namely, that the doubts that they have over their identity can stretch to their opinions and attitudes as well. Adolescents are still experimenting with themselves, still trying out their adult clothes so to speak, and by supporting causes and joining things they experience a sense of kinship that gives them confidence. If other people are rebelling against authority, this suggests that their own battles with teachers and parents must be justified too.

The adolescent's partial rejection of the authority of parents and teachers also makes him or her less inclined than hitherto to see them as role models. Alternatives are sought among cult heroes such as sports people and pop stars, and among their peer group. In fact, the peer group becomes increasingly important, especially in matters of dress, speech and behaviour. Acceptance by the peer group is of great moment. There is often an excessive concern to conform to its norms, and an acute embarrassment at anything, such as late physical development, that fails to do so. The sex drive, which in males appears to reach its peak at about sixteen to eighteen years of age, makes the adolescent take an increasing interest in the opposite sex. To prove unsuccessful in relationships can be a profound blow to both boys and girls, and may lead to negative self-concepts that will crucially affect decisions in later life about such things as vocation, friends, lifestyle and marriage partner.

Adolescence is also a peak age for delinquent activity. Although delinquency is a multi-causal phenomenon, whose origins often stretch back into faulty adjustment early in childhood, the majority of delinquent acts tend to occur in those who are in or near the final year of compulsory schooling, precisely the time when they are most irked by a continuing lack of adult status. Lower levels of aggression, greater dependency, more effective socialisation, and an earlier reconciliation to their role in life has traditionally made girls less liable to delinquent activity than boys – though over recent years delinquent acts in girls, particularly those involving violence, have been increasing proportionately faster than in boys. In America, the former ratio of one such act in girls to every five in boys is now reported to be down to one to three. This could well be a reflection of the changing status of women in our society.

Evidence from both Britain and America suggests that the personality of the delinquent adolescent is characterised by hostility, suspicion, impulsiveness and low self-control. Usually there are poor self-concepts, feelings of inadequacy and rejection, and of confusion and conflict. In addition to being frequently neglectful, parents of delinquents usually show those characteristics noticed by Cooper-smith in the family background of low self-esteem boys: that is, they are erratic, unpredictable and show little evidence of any genuine interest in their children. Frequently, the father is rejected as a role model by the son because of the father's weakness, drunkenness or harshness. The incidence of delinquency increases sharply as we move down the socio/occupational groups, and typically the delinquent comes from a deprived urban area, where, as we saw in Chapter 1, elements in the community may approve such values as toughness and a rejection of authority.

In delinquency there is probably also a temperamental factor at work. I mentioned in Chapter 1 that Glueck and Glueck have found a high proportion of mesomorphs among delinquents, and it may be that the high leadership and aggressive qualities that some studies have associated with mesomorphy turn, when denied socially acceptable outlets, to the gang subculture that features so prominently in delinquent activity. Further evidence for a temperamental factor comes from the work of Eysenck, who found that delinquent samples are significantly extraverted, which again suggests a higher level of aggression and an innate need for external stimuli and excitement (see Chapter 5 of this volume).

It is not difficult to make adolescence seem a somewhat unattractive stage in human development. But, in fact, many teachers and other professionals prefer working with this age group, and welcome the adolescent's potential for idealism and involvement. They also find it exciting to watch the personality develop in such a brief span from a childish to an adult one, and gain great reward from the help they can give to the process. Hart (1988) found that in the course of this development identity becomes more personalised in the sense that the core self is seen less in terms of social relationships (in spite of the importance of the peer group), and more in terms of the inner world of thoughts and feelings.

Part of the secret in dealing successfully with adolescents is an awareness of the experimental nature of much of what they do. Teachers who work well with them are able to show, through tolerance, but at the same time through the clear and consistent standards they maintain in areas where such standards are not negotiable, that their role is to help adolescents to answer the questions they are posing about their environment and themselves, and to understand the challenges, limits, demands and opportunities that exist in the adult world that they are entering.

Such teachers (and parents and other adults) also seem aware of the depths of feeling and vulnerability that underlie the sometimes brash and cynical adolescent exterior. Faced with the problem of achieving an identity in which the various parts of the personality enter into a consistent relationship with each other and are not lost in role confusion, the adolescent feels profound self-doubts, and needs the security of knowing that parents and teachers have confidence in the kind of person that he or she is becoming. The brashness and the cynicism are often no more than a defensive screen erected to hide inner sensitivities and to impress the peer group. Successful teachers see through the screen though they are careful not to puncture it, particularly in front of the adolescents' peers, because this kind of humiliation can lead to shame and loss of face, and often to a subsequent unforgiving hostility.

Adults who understand adolescents also seem aware of the continuing need to show an interest – though never an intrusive one – in their activities. This means activities outside school as well as inside, and in future prospects and ambitions as well as in present performance. Such adults also show an interest in, and a respect for, adolescents' attitudes and opinions, tolerate their desire to be different from their elders, and refuse to make glib judgements about personality from such externals as fashions in appearance, speech or dress. Adolescents certainly need stable relationships with parents, and need teachers who encourage them to discuss problems over personal and sexual relationships, and who are prepared to give clear answers to questions, and to indicate the difference between facts and beliefs.

Why Identity Is So Important

Notice how the verb 'to be' is used in speech. We say '*I am* 30 years old', or '*I am* a personnel officer', or '*I am* an honest person' or '*I am* making good progress at work' or '*I am* happy in (my new home, my partnership, my life)'. In these examples and in much of our speech and our thinking, the use of the verb 'to be' indicates that we identify fully with our age, our work, our values, our emotions, our physical surroundings, and our relationships. This indicates that in a psychological sense we really see ourselves as *being* these various things.

If we find ourselves in an unsatisfying job, a difficult relationship, an unsuccessful career, an unsuitable house and so on, imagine what it does to our sense of self. We literally see, value and experience ourselves adversely. Identity is, in fact, a rather fragile thing, and in most people requires positive life experiences if it is to become and remain at harmonious and life enhancing levels.

Conflict between the values of home and school can increase the pressures towards role confusion in the adolescent. Often the school can best reconcile these pressures by avoiding unnecessary rules and restrictions that give the impression that school is out of touch with the real world. In any community, rules are necessary if people are to live together in harmony, but these rules are more likely to be successful if they exist clearly and obviously for that end, rather than to serve outmoded customs, or the prejudices of those in authority. The more democratic the process that can be used to arrive at rules, the more point everyone sees in them, and the more likely they are to be obeyed. Bad rules, which are inevitably ignored as soon as those responsible for them have their backs turned, lead only to a loss of respect for authority, and a consequent flouting of many other rules that are there for a much better purpose (see, for example, Fontana, 1994).

Finally, adults who relate well to adolescents seem to understand that it is counter-productive to look for the obedience and dependency in them that they showed when they were younger. It is the failure to show such understanding that leads to many of the conflicts parents have with adolescent sons and daughters. Refusal to accept that adolescents are growing up is only likely to make them assert their right to independence all the more strongly. Adults who recognise this right take care to give them every reasonable opportunity to demonstrate their growing ability to take adult responsibility. Such opportunities are of far more value than any number of homilies on the *need* to develop this responsibility. Too often, when adolescents are lectured on the desirability of acquiring a maturer approach to life, we mean that they should acquire it only when it suits us, and at other times revert to the subordination of an earlier stage in their development.

Intimacy versus isolation This stage, which occurs in early adulthood, is the culmination of the years of childhood and adolescence. Intimacy is the ability to have full and satisfying personal relationships with other people of both sexes, relationships which culminate in successful partnerships or marriage, in lifelong friendships, and in close and sustaining contacts with the people in the workplace and the community. Researchers have noticed significant differences in the way in which men and women manifest their capacity for intimacy. Gilligan *et al.* (1990) note that males are more concerned with expressing their individuality in relationships, whereas females are more concerned with 'making connections'.

Such differences seem to have their roots in earlier developmental stages. Boys typically play in large groups, with the focus on activity and competition, while girls are more concerned with smaller and more intimate groups that focus on discussion and which are more open and responsive to feedback and to the feelings of others (Maccoby, 1990). The result is that women tend to become more interdependent in their intimate relationships, more gregarious, closer and more caring, and more willing to explore and share thoughts and feelings. Men, by contrast, are more likely to emphasise personal power, freedom and self-reliance, and to spend more time alone (Tannen, 1990). Not surprisingly, women emerge as better judges of other people's emotions, as being more emotionally responsive, and as more nurturing, intimate and enjoyable in their friendships than men (Grossman and Wood, 1993).

This does not, however, mean that women are invariably capable of deeper intimacy than men. The deeply expressive works of leading male poets is enough to convince us of this. But, in general, they are certainly more successful at expressing intimacy, and more sensitive of the need for intimacy in others. However, the intimacy stage of personality development is best discussed within the wider context of what psychologists refer to as the mature personality –

that is, the personal qualities that mark people out as having attained a balance and a richness in their development that allows them to live full and satisfying lives. Erikson wrote widely on the mature personality, but the psychologists who have done most work in the field are Gordon Allport (1961) and Abraham Maslow (for example, 1976 and 1987).

Allport saw the acquisition of a real sense of personal identity in adolescence as meaning that the individual has developed from being essentially a number of different 'selves' to being a single, or whole, person. In the early stages of our personality development, Allport recognised that we possess a wide range of 'traits' such as friendliness, honesty or bookishness, which we use somewhat inconsistently and arbitrarily in our dealings with other people (for example, as children, we may be honest with our friends but not with our teachers; bookish at school but not at home). As we grow older, many of these traits coalesce into a smaller number of better-integrated units that Allport called *selves* (for example, we may have one recognisable self for school, and another for home). With the discovery of identity, these selves come together in adolescence and through into early adult life to form the single unit of the mature personality.

To Allport, the mature personality in adult life is, therefore, characterised by co-ordination and consistency. If people are mature, we know that, whatever the situation in which we meet them, they remain identifiably themselves (within reasonable limits at least – all personalities may break down under extreme stress). They are not honest at home and dishonest at work (or honest and dishonest at both home and work in different circumstances), or pious at church and amoral at the local club, or humorous with friends and a wet blanket with the family, or confident with their own sex but awkward with the opposite one. They do not, in fact, still have several different selves, each of them capable of its own separate codes of behaviour and of values. An extreme example of people who failed to achieve this mature integration were those Nazi concentration-camp officers who were reputedly good husbands and fathers in the evenings, but spent their days sending innocent people to the gas chambers.

Of course, this is not all there is to maturity. Usually, when we talk of the mature personality, we imply a value judgement in that we expect those concerned to have qualities that make them desirable to the community as a whole. It is possible, in theory at least, for people to be entirely integrated in doing evil, which might mean that they meet Allport's criteria, but are hardly the sort of people we want to have as neighbours, employers, or teachers of children. We also usually think of mature people as being effective, and good at getting things done within their chosen fields. This was supported by studies such as that by F. Barron, who found that graduate students rated most highly on maturity of personality by their lecturers seemed to be particularly good at organising their work, at judging themselves and others, and at resisting stress. They also seemed to be high on integrity and to be energetic, adaptable, resourceful and well adjusted (Barron, 1979).

Allport recognized the need for a definition of maturity that takes into account these questions of value and effectiveness and, in summarising the views of a number of psychologists on the subject, he considered that the mature personality manifests the following qualities:

1   An extended sense of self, allowing one to transcend the self-centredness of childhood, and to identify with the concerns and problems of others.
2   A warm relationship with others, allowing one to love them for their own sakes as well as for one's own.
3   Emotional security, allowing one to withstand the problems and fears of daily life.
4   Self-insight, allowing one to laugh at oneself without loss of self-esteem, and at the things one values without valuing them any the less. (There is *some* correlation between self-insight and intelligence, though the one does not necessarily imply the other.)
5   A realistic orientation towards the world, allowing one to exercise sound judgement of people and things, and to take necessary decisions.
6   A unifying philosophy of life, either religious or humanistic, enabling one to interpret life's purpose, and to decide on long-term goals and standards of behaviour.

This makes the mature person sound like a paragon of perfection, but that is misleading. A respect for others, for example, does not stop one from sometimes feeling angry or impatient with them. Sound judgement does not mean that one never makes a mistake. Emotional security does not mean one never feels depressed or inadequate. Self-insight does not mean one never feels surprised at oneself, or never feels disappointment at failing to achieve a cherished ambition. The basic point about maturity is that the mature person is not constantly at the mercy of personal weaknesses, or constantly vulnerable to people and events in the world outside. There is a degree of self-knowledge and self-control that allows one to make the most of oneself, a respect for others that allows one to love them without smothering them, a tolerance for the world in general that allows one to respect the rights of other people, and a sense of purpose and of aspiration that give substance and direction to life.

Many of these qualities may not develop, of course, until the individual is well past early adulthood. The personality still has to face major problems of learning and adaptation in middle and later life. Erikson describes these as *generativity,* which is the ability to innovate, to bring in new ideas, and, in particular, to influence the next generation through parenthood and teaching, and as *self-acceptance* – that is, the ability to review one's life in mature years and old age with a sense of fulfilment, with a knowledge that one has done what one could to enhance the lives of others, and to make productive use of the abilities one has been given.

Maslow's writings (Maslow, 1976 and 1987) are very much in tune with both Allport and Erikson. His ideas are discussed in more detail in Chapter 4 of this volume, but his identification of the mature personality belongs here. By studying prominent individuals rated as being mature – or *self-actualised,* to use Maslow's preferred term – he found them to possess the following qualities (and it is interesting to tie these in with Allport's descriptions of the mature personality):

1   *Concentration,* that is, the ability to experience life fully, vividly, selflessly, and with total absorption. For much of our time we are distracted by the chatter of our own minds, and by memories, hopes and daydreams that prevent us from engaging fully, moment by moment, with life, whether it be with the small details of daily existence, or the grander experiences prompted by nature or the arts. The self-actualised person is more focused, more attentive, more aware – and therefore more effective and efficient in the workplace and in social living.

2   *Growth choices,* that is, an openness to new experiences, a readiness to take risks with ideas and challenges, rather than to stay always with the safety of the known.

3   *Self-awareness,* that is, a deep and accurate knowledge of one's own mind, and the readiness to show independence of thought and action in defence of one's beliefs and convictions.

4   *Honesty,* that is, a readiness to take responsibility for one's ideas and actions, rather than being governed by a desire to please others or to show ourselves in a favourable light.

5   *Judgement,* that is, the ability to make accurate assessments of situations and people (including our own abilities), and the confidence to trust such assessments.

6   *Self-development,* that is, a readiness to develop one's potentialities (Maslow pointed out that many highly gifted people fail to use their abilities fully, while others with only average talents achieve a great deal).

7   *Peak experiences,* that is, moments when we think, act and feel most clearly and accurately, are more loving and accepting of others, and perhaps gain profound insights into the real nature of existence.

8   *Lack of ego defences,* that is, an awareness of the way in which we distort our images of ourselves and of the external world, and use such distortion to protect our egos (see Chapter 3 of this volume for a fuller explanation of ego defence mechanisms).

An understanding of the mature personality and of self-actualisation is essential if we are to continue the process of growth and development throughout our lives. The majority of our years are passed in adulthood, and we often face particular problems of adaptation in middle and later life. The middle-aged parent who finds that children have grown up and left him or her feeling isolated and alone; the fifty-year-old worker locked into a profoundly unsatisfying job and way of life; or the retired couple who have leisure they do not know how to use. The mature personality is able to meet the challenges of the passing years, and to adapt and grow right through into old age. We referred in Chapter 1 to the fact that Carl Jung, one of the greatest explorers of the human mind, took the view that the later years of life (perhaps the final third of life) are perhaps the most important of all. Free from the responsibilities of learning and of obtaining qualifications, of bringing up children, of forging a career, the individual in the last third of life can turn increasing attention to fundamental questions on the meaning of life and the final destination of the human spirit.

Men, women and maturity in the workplace

The question now arises: what do the various qualities we have been discussing in this chapter tell us about the performance of adults in the workplace? Their implications for those who work with children are clear, but are the qualities that go with the mature personality and with self-actualisation desirable in adult workers, and does the greater openness to intimacy identified with women mean that they make better workers and managers than men?

Let us take the second part of this question first. Currently, psychologists are taking increasing interest in what is called *emotional intelligence* (for example, Goleman, 1995) – that is, having the ability to recognise, manage and harness one's own feelings, and to be adept at recognising, empathising with and responding appropriately to the feelings of others. The development of emotional intelligence through life links closely with the Eriksonian learning tasks of trust, identity and intimacy that we have been discussing. It also links to the extended sense of self, to the ability to create and maintain warm relationships with others, with the self-insight emphasised by Allport, and with many of the qualities of Maslow's self-actualised person.

The development of emotional intelligence seems to depend significantly on the kind of positive parental qualities to which we have already drawn attention, and which we shall be emphasising further in subsequent chapters. Parents who take their children's feelings seriously try to understand what is upsetting them, and acknowledge that things regarded as unimportant to adults may matter a great deal to children. Emotional intelligence plays a vital part not only in self and self-other awareness but also in the ability to handle life generally. For example, Brazelton (see Goleman 1995) found that children who do poorly at school almost always lack one or other of the main expressions of emotional intelligence, whether it be self-assurance; a realistic appraisal of appropriate behaviour; impulse control; or how to express need and request help.

The greater ability of women (generally, though not always) to read both verbal and non-verbal emotional signals, and to express and communicate their own feelings, obviously indicates higher levels of emotional intelligence than those found generally (though by no means always) in men. From boyhood, men – as a consequence of upbringing as much as anything – tend to minimise emotions that have to do with vulnerability, guilt, fear and hurt (Brody and Hall, 1993), which clearly inhibits the development of this important area of human (and humanising) ability. From this, it is clear that in all posts requiring high levels of emotional intelligence, women are likely to be better-equipped than men. Unfortunately, many posts seem likely to penalise rather than to reward this ability. An arrogant, dominating leader (man or woman) is likely to misconstrue emotional intelligence as weakness in his subordinates. Jobs requiring a task-centred rather than a people-centred approach might also lead to less obviously effective behaviour in those with high rather than low emotional intelligence. The wrong kind of job assessment (as, for example, once obtained pretty generally in the medical profession) can in fact place a professional premium on low emotional intelligence, leading those who score highly finding themselves forced to suppress their talents.

In addition, good leadership, as we shall discuss at various points in the chapters that follow, requires other qualities in addition to emotional intelligence. For example, it may need particular levels of knowledge and ability (such as mechanical knowledge) that are more likely to be present in men than in women. At times it may require a single-mindedness which women, with their broader interests in other people, may be less willing to manifest than men. It may also require the ability to work on one's own, and even to put up with the temporary unpopularity that might follow certain unavoidable decisions, however sensitively they are presented and explained. And it may require a competitive spirit, and even a certain ruthlessness when dealing with rival organisations. Many women are well able to show these various qualities, but are more likely to find them distasteful than do men, and contrary to the dictates of emotional intelligence.

However, the importance of emotional intelligence is now being recognised increasingly in the business world. Harsh and unfeeling criticism, sarcasm, contempt for the emotions of others, deliberate attempts to belittle and to disempower, refusal to give credit or to recognise effort, or to give appropriate responsibility, are quite the worst way to motivate people, to keep good staff, or to get the best out of them while they are employed. Baron (1990), in a study of 108 managers and white-collar workers, found that inappropriate criticism, followed by mistrust, personality conflicts and disputes over power were, in fact, the main reasons for job conflicts. Other studies suggest that good criticism, something referred to now as *artful (art-ful) criticism,* focuses on what a person has done and can do, rather than on personal labelling (shades of the behaviour of the good teacher and parent!). Criticism should therefore be:

(i)   *Specific*, so that people know exactly what needs to be remedied;

(ii)   *Contain a preferred solution*, so that they know ways in which this can be done;

(iii) *Given personally*, so that an opportunity exists for response and clarification (the growing trend to hand out criticism via e-mail even to someone in the next room is hardly a sign of emotional intelligence!); and

(iv)   *Given sensitively*, so that those on the receiving end are aware that their difficulties are fully understood, and that they are not left feeling resentful, hostile and unheard.

If all this sounds as though women inevitably make more popular managers than men, we must enter a note of caution. While no exact figures are available, many people (men and women) profess to preferring to work for a male than a female boss, so men must be able to get some things right. In addition, it is right to point out that the ability to express one's feelings is not, in itself, a sign of emotional intelligence. Some women may be expert at doing so, but may lack the ability to see the effect their behaviour has on the feelings of others. Emotional intelligence – it cannot be stressed too strongly – is the ability to be in touch with both one's own feelings and the feelings of others.

Turning now to the mature or self-actualised personality, it is clear that a number of the qualities involved are likely to enhance managerial effectiveness. The ability to concentrate, to show sound judgement and realistic appraisals, to maximise one's talents, to be open to new experiences, to relate warmly to others, and to remain emotionally secure are all likely to prove to be valuable assets. On the other hand, honesty and a readiness to show independence of thought and action may run counter to the willingness to compromise personal standards and beliefs that sometimes (regrettably) appears to be demanded in the workplace. Acquaintance with peak experiences can also mean that the individual's mind is often on so-called 'higher things', which may lead to a feeling of lack of fulfillment in many areas of business and professional life.

However, it reflects badly on our culture if maturity of personality is not required in our leaders and managers. If nothing else, it provides us with food for thought about the standards and values required in the workplace. And for the moment, we must leave it at that.

Can work help personality development?

Having looked at some of the qualities that go with success in the workplace, we must now ask whether work can assist the personality development of those who have missed out on some of the developmental tasks identified by Erikson. If one has failed to learn lessons such as trust, identity and intimacy, can work experiences help to put things right? Though it is unwise to generalise too freely, the answer is yes, but it must be kept in mind that the workplace is not a clinic. Its *raison d'être* is not to compensate for the inadequacies of the past experience of staff, but to operate as a successful, productive unit. Busy managers and colleagues cannot be expected to devote most of their time to providing therapy for their workmates, even had they the skills to do so.

Nevertheless, it is a good rule in human psychology that if we want others to develop desirable qualities, we must show these qualities ourselves. We must trust others if we want them to learn how to trust, and give them responsibility if we want them to act responsibly. However, it is a sad fact of life that this by no means works in all cases. People can abuse our confidence in them, and take advantage of our willingness to take them at their word. So, here again, emotional intelligence is needed. With its help, we are better able to know just how far to go with each individual. Some workers or colleagues can be trusted only in small things, with appropriate checks always ready to hand, while others can be given far more scope.

It is helpful, however, to remember one of the adages of the good teacher, namely to offer everyone the chance of success, no matter how low the initial level. We can always build up from this starting point as people show themselves able to learn the advantages to themselves and to others of becoming worthy of trust, and to learn the disadvantages of betraying that trust. Similarly, with lessons such as autonomy and competence. If people are given the chance to show what they can do – and to be praised and encouraged for it – their self-confidence will increase accordingly, as will their ceiling of achievement. Most people in most jobs are capable of far more than is asked of them, or allowed from them.

Intimacy is more difficult. In adult life, people who have not learned the lesson of intimacy are often so used to keeping others at a distance that they have little conscious wish to change things. The answer is simply to make intimacy, as far as possible and always in an appropriate professional context, available to them. Opportunities can be given to work with sympathetic team-mates (here again, women, from girlhood onwards, are usually much readier to make others welcome than are men, and are much more skilled at doing so), while demonstrations of friendship can be forthcoming from those in authority. For example, smiling at those with whom we work or who work for us is one of the most effective social signals we can give. Smiles show that we are pleased to see people, that we value their presence, and that we offer them our friendship – and there is evidence that smiling is equally good for those who smile, releasing into the bloodstream the same beneficial hormones released by laughter.

Generally, a happy workplace, whether it is a classroom, a shop-floor or a boardroom, is an effective and productive workplace. For many people, particularly those in rather dull and repetitive occupations, the company of congenial colleagues is the most attractive part of being at work. The feeling of being valued by superiors, of having access to them when necessary, of being confident that one will be heard by them with sympathy, and will have one's difficulties understood and one's ideas appreciated, adds further to the congeniality. Maturity of personality helps to make people congenial, reliable, honest and open, and into the kind of people we want to have as our friends. While many of the conditions and constraints are different, the workplace still resembles the world outside. The things that make society work smoothly and successfully help to make the professional world and the world of business do the same.

Chapter 3

Psychodynamic Approaches to Personality

We have looked at the determinants and the development of personality, and we now turn our attention to the nature of personality itself. That is, to the processes within the individual that go to make up what we call personality, and to the way in which these processes interact with each other and with other people. Psychologists have put forward various descriptions and explanations of these processes, often in sharp conflict with each other, but in the following chapters I shall attempt to show how many of these descriptions and explanations carry, in their different ways, considerable practical implications for the workplace.

We start by looking at what is called the *idiographic* approach, which holds that, since each person is unique, personality can best be studied by in-depth investigations of individuals or small groups. Idiographic theories originate mainly in clinical psychology, where the psychologist (or psychiatrist, if he or she happens to be a medically qualified psychologist) works with people suffering from personality problems, such as excessive anxiety, which make it hard for them to cope with even the ordinary stresses of everyday life. From the perspective of the workplace, the interest of these theories lies in the fact they provide us with models that help us understand something of the motivating forces that underlie human behaviour, particularly where these processes are linked to so-called unconscious factors. The best-known idiographic theories are those given the general title of *psychodynamic theories*.

Many writers on personality see modern psychology as being dominated by three schools of thought: *psychodynamics; behaviourism;* and, more recently, *humanistic psychology,* the last two of which we shall look at in subsequent chapters. The logical point at which to start a discussion of psychodynamics, the school of thought which first focused systematic attention on personality, is with Sigmund Freud, its founding father.

Sigmund Freud

If one had to make a list of the people whose thinking has altered most radically the way in which modern Western people view themselves, Freud's name would come near the top of the list. He certainly remains for the layman by far the best-known psychologist (Stanovich, 1996). The originator of psychoanalysis, the first and for many years the most influential of the various psychodynamic schools, Freud (1856–1939) was born of Jewish stock in Moravia in the modern Czech Republic, but lived most of his life in Vienna until fleeing to London in 1938 to escape Nazi persecution. During his fertile career he published so many books and papers (his collected works run to twenty-four volumes in the standard edition), introduced so many theories and ideas, and fought so many battles with his fellow psychologists and psychiatrists, that it is never easy to know where to begin an account of his work. Further, since Freud was constantly refining and developing his theories, it is sometimes hard to find one's way through the apparent contradictions in his writings (see, for example Gay, 1988 for an excellent account of his life and ideas).

Nowadays, many of Freud's theories are accepted in their literal form only by the most devoted of his followers, but his influence has been such that many of his concepts are in everyday use not only by psychologists but by lay people as well, and the same holds for many of the terms he invented. Probably no other psychologist's work has sunk more deeply into the texture of Western thought. In spite of the fact that many of his ideas have long been superseded (and often disproved) by modern scientific psychology, his influence has been such that no one who wishes to discuss personality with any authority can afford to be without some accurate knowledge of them. In addition, these ideas still have great resonance with many people. They carry intrinsic interest, and *seem* to the listener to tell him or her things that accord with personal experience. In consequence, many people identify very readily with Freud's model of personality (hence his continuing popularity), and it can still offer us useful insights into many areas of behaviour within the workplace, whether we are working with children or adults. In fact, Fadiman and Frager (1994) put it that Freud's 'ideas are of no less urgent concern today than they were during his lifetime. At the very least, we need to be in an informed position to criticise them'.

To go back to the beginning, Freud gave us new ways of looking at childhood, ways that were in stark contrast to the belief that misbehaviour and other personality problems in children are the work of the evil one, to be corrected by stern and rigid discipline. To Freud, the child is very much more sinned against by the adult world than sinning, very much more a victim of the mistakes of parents than of mistakes of his or her own making. But Freud did more than simply focus attention on childhood experiences. He suggested that the way in which these experiences influence later personality development can only be understood if we explore the unconscious as well as the conscious mind.

Belief in the power of the unconscious mind to determine human behaviour is now so widespread that it can come as a surprise to know how different things were before Freud. Freud did not originate the idea of the unconscious, which had been with us from antiquity; but to most thinkers before Freud the unconscious was simply a 'waste paper basket of ideas and memories which had fallen below the threshold of awareness because they were relatively unimportant and lacked the mental energy to force their way into consciousness' (Brown, 1964). Freud took precisely the opposite view. After qualifying as a medical doctor at the University of Vienna in 1881, his interest in what was then called nervous disorders (psychological problems such as irrational fears and anxieties, depression, obsessive-compulsive behaviour and so on) took him to work first with the hypnotist J. M. Charcot in France, and later with Joseph Breuer back in Vienna. It was during this time that he became convinced that all aspects of human behaviour have a source much deeper than the conscious mind. Breuer had devised what he called a 'talking out' technique, in which the patient's nervous disorders were much improved simply by talking about them to the physician, and adding any additional memories and thoughts which happened to come into his or her head at the same time.

Freud was very impressed with the effectiveness of this technique, and, as he had become increasingly dissatisfied with hypnosis, he experimented extensively with it himself, eventually developing from it what is now called the technique of *free association*. In free association the patient is invited to report, without reservation, the thoughts that come to mind in response to stimulus words or ideas presented to him or her by the psychologist (or *psychoanalyst*, as the Freudian psychologist is more correctly called). The theory is that gradually, through one thought leading to another in a stream of consciousness, the patient will uncover long-forgotten memories of the experiences that are the original causes of present nervous disorders.

It was the astonishingly complex network of thoughts and recollections his patients revealed during free association, many of them stretching back into early childhood, that convinced Freud that the conscious mind is only the tip of the iceberg of mental life, with the more important part lying beneath the waters – that is, deep down in the unconscious. Far from it being simply a 'waste paper basket of ideas and memories', the unconscious is, he felt, energised by powerful instinctual drives such as sex and self-preservation which act as the main impulse behind human behaviour. And, far from lacking the mental energy to force themselves into consciousness, Freud saw much of the contents of the unconscious as being kept out of awareness (repressed) by the conscious mind precisely because its significance and power form too great a threat to the individual's precarious socialised self.

To understand this part of Freud's theory, we must remember that he was writing at a time when deterministic ideas were gaining strength in the scientific world. Everything had to have a cause, a source of energy, which produced its visible effects. In the case of human psychology, it seemed to Freud that the unconscious was this cause. The powerful unconscious instinctive drives his patients revealed during free association seemed to him to be the dynamo (hence the term *psychodynamic psychology*) that provides the motivational energy for all mental activity. True, in the course of man's evolution, the unconscious has become overlaid with the thin veneer of civilised thinking that we call the conscious mind, but the conscious mind has no mental energy of its own. Within the dynamic system of human psychology, energy has to be transferred continually from the unconscious to the conscious (often in a disguised form – for example, sexuality may become creativity; and self-preservation, ambition) if the latter is to function. As we shall see shortly, he considered that it is when there is a breakdown in the orderly way in which this energy transfer takes place that personality problems arise.

Although Freud remained satisfied for most of his career with this division of the mind into the unconscious and the conscious, in 1922, at the age of twenty-six, he published *The Ego and the Id*, which proposed a division of the mind into three systems, with the terms 'unconscious' and 'conscious' now used only to describe the kinds of mental phenomena which each of these systems contains. We need to discuss these three systems: the *id*; the *ego*; and the *super-ego*, separately.

The id   At birth, Freud claimed that the mind consists only of the id. The id contains everything psychological that we inherit, a fixed amount of mental or 'psychic' energy. This energy is in the form of *instincts,* that is, of irrational drives whose only aim is to seek gratification for the individual's instinctive, animalistic needs. Since the newborn baby is therefore psychologically on the level of an animal, the baby is literally an 'it' (Latin *id*) rather than a person.

As the id remains the only source of psychic energy throughout life, we can never free ourselves entirely from its power. The id is the primitive side of us, the 'dark force' that novelists such as D. H. Lawrence wrote about. The id links us, through the long chain of our evolutionary history, with the basic forms of life from which we have arisen. Since the id is entirely unconscious, we are never directly aware of it, but it is always there, seeking the satisfaction of its powerful needs. Beneath the reach of consciousness, and of ethical and rational thought, the id can never be other than a blind, unsocialised, amoral force. Left unbridled, its drive towards selfish satisfaction would reduce human behaviour to that of the beasts.

Freud considered that the instincts within the id fall into two groups: *eros* instincts; and *thanatos* instincts. The eros instincts are the life wish, and consist both of those drives directed towards self-preservation (flight, hunger, thirst and so on) and towards preservation of the species (the sex drive, or *libido*). The thanatos instincts are the death wish, and take the form both of aggression directed outwards towards others, and of aggression directed inwards towards the self.

Freud referred to the instinctive drives of the id as *primary processes,* while the selfish objectives of these drives he termed the *pleasure principle*. During the first year or so of its life, the child is entirely dominated by the primary processes and by the pleasure principle. He or she lives only for the satisfaction of primitive needs, and is unconcerned about the convenience or the wishes of other people, as many a parent dragged from the depths of slumber in the small hours of the morning by a baby's crying knows only too well.

Presumably, if the small baby went on having all its needs instantly gratified, it would go on being dominated by the id throughout life, but, thankfully for the rest of us, the child gradually comes to realise that not all of these needs are exactly in tune with reality. People don't come running every time you cry; a bottle of milk isn't always enough to satisfy you; and the discomfort of colic won't disappear just because you want it to.

In consequence, part of the id begins to learn a more rational way of looking at things, and gradually separates itself off from the rest to form what Freud called the ego. The socialisation of the baby has begun.

The ego From the second year of life the ego becomes an increasingly important part of the child's mental functioning. It serves as the mediator between the needs of the id and the restrictions reality places on the gratification of these needs. Unlike the id, which obeys the pleasure principle, the ego therefore obeys the *reality principle*. It contains all the child's rational thinking, sense of self, and all conscious thoughts. By means of the ego, the child becomes more of a person and less of an animal (*ego* = 'I'). Freud called ego processes *secondary processes* to distinguish them from the primary processes of the id. Because these secondary processes prove successful in mediating with the outside world, and in seeing to it that the id's needs are satisfied wherever possible, the id allows the ego to syphon off more and more of its psychological energy, until soon the ego has a surplus it can turn to more social pursuits and the development of general interests and skills. However, the id always remains ready to cut off the flow of energy to the ego and to reassert itself should the latter fail in its primary task of satisfying the id's needs. To put it somewhat melodrama-tically, the animal in us always lurks just under the surface ready to take over if more civilised means fail to gratify its drives (a point that has been exploited to good effect by many a science-fiction writer, to say nothing of such novelists of childhood as William Golding in *The Lord of the Flies*).

To Freud, the diversion of energy from the id to the ego is the major dynamic event of personality development. However, it is not the final event. From the age of about six, part of the child's ego separates itself off in turn and becomes the third system of the mind, the super-ego.

The super-ego One of the ways in which the ego learns about reality is by identifying itself with other people, particularly with parents (we have already had something to say about this in the previous chapters). In the process of this identification, children take on many of the moral precepts of the adults in their lives. But these moral precepts often owe far more to the beliefs and prejudices of these adults than they do to reality, and therefore cannot be accommodated within the ego itself, which obeys only the reality principle. A section of the ego therefore has to break away to deal with them, and this becomes what Freud called the super-ego.

The super-ego is a very important concept in Freudian theory. It will be remembered that in Chapter 2 of this volume it was said that children get their ideas of their own moral worth largely from what people tell them about themselves. Freud claimed that the super-ego provides us with a model of the mechanics of all this. Since the super-ego is created in response to the code of restrictions, admonishments and moral precepts that parents impose on the child, it also acquires parental powers of reward and punishment. It rewards by the feelings of pride that we get when we obey its promptings and strive towards the *ideal self* it holds up as a model in front of us, and it punishes by the pangs of *conscience* we feel when we disobey them.

The contents of the super-ego are partly conscious, but mainly unconscious. Thus most of it, like the id, lies beyond the range of rational thought. Early in life we are saddled with many of our parents' beliefs, and find it difficult, even as we grow older, to isolate them and submit them to rational scrutiny and debate. Thus often we behave even as adults in certain ways because we consider them to be 'right', but are unable to give a reasoned, objective argument as to *why* they are right. As we shall see shortly, if the super-ego contains many of these irrational values and beliefs, and if it becomes, as Freud put it, 'overdeveloped', it can cause almost as many personality problems (in this case, such things as rigidity of thought and emotion, authoritarianism, guilt and self-rejection) to the individual as can an unchecked id. However, a normal, well-balanced super-ego is an essential part of the socialisation of the child, and the essential repository of a moral sense in us all.

By the age of six or seven the three personality systems of id, ego and super-ego are in existence. For the personality to remain healthy, Freud considered it vital that these three systems remain in a state of balance, with a smooth transfer of energy from id to ego to super-ego. Where the balance is disturbed, and where one of the systems dominates the others and uses up more than its fair share of energy, the result is that the personality breaks down into excessive anxiety. Since any one of the three systems can dominate, this means that we can have three distinct forms of anxiety: *neurotic; realistic;* or *moral.*

Neurotic anxiety   In what Freud called neurotic anxiety, the id dominates, and the ego, the conscious mind, goes in fear of being overwhelmed by its dark, instinctive, unconscious forces. Since these are below the level of consciousness, the person concerned is not aware of the fundamental cause of his or her problems. Anxiety is felt as a vague, nameless dread, a 'free-floating' anxiety that persists even when the outer life is devoid of any real pressures. Neurotic anxiety is, in a deep sense, a fear of one's own drives and impulses, a fear of losing control over the beast inside oneself.

The causes of neurotic anxiety are complex, but they boil down to the fact that the adult was not helped in childhood to recognise and come to terms with instinctive energies (such as anger, fear, sexual arousal, jealousy and so on). Throughout life, there is therefore a part of one's own nature that remains a stranger to oneself, and the individual lives a kind of Jekyll and Hyde existence, forever on the brink of self-made catastrophe. Should the sufferer give way to the id, we get what Freud called *the acting-out of impulses,* as when a usually docile and well-controlled child or adult has a fearsome and unexpected outburst of rage, or a respectable middle-aged citizen goes impulsively on a shop-lifting spree. Far from helping the person concerned, acting out of impulses usually makes things much worse. He or she confesses afterwards to not knowing what came over them, and in the future goes in dread lest a similar thing should happen again.

Realistic anxiety   Realistic anxiety occurs when the ego dominates, typically when it is faced with so many real difficulties and terrors in the external world that it requires an undue share of psychic energy to deal with them. The person beset with realistic anxiety has little energy left to enjoy the pleasures of the id (for example, in extreme cases they may lose appetite and sex drive) or to devote to super-ego demands such as the welfare of others.

Extra-strong examples of realistic anxiety were termed by Freud *traumas,* and usually take the form of brutal emotional shocks or frightening experiences, but realistic anxiety is also caused in children by such things as excessive demands for academic success or standards of behaviour, by a background of domestic strife, or even by the uncertainties of having to start a new school or work with a new teacher. In adults the stress of undue pressures at work, or of emotional difficulties in relationships, or sudden bereavements or ill-health may be the precipitating cause. Temperamentally, some people are more prone to realistic anxiety then others, often because their autonomic nervous system is more readily aroused (that is, their bodies are quicker to manifest anxiety symptoms such as sweating, rapid heart beats, 'butterflies in the stomach' and so on).

Moral anxiety If the super-ego dominates, we get what Freud called moral anxiety, an anxiety in which the individual is trapped in an over-rigid value system taken over from parents. If it is the *ego-ideal* side of the super-ego that dominates, the individual is excessively high-minded and perfectionist, prompted by lofty ideals which have more to do with an unrealistic 'virtue' than with truth and compassion. If it is the *conscience* that dominates, he or she is compulsively on guard against anything that might arouse feelings of guilt, and prone to reject both the pleasure principle of the id and the reality principle of the ego, and inhabit instead an unreal world of taboos and forbidden things.

In both children and in adults, guilt feelings in the person who suffers from moral anxiety can be so threatening that, whenever they have done something which they conceive as wrong, they may actively seek punishment in order to reduce them. Where punishment is not forthcoming, they may torture themselves with ideas of unworthiness and inadequacy, even developing ritualistic gestures such as excessive (*obsessional-compulsive*) handwashing in order symbolically to rid themselves of the guilt feelings.

Ego-defence mechanisms
Although these three forms of anxiety stem from different systems within the personality, it is possible for the same person to experience all three of them at once. But, whether we experience one or all three, it is always the ego that does the experiencing. The id and the super-ego can cause anxiety, but they never suffer it themselves. It is the ego, with its conscious processes, that is the battlefield upon which the personality fights out its civil war. And, whenever the ego is weakened by one of the three forms of anxiety,

it has less psychic energy left to fight a possible battle against one of the other two. Thus, to take up again our example of the normally well-controlled individual who suddenly surprises us all with temper tantrums, it may be that he or she has recently suffered a bout of realistic anxiety, such as the break-up of an important relationship, which draws off so much psychic energy that the person is unable to maintain their customary defence against ever-present neurotic anxiety. The id breaks through these defences, and the sufferer behaves in what seems to be an utterly uncharacteristic way.

It is fair to point out that in all three forms of anxiety, there may be no symptoms obvious to the onlooker right up to the moment of breakdown. Individuals may control anxiety so well that it is not until the ego is suddenly overwhelmed by having to fight a battle on yet another front that we get any idea of the pressures they have been under. But, of course, the better we know people, the more sensitive we generally are to their symptoms, or the more aware we are of the excessive workload they are carrying.

Freud considered that the ego possesses certain weapons it can use in its fight to retain control over the personality. These weapons he termed *ego-defence mechanisms*. We all of us unwittingly develop them to some extent in childhood, but they require a large amount of psychic energy to maintain, and normally as we grow older we develop more rational ways of coping with ourselves. Where we fail to do so, we tie up so much energy in ego defence mechanisms that little is left for more productive activity. Chief among these mechanisms are the following.

Repression   The ego tries to blot out the cause of the anxiety, to put it out of the conscious mind altogether. Repression is one of the commonest defence mechanisms, but its shortcoming is that repressed material is not really forgotten at all, but merely sinks down into the id, making neurotic anxiety even more likely in the future. The example of the individual with temper tantrums would be an instance of repressed material, in this case aggression, suddenly flooding back to take control of conscious behaviour. Repressed material can also re-emerge in disguised form, as when a child's repressed hatred of a sibling shows itself in antagonism towards the things at which the other excels.

Projection   The ego attributes to other people those urges – and failings – it is fearful of recognising in itself. Thus the individual who is hostile to others escapes facing this hostility by claiming it is they who are the hostile ones, or the person who is dishonest avoids confronting the fact by accusing others of untruthfulness.

Rationalisation The ego advances an apparently reasonable argument to explain away something that it finds too painful to explain honestly. Thus a sadistic adult may rationalise the use of corporal punishment by insisting it is for the good of the child, or a sadistic employer may claim one has to treat people badly in order to get the best out of them.

Reaction formation The ego defends against one of the id's disturbing urges by placing undue emphasis upon its opposite. Reaction formation is used particularly when this urge outrages the super-ego, thus causing moral anxiety. The child, for example, who feels hatred for parents may become an excessively dutiful and apparently loving son or daughter. The adult who has a troublesome sex drive may become an anti-pornography campaigner. Reaction formation is always distinguishable from genuine emotion by the fact that it is *exaggerated*.

Regression The ego regresses to a form of behaviour that was successful in gaining attention and sympathy, and thus in lowering anxiety, in the past. Thus a child who feels threatened by the arrival of a new baby may revert to babyish behaviour himself, or a child who is unhappy in a new school may revert to tearful, over-dependent behaviour at home, or the adult who feels badly treated may revert to childish spite and revenge.

Compensation The ego substitutes a drive that can be satisfied for one that cannot. The adolescent, for example, who fails to attract the opposite sex, may compensate by overeating. Closely allied to compensation, but more life-enhancing, is *sublimation*, when the ego directs frustrated energy into higher social or cultural goals. Freud saw much artistic activity as being an example of sublimation.

Various other ego-defence mechanisms have been recognised as important since the time of Freud, many of them readily recognisable. We have already looked at one of these in Chapter 2, when we said that a child who is unsuccessful in school may protect his or her self-esteem (which is part of the ego) by rejecting the standards the school sets. Another child or adult may protect self-esteem by withdrawing from anything that has to do with competition, or may make the excuse of imagined illness. (Hypochondria, as this process is called, may also be an example of attention-seeking behaviour in someone who feels socially neglected.) Another form of defence, used against recognising one's disappointment at personal failures or at the loss of cherished ideals, may be excessive cynicism, or a hypercritical or dismissive attitude towards the efforts of others.

Normal development

From what has already been said, it should be clear that Freud saw normal development taking place when the id, the ego and the super-ego are in a state of balance, and when the ego-defence mechanisms are being steadily replaced by more mature and efficient ways of dealing with personal psychological problems. As normal development progresses, the individual also outgrows excessive dependence on the primitive primary processes of the id, and learns to displace the energy associated with these processes into the socially acceptable secondary processes of the ego. This *displacement*, according to Freud, explains all the interests, attitudes and aspirations of the mature personality. Through orderly displacement, the id's drives are channelled into developmental stages such as those proposed by Erikson (see Chapter 2 above), aggressive drives becoming, for example, autonomy, determination, and leadership, while self-preservation drives become industry and competence, and the libido drive becomes marriage and parenthood.

One of the best known, and most controversial, aspects of Freudian theory is that this normal development proceeds through a number of what are called *psychosexual stages*, during each of which the instinctive drives that have to be displaced and socialised are centred on a separate erogenous zone of the body, and the individual is therefore maximally sensitive to experiences associated with it (the so-called oral, anal and genital phases). Perhaps because of its frank treatment of the sex drive, this part of Freud's work always attracts great interest, but it is of doubtful relevance to us. Few psychologists would accept it as a very accurate picture of what really happens to the personality during the years concerned. However, we can derive certain broad generalisations from it, which, taken together with the rest of Freud's work, suggest the sort of things that should be kept in mind if we want to help children to avoid some of the excessive forms of anxiety examined above.

Basically, children should not be set at war with themselves. We risk doing so by forcing them to reject the drives of the id, particularly its extra-strong drives such as anger, fear and sexual desire. These drives are present in children from early in their life, and they need help in recognising, accepting and learning to channel such drives into socially acceptable forms. We also risk setting them at war with themselves by endowing them with overdeveloped super-egos which demand impossible things of them, or fill them with guilt about the drives of the id. The super-ego should contain only necessary moral and social restraints, and by explaining the reasons for these restraints we help children to keep them within the range of their conscious thinking, so that they can be subjected to rational debate now and in the future (much as we said in Chapter 2, that the adolescent should be encouraged to talk about such things as values and restrictions in a properly open and supportive atmosphere).

Freud reminded us that many of the things we lead children to reject or repress are not necessarily bad in themselves, but simply make us as adults feel uncomfortable, perhaps because we find them inconvenient or embarrassing and were not allowed to come to terms with them in our own childhood. It is not easy for us to accept that children may at times feel intense hostility towards a parent or a teacher, or that they may have strong sexual desires, or that they may want to run away rather than to stay and face a threatening situation, but all these responses are perfectly natural. Children should not be made to feel guilty because of such feelings. Instead they should be encouraged to bring them into the open, to discuss and confront them. Only by a frank recognition of their existence can children be helped to control them, and to integrate them into the developing personality. If children are forced to repress these drives, they will remain unacknowledged in the id, repressing a source of creative energy, forcing the erection of rigid defence mechanisms, and awaiting their chance to burst back into con-sciousness and cause personality problems in later life.

Criticisms of Freud

I have devoted space to Freud because of the great attention his work has attracted over the years. In addition, he provides us with a vocabulary in which to discuss personality theory, since, as I suggested earlier, many of his terms are now part and parcel of the language of psychology. I have avoided most of his more controversial ideas, and presented only those that have most relevance, direct and indirect, to the workplace. This does not mean that all the aspects of Freudian theory covered in this chapter are based on scientific evidence. Freud derived many of his ideas from case studies and – like many innovative thinkers – from intuition, and these ideas represent a groping towards a theory rather than a finished one. There may not literally be such sharply divided levels of the mind as Freud believed, yet his id, ego and super-ego divisions provide us with a useful model for discussing the personality, for seeing how heredity and environment may interact with each other, and for isolating some of the causes of personality problems.

There may be many more ego-defence mechanisms than the ones identified by Freud, and they may operate differently from the ways in which he suggested. Some psychologists (for example, Christianson, 1992) claim that far from repressing many of the unpleasant things that happen to us, they remain all too obtrusive in our memories. However, while this may be true of later childhood and adult life, Freud's point was that the majority of repressions take place in early childhood, and in consequence have a particularly strong formative influence on personality thereafter. And there is important experimental evidence in favour of his theories (see, for example, Fisher and Greenberg, 1985 for an excellent survey). In any case, it seems that from personal experience the great majority of well-informed people believe that we frequently do push painful memories out of our awareness and into the unconscious (Garry *et al.*, 1994), and there have been a number of interesting experiments that reveal the workings of unconscious processes, and the way in which such processes may sometimes prevent people from correctly perceiving or remembering material that is painful to them (Fonagy, 1981). And there is little doubt that the ego-defence mechanisms Freud described help us to understand the methods we frequently use to protect our egos from anxiety, and the damaging and inappropriate role such defences may play in our lives.

In addition, work with factor analysis lends at least some weight to Freud's conceptualisation of id, ego and super-ego, though it suggests that his ideas may need some modification (Kline, 1983). Moreover, although it appears now that Freud's three forms of anxiety may not be as clearly differentiated as he thought, they certainly point to some of the most important ways in which long-standing fears and worries can be created, and the different effects they can have on our personalities.

Freud accepted that his ideas would be altered in the light of new evidence, and his own frequent tinkerings with his theories highlight this point. Many psychologists claim that this very flexibility is a weakness. They argue that because Freudian theory can be adjusted to accommodate virtually any new findings, it is impossible ever to prove or disprove it. Like a piece of putty, it can be moulded to take on the right shape to accommodate any criticisms levelled at it. This is true up to a point, but it fails to take account of the advances in our thinking that have stemmed from Freud. As already indicated, he stressed that early childhood experiences help to mould personality; that much of our mental life is unconscious and influences, unbeknown to us, a great deal of our conscious behaviour and motivation; that our personalities are often the scene of conflicts between our conscious and unconscious wishes, fears and values; that such fears and values are often dictated by a super-ego internalised from the attitude of our care-givers early in life; and the fact that normal and abnormal behaviour are on a continuum, with all of us suffering from some level of personality problems.

On the other side of the coin, Hans Eysenck (most recently in Eysenck, 1985) argues that, in addition to lacking much in the way of experimental support, Freudian theory has been actively harmful to psychology in that it has diverted us from a properly scientific investigation of the causes of personality problems, and has provided us with a technique (psychoanalysis) of doubtful value in treating these problems. Exploring the unconscious by means of free association and other Freudian techniques may be all very well, but Eysenck considered that in the long run there is little hard evidence that it does the patient much good.

In Chapter 6 we shall look at the personality theories put forward as alternatives by Eysenck, but we must leave the debate on the value of Freud's work to rumble on. For the present, the best conclusion is still that of Brown (1964): namely that, without knowing all the answers, Freud at least knew the kinds of question that psychologists ought to be asking.

Other psychodynamic approaches

Two of the most eminent of Freud's followers, whose work continues to attract increasing attention, were Carl Gustav Jung (1875–1961) and Alfred Adler (1870–1937). Both men introduced so much new thinking into psychology that they deserve more space

The Nature of the Unconscious

Many psychodynamic psychologists think of the mind as operating at four different but interconnected levels:

(i)   The conscious level, which is whatever is actively in one's mind;

(ii) The preconscious, which is all the material that can readily be called to mind when needed;

(iii) The personal unconscious, which is all the material from one's life experience which lies below the level of immediate recall, but which nevertheless exerts a profound influence upon personality – this is the level of Freud's id and of part of the super-ego, of the ego defence mechanisms, and of repressed traumatic experiences; and

(iv) The collective unconscious – a level proposed by Jung, which is a reservoir of our psychological possibilities, our shared genetic psychological inheritance.

In view of its influence on our personality, our motivation, our fears, our hopes, our values and our emotional life generally, the more readily we can access our personal unconscious and bring its contents into the preconscious, the more we are able to understand, change and develop ourselves.

than can be given to them here. But from the point of view of an understanding of personality in the workplace, the most important aspect of their thinking is that, while both men accepted the existence of id, ego and super-ego, the importance of unconscious processes, the shaping of personality in childhood, the dynamics of the ego defence mechanisms, and the part played in personality development by our basic, animalistic drives, they rejected Freud's notion that these drives are the only innate motivating force behind human behaviour. Eventually, although originally closely associated with Freud, they each broke away from him, and developed their own movements within psychodynamic psychology.

Jung, the more complex and mystical thinker of the two, and the founder of what is known as *analytical* psychology (see, for example, McLynn, 1997 for an excellent account of his life and work), saw human beings as being motivated over and above our Freudian, animalistic urges by a drive towards self-discovery. As we grow older, by studying ourselves and exploring our unconscious through observing our dream material, our memories and our thought patterns, we can come to know more about ourselves, and to better understand our own motivation, aspirations and strengths. Unlike Freud, Jung held that the personality is potentially whole at birth, and only breaks down into conflicting systems in the face of adverse experiences. The search for self-discovery is therefore really a search for the potential wholeness with which we are born, and which we carry with us throughout life. When we find this wholeness, we become what Jung called *individuated,* and he would have agreed that the individuated man has those qualities we listed in Chapter 2 as belonging to Allport's mature personality and Maslow's self-actualised person.

One of Jung's most interesting concepts is that one of the main reasons people fail to find themselves is that through their environment, and their early experiences with parents, teachers and society generally, they create a *persona,* a kind of public mask that hides their true feelings from others and from themselves. This persona is often a particular feature of people in business life, who, willingly or not, hide their real selves, even from themselves. A strong persona and emotional intelligence (Chapter 2) would hardly seem to go together.

The mechanisms behind the persona are not unlike those that Freud suggested are behind the super-ego, with individuals constrained to reject much of the true self and to assume the social mores, prohibitions and conventions of other people. Jung took a great interest in formal education, and saw sensitive and emotionally aware teaching being as of almost equal importance to good parenting in helping the child to avoid an over-strong persona, and to develop individuation. Teachers and parents can best provide this help, Jung argued, if they themselves possesses the self-knowledge that goes with individuation, and can thus avoid inflicting their own psychological shortcomings on their children. He considered that teachers, like parents, should encourage children to express themselves not only through discussion but also through the creative arts and the sciences, since creative expression stems largely from the unconscious. And in every subject in the curriculum teachers should as far as is practical encourage individuality. Each personality is unique, and can only achieve individuation in its own way. Where conformity and rules are essential, the child should be helped to see the purpose behind these rules, and the distinction between social convenience and moral imperative.

Jung also developed (though he did not originate) the idea, of particular importance in the workplace, that some people are *extraverted* in their personalities (that is, orientated, probably innately, towards other people and towards the stimuli of the outside world), while others are *introverted* (that is, orientated more towards their own inner states of mind). These terms were developed further by Eysenck, and are proving very influential in our understanding of personality. We shall be returning to them when we discuss Eysenck's work in Chapter 6. Jung also identified four fundamental psychological functions, *thinking, feeling, sensation* and *intuition*, each of which may be experienced in an extraverted or introverted fashion. In most people, one of these functions is dominant over the others, while one of the remaining three is usually deep in the unconscious (perhaps repressed) and consequently undeveloped.

Thinking is concerned with objective truth, with judgement and impersonal analysis (and asks the question 'What does this mean?'); *feeling* is focused on value (and asks 'What is its value?'); *sensation* is directed towards sensory experience ('What am I experiencing?'); and *intuition* towards possibilities, past experiences and future goals ('What is possible?'). In the workplace, individuals whose dominant function is thinking are planners, but may be so bound up in their planning that they tend to be difficult to budge even when confronted by new and contradictory evidence. Feeling types tend to make decisions on the basis of right and wrong rather than of logic or efficiency. Sensation types favour tangible, concrete experience over discussion or analysis, and can be very effective at dealing with crises and emergencies. Intuitive types are good at integrating present with past experience, and are often bold and imaginative if sometimes rather impractical thinkers. For Jung, the individuated person is able to call upon all four functions, as and when required.

Adler (see, for example, Manaster and Corsini, 1982), the founder of what became known as *individual* psychology, was not strongly at variance with Jung on most of these points, but he laid particular stress on the extraverted side of human beings. Individuals are motivated throughout life, he claimed, over and above basic needs and the drive towards self-discovery, by *social* drives – that is, by the desire to interact with other people. It is primarily from other people, Adler argued, that we receive the major experiences of our lives, and from other people that we learn how to understand and eventually to control ourselves. In common with Jung, Adler saw us as having much more say in our own destiny than did Freud. We have a *creative self,* a kind of innate ego, that helps us from an early age to start making sense of the world, to seek out new experiences, and to create from them and from our self-knowledge a *lifestyle,* a characteristic and unique way of coping with the world that is always open to further development in the light of new findings.

Adler's concept of lifestyle is an important one for the workplace, as it determines how we react to our experiences. Moreover, the lifestyle contains *complexes* – that is, associations of ideas and feelings that we have about ourselves and the world. The best-known example of these complexes – one of which has passed very much into the language – is the *inferiority complex* (which Cooper-smith's low self-esteem boys discussed in Chapter 2 of this volume certainly possessed). The inferiority complex means that the ideas and feelings we have about ourselves typically contain the belief that we are less effective than are the people around us. This belief colours our whole approach to life. It affects our work, our life goals, our interpretation of concepts such as fairness or authority, and our relationships.

Adler's followers have expanded the idea of complexes to cover all aspects of the lifestyle. We can, for example, talk about someone's negative complex about work or school, which leads them to become hostile or rejecting, and even to despise everything associated with learning or qualifications, or associated with co-operation and teamwork. We might also have a negative complex about sport, or the opposite sex, or racial minorities, or employers, or anything else. (Useful as the notion of complexes is, it need not be pursued further as it is similar to George Kelly's even more comprehensive theory of personal constructs, which we shall be discussing in Chapter 7).

Adler saw the possession of an inferiority complex as indicating that the individual has failed to achieve the *superiority* that Alder held to be an essential part of the social urge. In the well-adjusted person, this superiority means power over oneself rather than over others, and the ability to use this power for social good. Anyone handicapped in the drive for superiority – by, for example, a physical or environmental disability – may compensate (Adler borrowed the term from Freud and further developed it) by trying extra hard, and may achieve spectacular success, as when the stammerer becomes a great orator, or the sickly child a great athlete.

But some kinds of compensation can be overdone, as when the socially deprived child develops in adult life into the political extremist, or the bullied child becomes the tyrannical boss.

Jung and Adler provide a useful counterbalance to Freud within psychodynamic psychology in that their picture of humankind is a broader, more optimistic one. Both saw people as having the power to change aspects of their personalities even into old age, instead of being imprisoned in the experiences of childhood. Jung in particular stressed that we have creative, mystical depths, while Adler saw us as seekers and instigators of social experiences rather than primarily as victims of them.

The implications of psychodynamic theories for those working with children have been made clear at appropriate points in the chapter. However, those working with adults need to identify from the various aspects of personality described by each personality theory those that are most relevant to any given work situation. Different situations require different qualities. For example, Jung's ideas help us to recognise the importance of identifying which particular mode – thinking, feeling, sensing, or intuiting – is needed in a given job situation. An individual whose characteristic mode is that of thinking is likely to be much more successful in a highly structured formal and analytical environment such as a solicitor's office or a research and development unit than in a fluid and open-ended situation in which there are no predetermined right or wrong answers and where there is a premium on intuitive modes of behaviour, such as in journalism, or in art and design workshops. In situations where many practical problems may have to be solved at short notice, such as in the police or the military or public relations, a sensing mode may be most appropriate. Feeling types may be at their best in the caring professions or in public relations or personnel work. But the ideal, whatever one's working milieu, is to be sufficiently perceptive to recognise which of these various motives is most appropriate in any given context and, as we all have the potential to display all four modes, to respond accordingly.

This kind of flexibility can present problems, however. We may find it difficult to shift from our habitual mode or modes into those with which we are less familiar. If this is the case, it is helpful to try to analyse – with the benefit of hindsight – any situation where we consider that we may have acted less than successfully. What mode did the situation ideally require? Were we in that mode or not, and, if not, why not? Was there a failure to judge the correct mode on our part, or was our ability to switch into it self-inhibited? If this was the case, what might have prompted this inhibition? Did we see the feeling mode as being a form of weakness? Did we consider the thinking mode to be too detached and perhaps lacking in compassion? Did we regard the intuitive mode as being too risky, or did we have too little confidence in our own experience to operate from the sensing mode? Often all that is required is self-insight of this kind. In many situations we are not held back by any intrinsic rigidity of personality, but simply by a failure to apply our powers of judgement, or by our lack of practice at making fuller and better use of the richness of our own natures.

Adler's *complexes* are also of practical relevance to the adult. The possession of a complex of any kind means that we approach situations with a bias that inevitably interfaces with our judgement. For example, if we have a superiority complex we assume – without sufficient evidence – that others are likely to be less able or less worthy than we are. We fail to allow ourselves to judge them on their merits, often with undesirable consequences for personal relationships and for task effectiveness, and for our ability to develop a realistic assessment of our own strengths and weaknesses.

By the same token, an inferiority complex will lead us to regard others as being consistently better than ourselves, whether professionally or personally, and to expect failure rather than success when tackling a new task. An inferiority complex thus leads us to make what are, in effect, self-fulfilling prophecies. Our expectations inhibit our performance, contributing to the very failures that we fear. It is not difficult to recognise complexes in ourselves and in others. They may be based on past experience, or simply on what others told us about ourselves during our early years, when we were too young to judge accurately for ourselves.

The remedy for an inferiority complex is to *catch ourselves being successful*. That is to note (and reward ourselves with silent praise or with something more tangible) each time we succeed at something, rather than noticing only those times when we do less well. We can supplement this by actively seeking those things at which we are competent. We should also apply to ourselves the same standards we apply to others. Typically, people with inferiority complexes consistently judge others much more leniently than they judge themselves, and are much readier to excuse the mistakes of others than they are to excuse their own. Effectively, what is needed is an improved sense of realism.

A similar sense of realism is necessary for those with a superiority complex (though, unfortunately, those with such a complex are curiously reluctant to modify their way of seeing things!). Here the need is to *catch others being successful*, and to be more alert to our own shortcomings. In some cases a superiority complex hides genuine insecurity. The person concerned finds it difficult to face the reality that he or she is not good at something. One defence for fragile self-esteem is to become deaf to criticism – including self-criticism. Thus, paradoxically, a superiority complex can exist as a defence against an inferiority complex. All rather confusing. But then, no one has said that human nature is simple

Psychodynamic theories and personality testing

Psychodynamics psychologists assess personality through the techniques of the consulting-room, such as free association, but they have also developed a number of measuring devices that are of relevance to the workplace. The most long-lived of these are known as *projective techniques* (see, for example, Semeonoff, 1976), and operate on the assumption that people will project their conscious and often their unconscious personality problems into interpretations of ambiguous stimuli. This is rather akin to what happens when we see faces in the fire or pictures in the clouds. The kinds of faces and pictures we see may owe as much to our unconscious preoccupations as to the shapes that are in fact there. For example, a timid, frightened person may tend to see threatening things; someone who longs to be married may see things to do with a wedding; or a person with repressed aggression may see knives or guns.

The first projective technique to be developed – and still one of the most influential and widely used (Piotrowski and Keller, 1989) – was the Rorschach Inkblot Test (Rorschach, 1942). The test consists of ten symmetrical inkblots (rather like the 'butterflies' made by shaking paint on to a sheet of paper, folding the paper over and opening it out again), five in colour and five in black and white. Individuals being tested, who, it is claimed, can be as young as three years old, look at each blot in turn and say what it looks like to them. Their responses are scored in terms of such things as content, localisation (do they relate to the whole inkblot or only part of it?) and determinants (do they relate mainly to colour or to form?). It takes specialist training before psychologists are competent to use the test and interpret its results, but the test suffers from a lack of appropriate standardisation (though current computer-aided scoring methods are helping to enhance the test's validity – see Wood *et al.* 1996). That is, we have little idea of how the majority of people would respond to it, so it is difficult to say precisely how unusual an individual's responses may in fact be. And we have no consistent evidence about how much of a connection there is between these responses and how a person deals with real-life problems. Nevertheless, the theory behind it remains an important one, and there is no doubt that it does reveal interesting aspects of our conscious and unconscious preoccupations while at the same time providing suggestive leads that supplement other information.

A more straightforward projective test, which has influenced the development of many similar tests down the years, is the Thematic Apperception Test (TAT), devised by Henry Murray in 1943. The TAT consists of a number of realistic but enigmatic black and white pictures, mainly of social situations, about each of which individuals being tested are invited to tell a story. Their responses are then analysed in terms of Murray's concepts of *need* and *press,* a need being a primary organic force (such as Freud's instincts or Adler's social drive), while a press is anything within the environment that helps or hinders the satisfaction of that need (for example, a need for social approval can be aided by the press of an attractive appearance). The theory is that, in telling a story about each of the pictures in the test, individuals will attribute to the characters and situations their own needs and presses. They may suggest, for example, that a pensive man in one of the pictures is 'worrying about failure at work', and suggest that this failure is because 'everyone is against him'.

The TAT has been supplemented by extra pictures for use with children aged from eight to fourteen, while for children even younger than this there are special tests such as the Children's Apperception Test (first devised in 1955), designed to test for problems associated in particular with school. In all these tests, Murray's original marking scheme has been added to, and there are now many alternative schemes available.

Another set of projective techniques utilises the notion that people project something of themselves into their drawings and their stories. The well-known Goodenough Draw-a-Man-Test, originally a test of intelligence, has been widely used in this context. Yet other tests such as the Lowenfeld World Test are designed to allow the

---

Psychodynamic Psychology and the Complexity of Personality

One of the major virtues of psychodynamic psychology is that it recognises just how complex – and complicated – our personalities are. Science generally seeks to simply whatever it studies – in other words, to reduce it to the fewest possible components and explanations. Psychodynamic psychology recognises that we cannot do this with human personality. Jung once said that we do not know where the mind ends – that is, we have never been able to plumb its depths. These words are as true now as when he said them.

The complexity of human personality is one reason why the many different approaches touched on in this book have something of value to tell us. Each approach looks at personality from a different angle, and emphasises different areas of importance. But only psychodynamic psychology attempts to address the vast, untapped areas of the human unconscious, and to show some of the ways in which our unconscious influences our conscious lives. Because of the difficulties in exploring the unconscious, we cannot expect psychodynamic psychology to be as precise as the more scientific theories we describe in other chapters. But if we want to look deeply into what it is and what it means to be human, then the psychodynamic approach is an essential part of our exploratory repertoire.

---

psychologist to watch children playing with dolls, and to see what roles they assign to them and how they make the dolls interact with each other. Tests of this kind can also be of use in management training, to help individuals to recognise their own preoccupations and patterns of social behaviour.

As with the Rorschach test, most projective tests lack standardisation. In some cases, there is also disagreement on how the results yielded by them should be assessed. Inevitably, this means that we must be cautious about the conclusions drawn from them. But there seems little doubt that they can give us valuable insights into personality. As Semeonoff (1981) points out, it is wrong to expect from projective techniques the kind of 'validity' we demand in questionnaire tests such as those we shall discuss in Chapter 5. Projective techniques are designed to assess the private world of the individual's *experience* rather than the public world of his or her *behaviour,* and as such they cannot be expected to show what we might term 'scientific precision'. Without such devices as projective techniques, we may have to accept that this private world remains inaccessible to the psychologist.

Implications for the workplace

The implications of psychodynamic theories for those working with children have been made clear at appropriate points in this chapter. However, those working with adults need to identify from the various aspects of personality described by each personality theory those that are most relevant to any given work situation. Different situations require different qualities. For example, Jung's ideas help us to recognise the importance of identifying which particular mode – thinking, feeling, sensing or intuiting – is needed in a given job situation. An individual whose characteristic mode is that of thinking is likely to be much more successful in a highly structured formal and analytical environment than in a fluid and open-ended situation in which there are no predetermined right and wrong answers, and where there is a premium on intuitive modes of behaviour. In situations where many problems have to be solved at short notice, a sensing mode may be most appropriate, and so on.

Overall, when we examine why people behave as they do, we may also need to take ego-defence mechanisms into account. This is particularly the case when studying the way in which people respond to criticism. For example, those who cannot accept legitimate comments designed to help them improve their performance, or who characteristically shift the blame on to others and deny responsibility for their actions, may be defending against their own sense of vulnerability. If we were always being sternly criticised as children, we may develop ego defences to protect our frail self-esteem which persist into adult life. And those with inferiority complexes – often developed in childhood as a result of similar kinds of criticism – may defend against any censure from others, no matter how well-meant, in order to protect their over-sensitive picture of themselves. Without such a defence they may become unduly daunted and disempowered by even the mildest of rebukes.

We can observe these various aspects of personality within ourselves as well as within others. Thus if we are conscious that we have over-reacted to a given situation, we need to identify what it is in us that has brought such an action about. What was it that prompted such defensiveness in response to quite reasonable opposition of one sort or another, or that goaded us into unnecessary anger, or that caused us to feel wounded or undervalued? Psychodynamic theories remind us that any over-reaction is usually a sign of a defensive mechanism at work.

Equally, we need to look at the value systems that we and others operate. Where we meet rigidity and irrationality in these systems we may suspect the operation of a super-ego that has not been brought fully into consciousness where its various moral imperatives can be examined and submitted to rational reflection. Where we find it hard to get to know another person, or when people seem to find it hard to relate well to us, we need to ask whether there is a persona at work that prevents real human feelings and reactions emerging, and genuine communication taking place.

If we think of the mind as an iceberg, with only a small percentage above the surface and in consciousness, this reminds us how important it is to be able to look deeper into the unconscious, so that we can recognise the extent to which hidden and hitherto unacknowledged motives and fears, and unfulfilled hopes and wishes, are affecting behaviour. Knowing oneself – an essential feature of the mature personality – means bringing more and more of the unconscious into the light of consciousness, where it can be understood, worked on, and if necessary put to rest or to more appropriate use.

It is said that failure to bring the conscious and the unconscious minds into fuller communion with each other means that we spend much of our lives as strangers to ourselves. Neurotic anxiety and moral anxiety, as we have seen, are said by psychodynamic psychologists to have their roots deep within us. Bringing them to the surface – by the expedient of asking ourselves *why* do I feel as I do? *Why* did I react as I did? *Why* do I have these irrational fears and anxieties? – can help greatly towards self-discovery. The answers to many of our psychological problems lie within ourselves. We are none of us immune from the effects of our life experiences, from the cradle onwards. Recognising that this is the case not only helps us towards self-understanding, it also helps us towards a greater understanding and tolerance of other people: two forms of under-standing that are essential qualities of the mature personality.

Chapter 4

Humanistic Psychology and Personality

Humanistic models of personality share similarities with psychodynamic ones, and are also primarily idiographic in approach, but they differ from them importantly in that they insist people must be studied as *individuals*, rather than as collections of neuroses or traits. They also differ from Freud, though not from Jung and Adler, in that they insist that personality is never complete. Men and women are regarded as being in a constant state of development throughout life, much as we saw that Erikson considers them to be. Far from having our personalities predominantly fixed in the first five or six years of life, humanistic psychology argues that from birth to old age we are in a constant state of change, or as it is sometimes put, of *becoming something else*.

We have already met two humanistic psychologists, Gordon Allport and Abraham Maslow, whose work we looked at in the discussion of the mature personality in Chapter 2. In many senses, Erikson could also be put into this category. Maslow (1908–70) founded the American Association for Humanistic Psychology in 1962, and in the following decades humanistic psychology achieved rapid growth, exerting in the process considerable influence on the application of psychology to the concerns of daily life.

Humanistic psychology recognises that we are motivated by a whole range of variables over and above the instinctive needs proposed by Freud, or even the need for self-discovery and social relationships (Jung and Adler). Maslow criticises psychodynamic psychologists for missing the essential diversity of human beings. While accepting that we are motivated importantly by the needs that they propose, he rejected the notion that sex or self-discovery or social relationships are the *overriding* drives behind all of us. In his view, there are individual differences that must not be overlooked, and that must be taken into account by psychological theory.

Maslow held that the psychologist can do no more than suggest a general framework of needs or motivation, within which each personality occupies a unique place. Such a framework must take into account the historical fact that men and women are motivated not just by personal needs but also by lofty ideals, by self-sacrifice, by the arts, and by curiosity and the urge towards scientific discovery. The framework he proposed (Maslow, 1970) is therefore in the form of a hierarchy of needs. Once the earlier, more basic needs such as those of the Freudian instincts are satisfied, we become free to develop higher-order needs, and it is these that make us most human. The hierarchy, working from the basic needs upwards, is:

1   physiological needs (for example, food, sex, shelter);
2   safety needs (for example, protection from neglect);
3   social needs (for example, social acceptance);
4   ego needs (for example, self-esteem, status); and
5   self-fulfilment needs (for example, creativity, insight).

The hierarchy is usually shown in the form of a triangle, illustrating the fact that few people progress to the higher levels.

Maslow's hierarchy of needs fits in well with Erikson's developmental stages (see Chapter 3 of this volume). Through the satisfaction of needs 1 and 2 we learn trust; through 3 and 4 we learn competence and identity; and through 5 we learn generativity and self-acceptance. Maslow argued that one of the main reasons why deprived individuals make less progress at school and in work (and indeed why deprived countries make less progress than more affluent ones) is that failure to satisfy basic physiological needs prevents individuals from progressing upwards to the higher-order needs (Level 3 upwards in the hierarchy) which lie behind educational and career motivation, and behind artistic creativity and scientific discovery. Maslow called these higher order needs *meta needs* to distinguish them from more basic ones, and insisted that, although Levels 3 and 5 in the hierarchy include the needs proposed by Adler and Jung respectively, they include much more besides. The individual who goes on to satisfy successfully the needs at the top of the hierarchy achieves the *self-actualisation* we discussed in connection with the mature personality in Chapter 2.

Maslow's theory does not tell us a great deal about how meta needs develop, however, or how we go about measuring them. Many people do not see this as a problem to our understanding, but

---

Work Enthusiasts and Workaholics

In the workplace some people are motivated to work hard because they enjoy what they are doing, while others are driven by the desire for success itself, irrespective of the task concerned. Some people are motivated by co-operation, others by competition. Generally, those who have advanced to Level 5 on Maslow's hierarchy are more likely to belong to the first category in each of these pairs, and to be enthused by work that is intrinsically fulfilling and of clear value to others.

Highly committed individuals who are at Level 5 will tend, in fact, to be what psychologists describe as work enthusiasts, while those at the lower levels may more typically be workaholics. The work enthusiast works hard because the job is worth doing, and if circumstances change he or she is just as able to enjoy leisure and find fulfilment elsewhere. The workaholic, by contrast, is more likely to work hard to satisfy a need for power, or to compensate for self-doubts, or to meet the expectations of internalised parents. If circumstances change, he or she tends to become increasingly restless and dissatisfied with life.

---

scientific psychology depends to a great extent on explanation and measurement. Thus psychologists want to know why one person wants to go fishing while another wants to study quantum physics, and yet another to write poetry; and to know why one person prefers to go out partying while another would rather stay at home with a good book.

Another humanistic psychologist, Carl Rogers, supplies us with some of the answers.

Carl Rogers

Carl Rogers (1902–87), like Freud and Jung, gained much of his experience from clinical work. Besides his influence within this field and within education, he has also had a marked impact on the fields of counselling, business studies and social work. His ideas are not easy to summarise in a few pages (see Evans, 1975 for one of the best introductions), and the interested reader is strongly advised to turn to Rogers' own work for further elaboration (for example, Rogers, 1980).

Rogers is sometimes called a *phenomenologist*, because he placed emphasis not on what actually happens in the individual's environment, but on what the individual *thinks* is happening. In childhood in particular – but also in adult life – the individual defines himself or herself through observing and evaluating his/her own experiences, and often obtains impressions of the world that are quite at variance with those of other people. We only have to listen to the conflicting accounts that two sincere witnesses give of the same event to recognise this. Rogers was thus emphasising not only that personality is unique, but also that each of us inhabits a unique world, a world of subjective experiences known only to ourselves. Certainly we can *tell* other people about these experiences, but, although others appear to understand, they may not do so in the way we do.

Rogers calls the subjective world inhabited by each of us our *phenomenal field*. Like Freud, he accepted that this field contains conscious and unconscious factors. The conscious mind deals mainly with experiences that can be symbolised (that is, put into language, talked about, understood) while the unconscious deals with those that cannot (for example, irrational fears and desires). The primary threat to personality, as Rogers sees it, is that sometimes we symbolise conscious experiences incorrectly – that is, we make sense of them in the wrong way. This happens when, for example, a child interprets the teacher's attempt to help as a sign that he or she is censuring the child, or when an employer interprets a friendly remark from an assistant as over-familiarity. It happens, in fact, every time we misunderstand someone else's motives, or misinterpret their behaviour, or fail to read a situation correctly, to understand the dynamics of the workplace, or to master concepts in an area of skills. As a result of incorrect symbolisation, we often subsequently behave inappropriately (for example, the child may be afraid to ask the teacher for help when he or she needs it; or the assistant may see his/her employer as being arrogant and unapproachable). We may all of us be unnecessarily at odds with people, or behave inappropriately or ineffectually in the workplace, or may mishandle the next step in skill learning. Sometimes these incorrect symbolisations are put right; but sometimes they persist. Where individuals possess a large number of incorrect symbolisations, Rogers says that they are out of *congruence* – that is, their phenomenal fields do not represent the real world.

Although accepting Freud's emphasis on the divide between conscious and unconscious experience, Rogers did not adopt Freud's model of the id, ego and super-ego. Instead, he talked of the *organism,* which is the total person including basic and meta needs, and conscious and unconscious processes; and the *self,* which is the part of the organism that contains all the ideas we have about ourselves – all the things, in fact, that we feel define us as a unique individual. The self also contains the *ideal self,* which, as in Freudian theory, is our picture of the kind of person we would like to become. Unlike Freud though, Rogers saw the ideal self as being sometimes learnt not only from parents and authority figures, but also created by our own meta needs and aspirations.

Just as there should be congruence between the phenomenal field and the real world, so Rogers insisted that there must be congruence between the organism and the self, and between the self and the ideal self. An example will show how this works. In an imaginary world where children can behave exactly as they like all the time, and receive praise for doing so, they would certainly not grow up incongruent. Their picture of the world as a place in which they can do as they like (that is, their phenomenal fields); their own desire to do as they like (that is, their organisms); their picture of themselves as children who always do as they like (that is, their selves); and their picture of themselves as children who ought to do as they like (that is, their ideal selves) would all be completely in harmony, and therefore in congruence with each other.

However, the world is not a place in which any of us can always do as we like. Inevitably, therefore, from childhood onwards we all develop some incongruence. We have to learn to avoid physical dangers, however enticing, and we have to study the wishes and the rights of others. Individuals who want to obey the dictates of their organisms and unfairly assert their will over others have to be prevented. The child who demands the constant attention of parents has to learn that they, too, have lives of their own to lead.

It is indeed Rogers' ideas on how we can best learn to live with some degree of incongruence, and function effectively socially and in the world of work, that represent his main contribution to applied psychology. Rogers agreed with Freud that we start life selfishly, but he attributed this not so much to the basic drives of the id as to the simple fact that in our early years we each inhabit our own phenomenal field. We do not have the experience to know that other people have different phenomenal fields from our own, and are not there simply for our benefit. We have to *learn* about the phenomenal fields of others. We do this best by imaginatively putting ourselves in their shoes and realising what it must feel like to be them. This holds good not just in childhood but throughout life. Good managers understand what it is like to be subordinates. Good subordinates understand at least something of what it is like to be a manager. A good teacher understands what it is like to be a child.

This illustrates the enormous importance of communication. The more people discuss how the world seems to them (that is, their phenomenal field) with others, the more readily does this understanding emerge. Communication and understanding are demanding processes. It is often much easier to blame others than to find out the strains and pressures and misunderstandings under which they may be labouring. Nevertheless, understanding leads not only to greater harmony in interpersonal relationships but potentially also to enhanced efficiency and effectiveness among all concerned.

As understanding grows, so the temptation to label others decreases. Labelling people in negative ways (for example, as incompetent or lazy or unintelligent) tends to fossilise – so to speak – our view of them within our phenomenal field. If children, subordinates and others who value our judgement learn that we are labelling them in this way they may incorporate such labels into their pictures of themselves, or may protect their self-esteem at the cost of downgrading their good opinion of us. The result of incorporating our labels into their self-image, explained Rogers, is likely to be a state of *incongruence* between the organism, which has an innate desire to see itself as being valued and effective, and the self, which now sees itself as unvalued and ineffective. This may lead to the creation of a series of ego-defence mechanisms, which Rogers agreed are very much the ones defined by Freud. Incongruent people, at odds with themselves, tend to be tense and anxious, afraid of losing control, defensive and often rigid in their thinking, and unable to discover the sense of identify on which Erikson placed so much stress. Ultimately, they are in danger of losing touch with important aspects of reality, and, should the repressed wishes of the organism break through into consciousness, may lose any consistent sense of self and be at risk of developing excessive neurotic anxiety.

Congruent people, on the other hand, are able to develop (that is, to actualise themselves) along the lines laid down for them by inheritance. They become, in other words, the people their inheritance 'intended' them to be. Freed from internal conflicts, they are able to turn their attention outwards, to empathise with other people, to enjoy art and beauty, to interest themselves in science and discovery. Through this broadening of the personality they come to experience the satisfaction to be gained from serving and helping others, from engaging in creative activity, and from improving their quality of life generally. Because they inhabit realistic and rewarding phenomenal fields they also have the courage to be themselves, even when this risks going against the opinions or behaviour of their peers.

Rogers described congruent people as *genuine* (open to their own feelings and ready to self-disclose); *accepting* (offering others unconditional positive regard); and *empathic* (ready to listen to others and identify with their difficulties). Not only are these the qualities of the congruent person, they are also the qualities that nurture growth and congruence in others, whether the relationship is between parent or teacher and child, therapist and client, leader and group, or employer and workers. Rogers claimed in fact that from childhood one of our strongest organismic needs is for the *positive regard* and *empathy* of the significant others in our lives, and ideally for their love and approval. It is this need that makes us obey teachers and parents in our early years, even when this obedience means forgoing other organismic wishes. Many of our self concepts – including our ideal self, the person we want to become – are formed in response to the need to gain and to keep this positive regard. Where such regard is only given to us conditionally within the important relationships in our lives (parents, partners, colleagues, superiors), and where there is the constant risk of its being withdrawn as a punishment for unwanted behaviour, there is a strong tendency to sacrifice more and more of our organismic wishes in order to retain it – at the risk of becoming less and less congruent. This point was referred to in the discussion of self-esteem in Chapter 2 of this volume. Satisfactory personality development and maintenance is unlikely if we go in constant fear that the important people in our lives are ready to turn their positive feelings for us on and off as they please.

Rogers' insistence on this point, and on the uniqueness of each person's phenomenal field, is evident in the techniques of counselling developed by him and by his followers. Counselling is now widely used within the workplace, and Rogers' methods have been particularly influential here. Known as *client-centred* (see, for example, Rogers, 1957), these methods place emphasis on helping clients to work out the solutions to their own problems in an atmosphere of positive regard and empathic understanding, rather than on the counsellor acting as an authority figure and telling clients what is 'wrong' with them and what they should do to put things right. Because each client is unique, client-centred therapy insists there can be no ready-made formula to offer them, as tends to happen in the forms of counselling derived from psychodynamic theories. The fact that the counsellor is prepared to listen to clients; to accept them for what they are; to prompt them gently when they have difficulty in self-expression; to help them to identify what is happening within their phenomenal fields; to locate areas where incongruence has occurred; to support their attempts at dealing with their problems; to show understanding of their difficulties; and to be generally non-judgemental and encouraging, are in Rogers' view the keys to successful counselling. And the warmth and friendliness of the Rogerian therapist and counsellor is often in marked contrast to the more remote, objective approach of the Freudian.

Rogers' description of the correct counselling interview (whether it takes place between therapist and client, or between manager and employee) can be summarised as follows:

(i)   The client, employee or child comes for help;
(ii)   The counsellor encourages free expression;
(iii)   The client describes the situation with which he/she needs help;
(iv)   The counsellor accepts and helps clarify the situation;
(v)   Positive feelings are expressed;
(vi)   Positive impulses are recognised;
(vii)   Insight into the real reasons behind the situation is developed;
(viii) Choices for handling the situation are clarified;
(ix)   Positive actions are decided upon; and
(x)   Client insight into self increases.

In even the most difficult child or the most hardened adult, Rogers claimed that the need to be heard empathically and with positive regard is always there. The experienced counsellor can usually spot the form this need takes, and use it supportively in order to increase the client's self-understanding and rehabilitation.

Rogers has shown that a simple technique called *Q-sorting*, can be a further help in exploring this need and other aspects of the individual's phenomenal field. So simple is the technique in fact,

---

The Good Listener

Rogers' work emphasises the importance of being a good listener. The ability to listen is, in fact, the secret of good counselling – and also much of the secret of good management practices in the workplace. The world is not short of people who want to talk, but it is rather less well supplied with those who can – and are prepared to – listen.

Good listening involves two particular qualities. The first is a genuine interest in other people and in their concerns, worries and ideas. And the second is the ability to concentrate on what the other person is saying without allowing the mind to wander or to succumb to the temptation to interrupt with one's own experiences, judgements or conclusions. Good listening is the quickest way to get to know another person, and to understand and appreciate their strengths and weaknesses. Good listening also signals to the other person that they are valued and respected, and that one does not pretend to have a monopoly of the truth – other people also have ideas and opinions that are worth hearing.

---

and so non-threatening, that it can be used without specialist training, and is of particular value in the workplace.

In Q-sorting, a number of cards are prepared, each with a statement relating to the area of the client's life being explored. For example, the cards may carry self-descriptive statements such as 'I try hard at most things I undertake', 'I am popular', 'I like my own company', and the client is asked to sort them into five (more rarely seven) piles, ranging from a pile which contains the descriptions that are 'most like me' down to one containing descriptions which are 'least like me'. To take a further example, the cards may carry statements to do with attitudes to work such as 'I prefer working alone', 'Generally I am undervalued by my superiors', I don't feel my job is secure', and the client asked to sort them into piles ranging from 'statements with which I most agree' down to 'statements with which I least agree'. The number of cards a client can place in any one pile is usually restricted, so that we get a fair spread across the piles (often what is known as a *normal distribution* is used, with most cards being placed in the middle piles, tapering off to the least cards at the two extremes). The total number of cards is not critical, but a minimum of twenty-five and a maximum of fifty is about right.

Q-sorting gives us a useful picture of how people view themselves, and, of course, we can repeat the process, using different cards, for any part of their phenomenal field we wish to explore (for example, 'the job I would like', 'my ideal person', 'the things I find most difficult in my work').

Another versatile and equally simple test is Osgood's Semantic Differential (Osgood *et al*. 1957), in which a relevant concept is written at the head of a sheet of paper (for example, 'the person I am'), and the bi-polar pairs of adjectives that might define this concept are listed below, for example:

The person I am

strong . . . . *weak*
sad . . . . *happy*
honest . . . . *dishonest*
cruel . . . . *kind*
active . . . . *passive*

The individual is asked to place a tick in the appropriate position in the continuum between each pair of adjectives. For example, people who conceive themselves as being very strong would put a tick nearest to 'strong' (furthest from 'weak'). At the end of the exercise, a useful profile of the individual's self-concept emerges. If required, the exercise can be repeated for 'the person I would like to be', and correlations sought between the responses to the two concepts in order to examine the degree of congruence between the individual's self and his or her ideal self.

The Semantic Differential can also be used to explore concepts relating to professional issues. For example 'my job' or 'my professional goals'. In the case of children, each subject in the curriculum can be used as a concept, and pairs of adjectives or descriptions such as 'easy–difficult', 'interesting–dull', 'relevant to my future–irrelevant to my future' used. Colleagues, friends or, if appropriate, partners can also be asked to rate the individual on the same concepts so that the extent of congruence between how individuals see themselves and how others see them can be ascertained. As with Q-sorting, the Semantic Differential can be used to explore any aspect of an individual's phenomenal field.

Criticisms of humanistic psychology

Nothing is more confusing than a book that constantly describes theories only to knock them down again a few pages later. But in a field such as personality, with all its perplexities and imponderables, a certain amount of knocking-down is unavoidable if an accurate picture is to be presented. So, as with psychodynamic theories, some reference must be made to the drawbacks of humanistic psychology.

The most obvious criticism is that none of the measuring techniques that humanistic psychologists use really takes into account unconscious factors. And, of course, techniques such as Q-sorting allow people to give deliberately inaccurate responses in an attempt to show themselves in a favourable light. At other times, individuals may strive for accuracy, but be unable to make perceptive distinctions between the people or events with which we are confronting them.

Humanistic theories present a more optimistic picture of personality than do psychodynamic ones, but is this picture necessarily true? It is sometimes suggested that writers such as Maslow provide us primarily with an exercise in raising self-esteem. This is inaccurate, but concepts such as Maslow's meta needs are difficult to demonstrate scientifically. We know that men and women have an inbuilt urge to meet basic survival needs, and that they will go to great lengths to satisfy this urge, but it is much harder to demonstrate that they have an inbuilt, as opposed to a purely acquired, need to seek self-fulfilment and the deeper meaning of life. Nevertheless, research into humanistic theories, as summarised for example by Smith (1981) indicates that even difficult areas such as self-actualisation can be subjected to research investigation. Both here and in terms of Rogers's theory of the self, such research has tended to support the ideas concerned, and the various practical techniques derived from them.

Rogers' phenomenological approach nevertheless attracts another criticism, which is that, if we each inhabit a *subjective* world, no one can really know what the *objective* world is like, and it thus becomes nonsense to talk about whether the client's constructs approximate to it or not. This is the kind of problem philosophers like to argue about, and we had better leave them to get on with it. Common sense tells us that there appears to be a workable consensus among us as to what everyday reality is about, and we have to get on with the job of helping each other to cope with this reality. On balance, the humanistic approach seems to be one of the most useful ways we have of thinking about personality, and of studying individual differences within the framework of the whole personality.

The final criticism levelled at humanistic psychologists, and one that leads us on to Chapter 5, is that they neglect the social context in which much human behaviour takes place, and which seems highly instrumental in helping to shape behaviour. True, they lay great stress on the importance of social relationships, and Rogers has shown how groups of people can help each other to tackle individual problems through the open communication of feelings and ideas. But humanistic psychologists as a whole often seem to take insufficiently into account the fact that psychological conflicts on the one hand, and many short- and long-term goals on the other, can result less from such things as personal inadequacy or ambition than from the daily pressures that come from working with other people. It may be that these pressures make personality less consistent than the humanistic psychologists assume it to be, and that even people with mature personalities change more from day to day than humanistic psychology suggests.

In the next chapter we shall look at what are called *field theories* of personality. Like humanistic theories, their emphasis is on the individual, but in this case they place the individual within a social field that contains forces and pressures which pull first in one direction and then in another. They are of particular value to those studying the workplace, where much of what happens takes place within the social context.

Chapter 5

Field and Social Models of Personality

Field models are similar to humanistic models in that they take into account the whole person, but differ in maintaining that variations between people in personality are occasioned less by inner processes than by the individual's psychological or life 'space' – that is, the context, primarily social, within which we live our lives. One of the first, and still one of the most useful, field theories was advanced by Kurt Lewin (1880–1945), widely regarded as being the father of group dynamics. Lewin's theory is represented diagramatically by three ellipses, one inside the other (Figure 5.1). The innermost ellipse and the second ellipse represent the *person* (P), with the former being the inner world of thoughts and fantasies, and the latter the perceptual and motor faculties with which we make contact with the external environment. The outer ellipse represents the immediate aspects of the environment (the *psychological environment*, or E), while all the space outside this represents *the foreign hull*, the rest of our environment, which is too remote to touch us much as people. Together, the three circles form our *life space*, the psychological limits of our existence. Within this life space, the personality is formed, but Lewin rejected the notion of personality as a constant entity, or as necessarily following a set developmental path. As a result of the dynamic forces at work within the life field, the individual is subject to constant change, both influencing and being influenced by the environment at all times.

Lewin elaborated his theory to deal with the mechanics of how P becomes modified and developed in response to the events that take place in E, but for our purposes this adds little of practical value to the insights into such matters that we have already gained from psychodynamic theories and humanistic psychology. What concerns us is the interaction between P and E, and to understand this we must first look at how E is structured.

Lewin (1935) saw E as being divided ('differentiated') into a number of regions, each of which has relatively greater or lesser influence on the individual. Early in life, these regions are few, consisting of the family and the immediate home environment, but, as individuals grow older, new ones are added. Progressively, we start school, make friends, join organisations, study for qualifications, pursue careers, marry and have children. In consequence, our worlds become increasingly complex. Each of these regions has boundaries between it and the others. In the case of children, school is a different social environment from home; home is different from the peer group or the youth club, and so on. Each of these regions is likely to have different values, operate different standards, and expect different behaviour from the individual. In adult life, the expanding number of regions in which we operate may each have their own unique characteristics and (perhaps mutually conflicting) ways of being Even different sections or departments within the same workplace may represent very different regions.

Where the boundaries between regions are low, the regions are said to be in *communication,* and individuals can move easily through their life space, or, as Lewin puts it, they can experience satisfactory *locomotion.* The mores of work and home, of the peer group, and of interest and cultural groups may be in broad agreement with each other. In this case, the individual finds it relatively easy to behave in much the same way in each environment, so providing a consistent view of self and of the world.

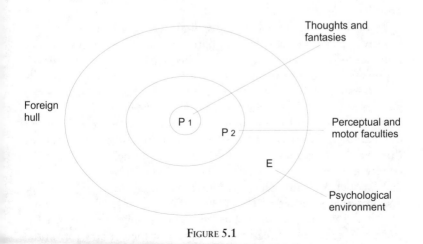

FIGURE 5.1

Obviously, locomotion between regions can be of several different kinds – social, vocational, intellectual, sporting, spiritual and so on. A *valence* is the degree of importance that individuals attach to each region (positive if the region is well-liked or useful; negative if it is unpopular or threatening), and a *vector is* the force that makes them want to move into, or out of, a region. The stronger the valence, positive or negative, the stronger the corresponding vector, positive or negative (for example, we may have a strong positive valence to move into employment if we are job-hunting, and a negative valence to keep us out of courts of law).

Psychological problems within P, such as Erikson's 'search for identity' (see Chapter 2 of this volume) stem in Lewin's view largely from the individual's inability to move easily between the regions in E, and particularly from conflicts that arise between these regions. These conflicts are of three main types.

Type One occurs when the individual is confronted by two positive valences of equal force, but the barrier dividing them is too high, as for example, when home and work (or school) teach value systems that are in conflict with each other, or if success at work can only be obtained by neglecting one's family, or vice versa. A Type One conflict can be resolved by moving out of one of the regions concerned, if this is possible (for example, by changing jobs), or by changing oneself in some way (for example, by lowering one's aspirations at work so that more time can be spent with the family), or – as we shall see in due course below – by developing two quite different sets of values and behaviour, one for use in each of the groups.

Type Two occurs when individuals are confronted by two negative valences of equal force, both of which they wish to avoid. For example, a man may desperately want a transfer from a department where he dislikes the work, but finds that a transfer is only possible if he moves to a department where he dislikes the people. A Type Two conflict can only be resolved either by rejecting both alternatives (for example, by resigning one's post), or by downgrading the importance of one or other of the alternatives (for example, by abandoning the need to like one's work or one's colleagues).

Type Three occurs when the individual is confronted by positive and negative valences of equal force. For example, the individual may badly want promotion, but finds this is only possible if he or she agrees to move to a less desirable part of the country (or, in the case of a child, by moving into a class or a set with an unpopular teacher). Type Three conflicts can only be resolved by an objective assessment of the respective merits of the two alternatives, and the recognition that success in life often involves making hard career, social and personal choices.

Group decision-making

Lewin and later social psychologists have looked not only at how the individual moves between and operates within regions and groups, but at how groups themselves function. In doing so they have particularly identified both the strengths and weaknesses of group decision-making (for example, Fincham and Rhodes, 1992). Good decisions appear to depend to a great extent on the presence of:

(i)   *Group cohesion* – all members of the group share common aims and a common desire for successful outcomes;

(ii)   *Group participation* – each member of the group feels heard and valued, and feels able to make his or her contribution;

(iii) *Group communication* – each member of the group is subsequently kept fully informed of outcomes; and

(iv)   *Good group leadership* – the group has a leader who is able to define the identity and function of the group in a way that is, acceptable to group members, who responds warmly to each group member and protects their self-esteem and standing within the group, who gives appropriate rewards to group members (acknowledgement and praise), who keeps the group focused on essentials, and who operated democratically and delegates appropriate responsibilities.

However, research shows that groups are not necessarily better than individuals at decision-making. They typically take up a great deal of organisational time, are likely in some situations to be more conservative in their decisions than are individuals (the so-called *caution shift),* and in order to achieve group polarisation may put pressure on group members who dissent from the prevailing norm, thus creating a Type three conflict for them in that they may wish to disagree with the group, but know that doing so will lead to isolation within it, or expulsion from it. Pressures from the rest of the group can also be brought to bear on those individuals who prefer to work alongside the group but without becoming a member. The group can make things so difficult for such people that they may be faced with Lewin's Type Two conflict – they have no wish to join the group, but also have no wish to face the unpopularity and discrimination they experience as an outsider.

The term *groupthink* (see for example, Reason, 1987) is sometimes used for the kind of thinking that prompts groups to act in these ways. In addition to making life difficult for individuals, groupthink can lead to poor corporate decisions, particularly if the group feels so confident of its own superiority and powers of judgement that it disregards the warnings that may come from outside. It may also lead to conflict *between* groups. The build-up of strong groupthink loyalties and commitments to one's own group tend to lead to feelings of rivalry and even antagonism towards other groups and their members. Those who try to liaise between the groups may then be confronted by a Lewin Type One conflict, in that both groups may have equal valences for the liaison person, but the barriers between the groups may be too high. Unable to bring them together, he or she may have to resolve the conflict by siding reluctantly with one group against the other.

Depersonalisation and conformity

Groupthink may become so strong that it leads to the *depersonalisation* (or *deindividuation*) of individual group members – that is, he or she plays down personality characteristics, attitudes, opinions, interests, and even judgement, in order to conform to the group. A classic series of experiments demonstrating this was carried out in 1955 by Asch, who asked groups of university students to tackle a simple perceptual experiment that involved comparing the relative lengths of three straight lines. Before the experiment, all except one student in each group was secretly briefed to give the wrong answer, and attention was then focused on the naïve (non-briefed) students to see what their reactions would be. Although the error involved in the wrong answer was abundantly clear, no less than 37 per cent of the naïve students agreed with the rest of their group rather than take on the role of odd man out. In the case of this 37 per cent, *social control* proved strong enough to overcome *personal control*.

Subsequent experiments by Crutchfield (1955) showed that individuals who manifested this kind of conformist, depersonalised behaviour tend to be defensive, rigid and moralistic in personality, and intolerant of ambiguity (that is, they have a need for things to be cut and dried – in itself a sign of insecurity), while those who refuse to conform are more independent, open, confident and secure. Other research shows that conformers are anxious for social approval and tend to have low self-esteem. They are inclined towards authoritarianism, and thus prone to offer unquestioning obedience to the group and their superiors, and to demand unquestioning obedience from their own subordinates. Myers (1998) reports that the pressures towards conformity to the group are further strengthened when:

(i) Individuals feel (or are made to feel) incompetent or insecure when acting independently;

(ii) The group consists of three or more people (though increasing the group size beyond three does not add significantly to increases in conformist pressures);

(ii) The rest of the group are unanimous in their decisions;

(iv) The individual's behaviour and attitudes are public to the rest of the group; and

(v) The group has prestige and status in the eyes of the individual.

However, in experiments such as those by Asch, conformity to authority or to the group meant taking over values or judgements that were patently incorrect. When such values or judgements are clearly correct or have been arrived at by appropriately democratic processes, it can be a sign of personality aberrations to refuse to conform. To be the odd one out in such circumstances, particularly if as a result group action is inhibited or important decisions are delayed or abandoned, can be a sign of attention-seeking behaviour and a bid for significance. By controlling the debate and preventing forward movement the individual concerned demonstrates power over other people's actions and feelings.

Just as group pressures can lead to individual members becoming depersonalised, they can also lead to the group depersonalising other groups. Such depersonalisation means that other groups come to be seen as having no value, and thus are fair game for contemptuous or even cruel treatment – as happens in gang culture, in the treatment of ethnic minorities, and even in the rivalries between business organisations. Zimbardo (Zimbardo *et al.*, 1973) demonstrated this depersonalisation of one group by another all too graphically in an experiment at Stanford University in which he randomly divided male student volunteers into 'prisoners' and 'guards', with instructions that they role-play their parts. The two groups were placed in a simulated prison, with the former given prisoners' clothes and

---

Role Play

Used from early childhood to old age, role play is an excellent way of expressing emotions, of learning social skills, and of discovering new and often valuable areas of the self. It appears in fact to be a natural feature of our behaviour, as in the spontaneous role playing of young children. Increasingly, formal role play exercises are an important part of management training, of personal/social education, and of developmental activities such as psychodrama and dramatherapy.

The standard method of role play with adults and older children is to give each person a brief scenario and the outline of the character they are expected to improvise within it (for example, job applicant; angry shopper; employer breaking news of redundancy; anxious individual explaining his/her professional, financial or other problems). The work is done in pairs or in small groups, and essentially gives participants permission to act out personal qualities which for various reasons may have been repressed or left undeveloped. In addition, participants are able to experiment with interactive social strategies, and to benefit from the subsequent comments and feedback of the rest of the group.

Role play thus helps individuals to recognise that they have the potential for much desirable behaviour that hitherto they have felt to be beyond them, and to acquire the social and interpersonal skills necessary in both personal and professional life.

---

locked in barren cells, and the latter given wardens' uniforms, clubs, whistles and a set of rules they were told to enforce. After only one or two days of conscious role-playing the simulation became too real. The guards developed disparaging attitudes towards the prisoners, devised cruel and degrading routines for them, and became hostile and aggressive, while the prisoners became depressed, angry and genuinely distressed. The experiment, scheduled to run two weeks, was terminated after only six days.

Putting people in uniform or giving them other trappings of office can strengthen the depersonalisation process both for them and for their victims. In another experiment, Zimbardo (1970) found that women students from New York University, when dressed in Klu Klux Klan-style hoods, delivered twice as many electric shocks to a victim as did those not wearing hoods (in fact, the shocks were simulated, and the 'victim' was role-playing, but, crucially, the women delivering the 'shocks' were unaware of this fact).

Results such as these show not only the power of in-group and out-group norms, but the extent to which, frighteningly, people can become the characters they are playing. What we *do*, it seems, we risk *becoming*. Our behaviour – particularly when we are 'given permission' by group norms to behave in ways contrary to our original beliefs – can change our attitudes radically. However, it is fair to point out that the human tendency to behave in this way can work for good as well as for ill. Being placed with sensitive and caring groups, or being asked to role-play the part of people with these qualities, can be a powerful aid in turning round unwanted behaviour in both children and adults.

Group dynamics

As discussed earlier, on occasion, individuals may be members of more than one group, each with very different sets of values, and unless they can leave one of the groups they may develop two quite separate ways of behaving in order to resolve the Type One conflict involved. A classic piece of research by Hartshorne and May in 1928 showed that children vary their interpretation of values such as honesty depending on whether the context of their behaviour is their classmates or outsiders (for example, it is all right to be dishonest with a teacher but not with classmates). It would be unrealistic to suppose that adults necessarily behave differently, at least in cases where membership of both groups remains important.

Alongside his interest in individuals within a group, Lewin was also very interested in the group itself. As mentioned earlier, the whole subject of *group dynamics*, in fact, stems largely from his work. In group dynamics, the group (whether an organisation, a school, a class or a team) can be thought of as an enlarged version of the psychological environment, E, defined on page 82 in our discussion – that is, as an ever-changing field in which each individual represents a region. Some regions have stronger positive or negative valences than others (that is, some people are particularly co-operative, or popular, or disruptive), and individuals are pushed and pulled by various vectors, towards or away from the regions around them. The group thus builds up its own internal tensions and conflicts, such as subgroup rivalries and hostilities. It also builds up group norms, hierarchies and pecking orders. It develops group fads that come and go, and the popularity of individuals within the group can wax and wane.

Attempts by Lewin and others to find which qualities of personality mark people out from the rest of their group as stars (extra popular) or as leaders suggest that these qualities vary from group to group. A person who is successful in one group may be relatively ignored in another. Stars, however, tend generally to be above the group average in intelligence and in confidence, and Kelvin (1970) suggests that most leaders have the ability, as we have already seen, to define the group (that is, to give it direction, identity and standards), and to act as a source of rewards for group members (for example, by conferring approval or status).

Good leadership also goes with the ability to assess accurately the motives of individual group members (Maehr and Braskamp, 1986). Some members will be motivated by accomplishment and achievement, others by recognition, others by affiliation (that is, by strong feelings of belonging to the group or unit), and others by power. Having assessed motives, the leader can then adjust incentives and rewards accordingly. In addition, good leaders set goals for individuals which they recognise as being reasonable and achievable, and give group members good feedback and progress reports. Failure to achieve reasonable and realistic goals affects people's views of themselves, and inclines them towards self-blame, whereas failure to achieve unrealistic goals leaves them blaming and thinking less of their leaders (White *et al.*, 1995).

However, although leaders can to some extent act out the good leadership role, their individual personalities will mean that some leadership styles come more easily to them than others. There are many ways that leadership styles can be classified, and one of the simplest and most effective is into *task leadership style* and *social leadership style*. The former is typically goal-directed, task-centred, standard-setting and directive, while the latter is mediatory, more democratic and people-centred, and more concerned with building team spirit. Both styles of leadership are applicable in the right context though, not surprisingly, social leadership is usually better for morale (Burger, 1987). Again not surprisingly (this time in the light of our discussion of emotional intelligence in Chapter 2), women are more inclined towards social leadership, and men towards task leadership. Men, it seems, are more likely to distance their subordinates socially and to act out the role of a powerful other – that is, to talk assertively, to express opinions, to interrupt, to smile infrequently, and initiate social touching rather than allow subordinates to do so. Women, by contrast, are more likely to express support, to hear others out, and to invite their views (Eagly and Johnson, 1990).

However, in spite of the research evidence, we must not get too carried away by these gender and personality stereotypes. In any case, the truly effective leader is able to practise both task leadership and social leadership skills, and to do so not as sets of learned techniques but because they arise naturally from the kind of person he or she genuinely happens to be. Effective leaders will also have charisma, a quality difficult to define but unmistakable when we meet it. And he or she will also naturally favour what is called Theory Y of workers rather than Theory X (McGregor, 1960) – that is, he or she will assume that, when given a challenge and freedom, workers are motivated to achieve self-esteem and to demonstrate competence and creativity (Theory Y), rather than to assume that they are basically lazy, error-prone, interested only in money, and need driving from above (Theory X).

Lewin and group training

From the 1960s onwards, a movement has grown up around the ideas of Lewin and of humanistic psychologists such as Rogers, in which the group rather than an individual counsellor or trainer is used to help individuals come to terms with personality problems, or with social or occupational conflicts or misunderstandings. Such group work has been found to be an effective way of helping managers and workers to move towards increased mutual understanding, and to produce a more productive, goal-directed and effective working environment. Operating originally under such titles as 't-groups', 'encounter groups' and 'sensitivity groups' the spectrum has widened to include 'self-help groups', 'development groups', 'support groups', and even some specialised 'focus groups'. The main aim is to allow individuals to discuss their personal, professional or work-related problems in the presence of others, to observe how others react, to secure their understanding, and to explore new methods of responding, relating and organising in place of existing, less satisfactory ones.

Such groups are usually run on democratic or semi-democratic lines, and can be very effective in breaking down the barriers that separate people from each other, and in enhancing a spirit of mutual respect, sympathy and co-operation. Colleagues can become less self-centred, misunderstandings can be resolved, managers can become less remote, and workers can become more identified with the aims of their employers and better able to appreciate their problems. The end result of a successful group is that everyone feels more valued, understood, listened to, and empowered.

Under a trained leader, who remains largely unobtrusive but who monitors proceedings and acts skilfully to keep the discussion focused, to protect where necessary the more vulnerable participants and to ensure that everyone has an opportunity to speak if they wish, group work has proved highly effective in therapeutic and professional contexts, and in the training of managers, personnel officers, social workers and others involved in the field of human relationships. However, groups with inadequately trained leaders can do more harm than good. Outspoken personal comments can lead to hostility, resentment and unhelpful conflict, and can even inflict psychological wounds on sensitive people. On other occasions, people may disclose personal or professional details about themselves which they later regret, or which they find are used against them by unscrupulous colleagues. In addition, there is a risk that some people may use the openness of a group to to settle old scores, or to exercise personal power. For a group to work well, an atmosphere of mutual trust, positive regard and empathic understanding must be allowed to develop. To facilitate this, a clear set of rules needs to be agreed upon by everyone at the outset, and observed from then on. An example of five such rules is as follows:

Each group member agrees to:

(i)   Respect other group members and avoid giving deliberate offence;
(ii) Refrain from personal attacks on other group members;
(iii) Adhere to the timetable laid down for group meetings;
(iv) Observe strict confidentiality, and refrain from discussing group matters with outsiders; and
(v)   Allow everyone who wishes to do so to make their contribution, and to avoid monopolising the discussion.

On balance, group training is something that has to be handled carefully, and is often best left to the experts. The same is true of *family therapy*, which is a form of group therapy involving only the members of the nuclear family. The focal point here is that the personality and general behaviour problems of a child or adult family member can only be understood correctly if the individual concerned is seen and treated within the context of the home circle – that is, within the context of the immediate psychological environment. Thus the child is seen by the therapist in the company of parents, siblings, and any other members of the household. The family group is encouraged to speak freely about its tensions and difficulties, and about the way in which each person perceives and relates to the others, and gradually the causes of the child's problems (and of the problems arising in consequence) are allowed to emerge. With greater understanding of each other's difficulties and with the help of the therapist, the family becomes able to develop strategies of behaviour for improving domestic life (see Satir, 1972; Shadish *et al.*, 1993).

Values and conflict resolution

Research suggests that where conflicts arise with authority figures over such things as values, many individuals tend, as in their relationships with the group, to resolve them by conforming to the values of their superiors. In an important but controversial series of experiments Milgram (1974) produced evidence to show the lengths to which some people will go in inflicting pain upon a third person when they are told to do so by a prestigious lab-coated experimenter seen as representing scientific research. The individuals taking part in the experiments were recruited through a newspaper advertisement, and the protocol required each of them, working singly, to administer increasingly powerful electric shocks to an unseen subject (whom they had already been warned had a heart problem) in the next room each time he made a mistake in a memory experiment. As the shocks became stronger the unseen subject began to yell with pain and to demand the experiment be terminated. Nevertheless, the experimenter calmly instructed the individual administering the shocks to continue, even after the subject fell ominously silent and appeared unable to make a response of any kind.

Sixty-three per cent of those participating (men aged 20 to 50), while typically evidencing great reluctance and inner conflict, continued beyond the point of silence and right up to the administration of the final shock of 450 volts. Of the 35 per cent who withdrew from the experiment in disgust, none did so prior to administering 300 volts (enough to produce a very nasty shock indeed). The whole thing was in fact a set-up. The unseen subject was an actor, and the shock generator was a dummy. But the point was that participants were unaware of this, and so believed that real suffering was taking place. The main factor in their compliance with the instructions of the experimenter was what psychologists call *ideological justification*, that is, the willingness to accept a set of beliefs held by someone in authority which appear to justify – and give permission for – behaviour that normally one would regard as unacceptable. In the case of the Milgram experiments the ideology had to do with the semi-divine aura surrounding modern science. But it could just as well be an ideology associated with a professional or commercial organisation, a political party, or a religious leader. For many children, it can be to do with parents, teachers, or dominating friends – in fact, with anyone in the role of an authority figure.

In subsequent experiments, Milgram identified some of the situational factors most likely to lead to ideological justification.

(i)   The person giving the orders is close at hand and perceived to be a legitimate authority figure;

(ii)   The authority figure is supported by a prestigious institution, such as a top university;

(iii) The victim is depersonalised by being placed in another room; and

(iv) There are no role models for defiance (that is, no other people present seen to be defying authority).

Conformity

It is interesting to ask ourselves to what extent we are prepared to sacrifice our own values, beliefs and ways of behaving in order to conform to the demands of the organisation or the group, or those in authority over us. In making this sacrifice, we also sacrifice part of our personal identity. How much of this identity should we be prepared to lose?

We can ask the same question in reverse. To what extent do we expect the adults or the children for whom we are responsible to change their way of being in order to conform to our demands and expectations? Are we making unfair demands on them? Are we handicapping their individuality, and perhaps setting up role confusions for them? What is the right balance between conformity and individuality, between corporate or institutional identity and personal identity?

Achievement motivation

The readiness with which people change their behaviour to conform to group or authority norms leads one to question how strong is their basic motivation. Are they motivated primarily to obey personal values and to pursue personal goals, or primarily to obtain social acceptance? Maslow's hierarchy of needs which were discussed in the previous chapter, would suggest that the desire for social acceptance – the third level of the hierarchy – is a fundamental need for all of us, but that self-actualisation and maturity of personality imply the ability to move beyond this need once it has achieved basic satisfaction.

However, Lewin and other social psychologists place great stress on the continuing need for social acceptance and status for most of us. There is agreement therefore between Lewin's ideas and Adler's concept of the need for superiority (see Chapter 3). Lewin contended that most of what Maslow called our meta needs stem from the way in which the psychological environment satisfies our search for social acceptance and status. This is somewhat at variance with the insistence by humanistic psychologists that meta needs owe much of their strength to our innate psychological endowment, but clearly both personal and social factors play their part in these needs, with the relative strength of each varying from need to need, and from person to person.

The need for social acceptance and status – indeed, for all aspects of what is known as *achievement motivation* – can be studied in various ways, among which is a technique known as *content analysis*, a very useful one in the workplace. Content analysis identifies the number of times particular themes occur in the responses given by individuals during interviews or in written work. McLelland (1961), an early exponent of this technique, found that when people's responses to projective tests such as the TAT pictures (see Chapter 3) are analysed it becomes apparent that many give interpretations related to achievement goals (for example, when looking at a picture of someone sitting thoughtfully at a desk, they may say such things as 'He wants to succeed', or 'She is dreaming of becoming a doctor'). Responses such as these demonstrate high levels of achievement motivation (called by McLelland 'need for achievement', or 'N'Ach' for short), and follow-up studies indicate that the individuals concerned do set higher than average goals for themselves, even taking ability and intelligence into account. They also experience above-average success in attaining them. By contrast, those manifesting low achievement motivation either set themselves very easy goals which they know they can achieve, or very difficult ones which are out of their reach and which they will not be blamed for failing to reach (Geen, 1984; McCall, 1994).

More straightforward pencil-and-paper tests of achievement (such as that of Mehrabian, 1969) have also been with us for some time, and studies show the importance of social factors in prompting its development. Generally, individuals with high achievement motivation are those who are encouraged in childhood to be independent and to acquire new skills at a younger than average age. As children they seem relatively free from unnecessary restrictions, and are likely to receive physical affection as a reward for achievement. Rosen and d'Andrade (1959) found that even in very early childhood high N'Ach individuals are not only given more parental encouragement when engaged in such tasks as brick-building, they are also given more affection on the task's successful completion. They are also less likely to be offered over-detailed instructions on how the job should be done, and less likely to encounter parental irritation in the event of failure. (Certain obvious similarities suggest themselves between these parents and the parents of Coopersmith's high self-esteem boys described in Chapter 2 of this volume.) Later studies confirm these and similar findings, and suggest strongly that high achievement has emotional as well as cognitive roots in childhood (Dweck and Elliott, 1983).

This suggests that the foundations of strong achievement motivation, as with many other aspects of personality, arise in most cases from the early interaction of social reinforcement and natural ability. Goleman (1980) reports a study that followed 1528 children in the top 1 per cent of intelligence rating over the succeeding forty years. Those who achieved most in life were found to have had more active hobbies as children, and as adults to participate in more group activities and to show more inclination to participate in sport rather than to remain as onlookers. They were also found to be more ambitious, energetic and persistent throughout the time of the study. In fact, the importance of these last three qualities cannot be overestimated. Bloom (1985) reports that high achievers in the academic world, and in sport and the arts, are distinguished not so much by their natural talent as by their high levels of achievement motivation and by their extraordinary levels of self-discipline. Simonton (1994) notes, in fact, that high achievers in these fields and in areas such as politics have a passionate desire to perfect their gifts and are often continuously productive from an early age – so much so in fact that although natural ability in any given field appears to be normally distributed throughout the population, a small proportion of contributors is responsible for producing most of its achievements.

However, personality is capable of change and development throughout life, and achievement motivation can probably be enhanced throughout life if individuals are allowed to set themselves realistic and specific goals, to commit publicly to these goals, to think and talk about themselves in terms of success rather than failure, to recognise and acquire skills relevant to their work and interests, and to procure group support and encouragement.

Locus of control

Another important factor is what is known as *locus of control*. Locus of control (a term first associated with Rotter, 1966) refers primarily to the way in which individuals view the reasons behind their successes or failures. Those with an external locus of control attribute these reasons to external circumstances ('I did badly because my luck ran out', 'I failed because everyone was against me'), while those whose locus of control is internal feel the responsibility is generally their own ('I passed because I worked hard', 'It was my own fault I did badly'). The origins of locus of control may be partly innate (temperamental), but also owe much to the social factors and learning opportunities important for achievement motivation in general. Not surprisingly, people whose locus of control is external seem often to prefer undertakings in which chance plays an important part, while people with an internal locus prefer opportunities to exercise their personal qualities.

Clearly, an exaggerated locus of control in either direction can be a bad thing. The tendency always to blame others can be a way of avoiding our own inadequacies, while always blaming ourselves can lead to feelings of personal worthlessness. The ideal is to view each situation with the objectivity and clarity that enables us to see why things are as they are, and then to get on and make the best contribution we can. However, numerous studies (most recently Presson and Benassi, 1996) show consistently that internals achieve more in school, are less subject to depression, are better able to defer gratification in order to work towards long-term goals, cope better with stress and act more independently than do externals.

Working along similar lines to Rotter, Weiner (1979) developed what is known as *attribution theory,* which further explores how we conceptualise and attribute the reasons for success and failure in life. Weiner showed that the most highly motivated individuals are also those who prefer situations in which the consequences of their actions can be ascribed to themselves, who attribute outcomes to personal effort, and who are sensitive to cues that indicate the importance of the expenditure of effort in any area. One obvious conclusion to draw from this is that in professional (and personal) life, the tendency to blame others consistently for our own mistakes is not only unjust but may indicate low achievement motivation and in extreme cases rigidity, defensiveness, dishonesty, and an inability to live with a self-image which recognises that we are fallible enough to make mistakes.

Just as we attribute reasons for our own success and failure, so we attribute qualities, motives and even personality characteristics to others, often on the basis of the flimsiest of evidence. Even when we know people well, as within a marriage, attributions can still be made all too readily, and may have far-reaching and sometimes unfair consequences (Fincham and Bradbury, 1993). If we go back to the X Theory and Y Theory (page 91) that employers and managers may hold about their workers, we can see that attributions operate at a macro as well as a micro level. This links back to what we were saying earlier about the way in which groups can depersonalise other groups, attributing all kinds of negative qualities to them, often in the absence of any real evidence.

Other attributional styles

Several other areas of attributional style have been identified. One of the most relevant to the workplace, in that it influences the degree to which individuals can face challenge and cope with stressful situations, is the *pessimistic style* identified by Peterson, *et al.,* (1988). Peterson and his colleagues found that a pessimistic attributional style is associated with depression after failure, with a greater incidence of physical illness, and presumably with less willingness to try again after an initial lack of success (which resembles the behaviour of low self-esteem individuals discussed in Chapter 2). On the other hand, an optimistic style is associated with better school grades, with more success in areas such as salesmanship, and even with better physical health (Seligman and Schulman, 1986).

While not labelled originally as an attributional style, the quality identified by Kobasa and others (for example, Kobasa, *et al.*, 1982) known as *hardiness* is also of relevance. The research arose from the finding that some men reporting above average levels of stress suffer from below average levels of illness, while others with high stress are ill more often than usual. Comparisons between the two groups revealed that the former differed from the latter on three major variables. First, they were more actively involved in their work and their social lives; second, they were more orientated towards challenge and change; and third they felt more in control of their lives.

A longitudinal study of executives who had no previous history of illness was then carried out to determine whether the greater incidence of illness suffered by the low hardiness men in the initial investigation was itself responsible for their more negative outlook. Results over the two years of the study suggested that it was not. The qualities associated with hardiness emerged once more as the factors that helped to guard against susceptibility to physical illness when under particular stress. A sense of control over events and a commitment to personal goals emerged as being of particular importance (Cohen and Edwards, 1989), and once again we see the value of an attributional style which assigns to people the power to influence what happens around them, to engage with others, to develop and retain interests, and to have some impact on the nature and quality of our life space.

Chapter 6

The Trait-based Approach

The trait-based approach to personality is sometimes referred to as the descriptive approach because it is concerned to say what personality is *like*, rather than speculating on its underlying psychological mechanisms as is the case with psychoanalytical and humanistic approaches.

In everyday language, when we describe people's personalities, we tend to use such words as 'friendly', 'confident', 'worried', and so on. These are known as trait terms, and Allport (1961) identified no fewer than 18000 such terms in the literature, of which no fewer than 4500 are in common use. This is a huge number, and on close inspection it is clear that most of them are really only different aspects of a much smaller number of core attributes. For example, a person's timidity, hesitancy, defensiveness and nervousness may all be caused by a single attribute of anxiety. If we start hunting for these core attributes, we are said to be adopting a *parsimonious* approach, an approach much favoured in science, in which the observed facts are accounted for in terms of the smallest possible number of underlying variables.

Such an approach is not new. It stretches back at least as far as Hippocrates and the Graeco-Roman physician Galen, who in the second century AD saw all human beings as classifiable into four basic personality-types: the *melancholic* (sad and depressed); the *phlegmatic* (calm and stable); the *choleric* (irascible and quick-tempered); and the *sanguine* (cheerful and optimistic). It says something for the resilience of this classification that it was still going strong in the early twentieth century, when W. B. Wundt (1832–1920), one of the founding fathers of modern psychology, suggested that the four types could be explained by two basic bi-polar traits: namely, strength of emotion (strong versus weak), and speed of emotional change (volatile versus stable). Thus, to Wundt, the melancholic person shows strong and stable emotions; the phlegmatic weak and stable, the choleric strong and volatile; and the sanguine weak and volatile.

The importance of Wundt's theory is that for four rigid categories it substitutes two traits, which can then be expressed as scales or dimensions. Instead of being melancholic or phlegmatic, or choleric or sanguine, a person can now be placed at any point on the 'strong versus weak' and 'volatile versus stable' continuum.

While retaining the parsimony of Galen's approach, Wundt's model of personality was therefore much more able to explain individual differences. Instead of there being only four types of people, it gave us a wide variety spread out along the two dimensions, with only people at the extremes falling into one or other of Galen's four categories.

Eysenck's personality dimensions

One of the psychologists who did the most to develop Wundt's ideas was the late Hans Eysenck, referred to several times already. Eysenck acknowledged his debt to Wundt, but his work differed importantly in that it was based on strong research evidence, which we shall examine shortly. Eysenck, like Wundt, recognised the existence of two main personality traits or dimensions, but he considered them to be more correctly described by the terms *extraversion–introversion* (the 'E' dimension), and *neuroticism–stability* (the 'N' dimension). To these he later added a third dimension, namely high *psychoticism–low psychoticism* (the 'P' dimension). Since an understanding of these various terms is essential for a grasp of Eysenck's personality theory, they require some discussion (see also Eysenck, 1990 and 1992).

Extraversion–introversion

Broadly, Eysenck accepted Jung's definition of the extravert as a person who is orientated consciously towards the outer world of people and experiences. The extreme extravert is a person who makes social contacts readily, is fond of physical activity, likes change and variety in life, is easily aroused emotionally but usually not very deeply, and tends to be materialistic, tough-minded and free from social inhibitions. Eysenck also accepted Jung's definition of the extreme introvert as the direct opposite of each of these things, and far more inclined towards inner states of mind and social withdrawal.

What Eysenck did not accept (see, for instance, Eysenck and Eysenck 1969) is Jung's very complex view of personality, which he regarded as being impossibly elaborate and unscientific. He was particularly dismissive of Jung's theory that the extravert has repressed the introverted side of him/herself (and is therefore always unconsciously introverted), while the introvert has repressed the extraverted side (and is therefore unconsciously extraverted). In fact, apart from his acceptance of Jung's definitions, Eysenck had very little in common with him.

Neuroticism–stability

Neuroticism (sometimes referred to as instability) means a liability to excessive anxiety, while stability indicates a relative freedom from it. Eysenck made no attempt to subdivide anxiety (instability) into three different kinds, as did Freud (see Chapter 3 of this volume), and indeed remained very sceptical of most aspects of Freudian theory, because he took the view that they lie outside the scope of psychological proof. To Eysenck, who shared many sympathies with the behaviouristic thinking we shall be examining in the next chapter, concepts such as the id and the super-ego remain little more than speculations.

Psychoticism

Psychoticism refers to psychosis – that is, to mental illness (see Chapter 10). However, high scores on the psychoticism dimension do not necessarily mean that the individual is psychotic, simply that he or she shows certain traits that are a particular feature of the psychotic, but which are present in the normal population as well. People with high scores on the psychoticism dimension tend to be somewhat unfeeling, insensitive, solitary, and troublesome, and hostile, aggressive and even cruel towards others. They are generally high on sensation-seeking, enjoying arousal and danger, and may have something of the social misfit about them, with strong independence of behaviour and outlook (Eysenck and Eysenck, 1976).

Measuring Eysenck's dimensions

Few people come out at the extreme ends of Eysenck's dimensions (for instance, as extremely extraverted or introverted), and most tend to be located closer to the centre. Since the three dimensions are

---

Social Acceptability

A problem with all personality (and attitude and many other psychological) tests is that some people tend to give the answers they feel show themselves in the best possible light. This is known as the social acceptability syndrome, or 'faking good'. No matter how much the test instructions stress that honesty is required and that there are no 'right' or 'wrong' answers, a certain percentage of people will still resort to faking good.

Revealingly, this even happens when the tests are taken anonymously, which suggests that the individuals concerned not only want to present themselves in a favourable light to others, but also to themselves. To admit on paper to qualities or behaviour they think are reprehensible in some way clearly risks lowering them in their own estimation.

Generally, the Lie Scale (see page 107) will identify such people, and their results for the whole test are then regarded as being suspect, and usually discarded.

---

taken to explain all, or nearly all, of the observable differences in personality between people, it follows that everyone has a score of some kind on each dimension. Eysenck's results show that scores on the dimensions are not generally correlated, which means, for example, that an E score will tell us nothing about the score a person is likely to get on the N or the P dimensions.

In the light of this absence of correlation, the dimensions are said to be *orthogonal*, and in Figure 6.1 the two most frequently explored dimensions (extraversion–introversion and neuroticism–stability) are represented diagrammatically by orthogonal reference axes. It will be seen from the diagram that people with scores at the extreme ends of the two dimensions fall into four groups, characterised, as we proceed clockwise around the diagram, by extraversion, stability, introversion and neuroticism. By the same reckoning, people who have both their scores at the extreme ends of dimensions will come out respectively as stable extraverts, stable introverts, neurotic introverts, or neurotic extraverts. Eysenck suggested that these four categories correspond respectively with Galen's sanguine, phlegmatic, melancholic and choleric ones (which may lead us to wonder just how far psychology has advanced in 2000 years!).

The majority of people, even though their scores fall short of the extreme ends of the dimensions, will still tend to fall within one or

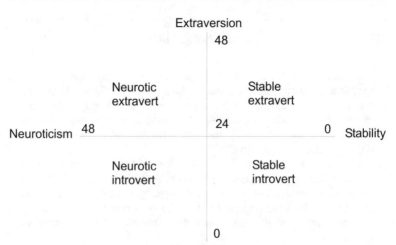

Figure 6.1

other of the four quarters of the diagram. A person will need to score high marks for extraversion and high marks for neuroticism to be the epitome of the neurotic extravert, but any score higher than 24 for extraversion and 24 for neuroticism will show that someone has a tendency in this direction. The only 'neutral' people will be those individuals whose scores lie at the precise mid-point of both dimensions (though it is possible to score high or low on one dimension and yet remain neutral on the other).

Leaving aside the P dimension for a moment, four distinct personality stereotypes thus emerge from Eysenck's work, with four relatively distinct patterns of behaviour. The stable extravert tends to be outgoing, sociable, usually positive in mood, fond of new experiences and new challenges, and of activity and travel, optimistic, good at relating to new acquaintances, and generally likeable and friendly. Stable introverts are equally positive and optimistic, but have a greater tendency towards intellectual and solitary pursuits. Usually good at making friends, they often prefer a few close companions to the wide circle enjoyed by the stable extravert. Sometimes rather reserved with new acquaintances, stable introverts are nevertheless at ease with people they know well. Their rich inner life can sometimes prompt them to periods of solitariness, and they are typically happy with their own company.

Neurotic or unstable introverts are often worriers and may be subject to recurring bouts of melancholy and depression for no obvious reason. Generally rather pessimistic, they may become loners and in extreme cases show reclusive tendencies. When troubled they seek solitude, and may find it very difficult to communicate their problems to others. Neurotic or unstable extraverts are similar in their tendency towards worry and depression, but seek company (sometimes almost obsessively) when troubled. Often almost frenetic in their search for new experiences and diversions they may have a short attention span and find sustained concentration difficult.

Like all stereotypes, these four descriptions represent extremes, and many people will in any case be at or near the mid-point on either the E or the N dimension, and thus not fall clearly into any one of the four categories. As we grow older, there is a tendency to become more introverted. The relentlessly extraverted adolescent and young adult may show distinct signs of calm introversion in middle life. Nevertheless, these stereotypes are useful. Research indicates that stable introverts tend to do best in higher education, partly because of their ability to sustain the long solitary hours of study upon which success often depends. Unstable extraverts tend to be at the most disadvantage here, because of their difficulty in adopting the necessary study habits, and their propensity to seek company and social diversion as their anxiety mounts.

In business and professional life, extraverts generally make better salespeople than introverts (who may be successful for short periods, but who can find the constant need to meet new people and make new contacts tiring rather than stimulating). On the other hand, introverts are often better in areas where long periods of concentration are required, such as accountancy, scientific and medical research, and probably certain kinds of information technology and journalism. Neuroticism, which up to certain levels may be an advantage in the arts – particularly the performing arts – may prove a handicap in professions such as engineering, medicine, law, financial services, and any other profession where crucial decisions have to be taken and where the consequences of error can be disastrous.

From the perspective of the workplace, the P dimension is less easily accommodated. Perhaps the best way of regarding it is to see it as a modifying influence on the four main stereotypes. Thus high P, which can carry with it a certain independence – even ruthlessness – plus a tendency towards originality and creativity, of thought and action, can be an advantage in some circumstances if allied to high stability, but may be disastrous when linked to high instability. It may also manifest itself in different ways in the extravert and the introvert, prompting the former towards the kind of decisive and perhaps unpopular action sometimes required in the effective leader, and the latter towards the single-minded determination of the successful artist, ideas man – and perhaps software wizard.

Either way, the quality may sometimes go to make a successful business person, though probably not a good family man or woman, or a loyal friend. Certainly it may be a factor in high levels of problem orientation as opposed to people orientation. The research evidence that has accumulated in support of Eysenck's dimensions comes not from devices with complicated and controversial methods of scoring such as projective tests, but from simple questionnaires which ask people for details about their behaviour and preferences, and which can be scored objectively. In this sense, they share some similarities with the measurement techniques of humanistic psychologists, but there the similarity between Eysenck and people such as Maslow and Rogers ends.

Measuring traits

As he did with the psychoanalysts, Eysenck tended to regard humanistic psychologists as also being somewhat short on experimental evidence. Meta needs may exist, agreed Eysenck, or they may not. In the light of present knowledge, we have no real way of knowing. Eysenck's own approach was to present large samples of people with batteries of questions about themselves, and then to factor-analyse their responses. Results convinced him that certain personality attributes tend to be found together (for example, the person who is sociable tends also to be impulsive, talkative and lively) and therefore all arise from a single underlying personality trait, and it is three of these groups or clusters of attributes that he identified as extraversion–introversion, neuroticism–stability, and psychoticism, respectively.

Following the Maudsley Medical Questionnaire of 1952, Eysenck produced the Maudsley Personality Inventory (MPI, 1959), the Eysenck Personality Inventory (EPI, 1964) and the Eysenck Personality Questionnaire (EPQ, 1975) together with variants of these tests for use with special groups (for example, the Junior Eysenck Personality Inventory, for use with young children). A shortened

TABLE 6.1　Short form of the Maudsley Personality Inventory

		Key
A	Do you sometimes feel happy, sometimes depressed without any apparent reason?	N
B	Do you have frequent ups and downs in mood, either with or without apparent cause?	N
C	Are you inclined to be moody?	N
D	Does your mind often wander while you are trying to concentrate?	N
E	Are you frequently 'lost in thought' even when supposed to be taking part in conversation?	N
F	Are you sometimes bubbling over with energy and sometimes very sluggish?	N
G	Do you prefer action to planning for action?	E
H	Are you happiest when you get involved in some project that calls for rapid action?	E
I	Do you usually take the initiative in making new friends?	E
J	Are you inclined to be quick and sure in your actions?	E
K	Would you rate yourself as a lively individual?	E
L	Would you be very unhappy if you were prevented from making social contacts?	E

Source:　Reproduced with the permission of H. J. Eysenck

version of the Maudsley Personality Inventory is given as Table 6.1. The scoring key by the side of each question indicates whether a 'yes' answer would gain a score on the E dimension or on the N dimension. This shortened version should not be taken to give an entirely reliable picture of how one measures up on the traits concerned, but it gives at least a pointer in that direction, as results correlate significantly with those obtained from the use of the full inventory.

The various versions of Eysenck's personality questionnaires have been used extensively in research in management and in areas such as education, criminology, sexual behaviour and belief systems. In addition to items designed to measure the three dimensions already discussed, these questionnaires also contain a Lie Scale (the 'L' dimension) consisting of questions which, for most practical purposes, have only one truthful answer (an example would be a question such as 'Have you ever felt fear in your life?). Anyone who gets more than a certain number of these Lie Scale items 'wrong' is assumed to be unreliable in their responses to other items in the Inventory. (Obviously, when attempting the questionnaire, the subject has no idea on which scale a particular question is marked, and may not even know that there is a Lie Scale.)

Research has shown that, although there is no correlation between L scores and either N or E scores, high L scorers do tend to be relatively lower in measured intelligence (IQ) and in self-insight. There is also evidence of a negative correlation between L scores and scores on the P (psychoticism) dimension (Eysenck and Eysenck, 1976). Interestingly, although the advantage gained by introverts holds for both artists and scientists at the higher-education level and in adult life generally, it is particularly marked for scientists, perhaps because even more of their work is solitary than is the case with artists. Successful scientists seem generally to have lower N scores than successful artists, however, suggesting that high N scores may go with the kind of sensitivity necessary for artistic criticism and expression (see Eysenck, 1983 for a review of relevant findings).

Anxiety (instability) and educational achievement

In spite of the possible link between above average N scores and success in certain arts subjects, high anxiety levels in children and adults are not conducive to academic or occupational success. A mild degree of anxiety can improve motivation and performance, but once anxiety increases beyond this optimum level it begins to have an increasingly inhibiting effect. The more complex the task, the more this inhibiting effect is likely to occur.

Thus anxiety-provoking situations such as tests and examinations may well prevent many children and adults from performing at their best, particularly where these tests and examinations demand the recall of detailed abstract material (as, for example, in science subjects and foreign languages). What raises anxiety to this inhibiting level in one person may simply act as a useful motivator to another, however, which often means that particularly stressful events such as public examinations are regrettably as much a way of testing our nerves as they are of testing our knowledge.

There is little we can do about the fact of public examinations, but those of us involved in preparing others for them can lessen the anxiety they cause by ensuring that students are well prepared, have had sufficient practice in examination technique, and are encouraged to discuss and come to terms with their anxieties. Such anxieties should never be dismissed as groundless or as signs of weakness. They are real enough for the person who is experiencing them, and his or her prime need is for a sympathetic and understanding mentor who recognises this and provides appropriate guidance, encouragement and support.

In addition, those responsible for designing tests at any level should first consider their purpose. Tests and examinations can be either of the summative or the formative kind. Summative tests are attainment tests designed to find out how much people know, and to compare them against a particular standard, while formative tests are aimed primarily at providing feedback on what has been learnt, and on establishing how learning can be made more effective in the future. In a summative test, individuals know that they are on trial, and will be subject accordingly to anxiety, whereas in a formative test they recognise that there is no pressure of this kind, and that the whole exercise is simply designed to further their own progress.

As pointed out by Bloom (1983) and other authorities, tests are too often simply summative, and are used as a way of trying to motivate learning rather than as a way of finding out how learning can best be assisted. The result is that such tests fail to provide maximum benefit, and serve only to produce experiences of failure and anxiety which inhibit future progress.

Research evidence on children and adults

The findings of a range of large-scale studies in both Britain and in the USA (see Kline, 1983 for a summary) show that, in the primary school, stable extraverted children tend to do best. The correlations between personality type and academic success seem to be consistently significant at this age level, though many other factors such as intelligence, self-esteem and socioeconomic background are also involved. At the secondary school stage, the picture gradually changes (more rapidly for girls than for boys), with introversion becoming increasingly important for academic success, particularly in science subjects. This change owes something to the fact that individual work is increasingly emphasised in the secondary school; the age-related trend towards introversion mentioned earlier doubtless also plays a part, with some successful extraverts in the primary school developing into successful introverts during their secondary school years.

As was suggested earlier in this chapter, introversion continues to be important for academic success in higher education. Studies from the USA suggest that it is the stable introvert who is most favoured, though in Britain the question of whether it is the stable or the unstable introvert has been more open to debate. Some evidence, as we have seen, suggests that stability may be a help in science and engineering (perhaps because these subjects handle precise complex data where high anxiety levels could be a handicap to performance), but less so in arts subjects (where sometimes greater emphasis is placed upon sensitivity towards the expression and communication of emotions). Be this as it may, it would seem to be in both science and arts subjects unstable extraversion tends to go the least readily with academic success (Wankowski, 1970). We have already identified a possible explanation for this in observing that the unstable extravert is likely to seek company as a way of forgetting worries. The extravert's need for social stimuli when faced with the anxieties of preparing for examinations may make it more difficult to submit to the lonely, sustained work which such preparation demands. As a consequence the unstable extravert may be found down in the student bar or calling on friends when the tensions mount, and this personality who may need particularly careful support by those in authority at stressful times.

These findings may also hold good in the wider workplace. Attention has already been drawn to the fact that high extraversion–introversion appear to go with success in different occupations respectively, and the same may hold true for stability–instability. Stability is obviously important in high-stress jobs where cool judgement and an equable temperament are needed, whereas the emotionality that goes with high instability has equally obvious advantages in the performing arts and in other creative occupations such as art and design and writing. Failure in the workplace is often as likely to be due to incompatibilities between personality and occupation as to lack of skills and ability.

The physiology of Eysenck's Dimensions

It was observed at the beginning of this chapter that trait theorists such as Eysenck have little interest in formulating theories on the underlying mechanisms of personality in the manner of the psychoanalysts and of the humanistic psychologists. However, with his belief that at least 70 per cent of the personality differences between people revealed by questionnaires such as his own EPQ are the result of heredity, Eysenck was concerned to isolate the innate physiological factors that go with the various personality types(see, for example, Eysenck, 1983). Briefly, he suggested that anxiety is particularly associated with the autonomic nervous system (that is, the system that controls and coordinates the body's involuntary functions such as heartbeat, breathing, the blood vessels, digestion, sexual arousal and glandular secretions), and with the hypothalamus area of the brain, which helps activate this system. Some individuals have autonomic nervous systems which are particularly quick to register the symptoms associated with anxiety (sweating, accelerated pulse, dry mouth, trembling etc.), while others have systems that are much less labile.

Individuals whose autonomic nervous systems are markedly difficult to arouse will generally have low N scores, and there is a suggestion that in some cases they may in fact experience a psychological thrill when such arousal is achieved, and may there-fore actively seek it by taking part in high risk activities such as dangerous sports, fast driving, extravagant gambling and, when linked to a low moral code and perhaps high P scores, even criminal activities. Less obvious forms of risk-taking, such as highly spec-ulative business or investment ventures, illicit love affairs, and the subtle goading of colleagues or superiors known to have poor self-control may provide further examples.

On the other hand, those with readily aroused autonomic nervous systems will tend to find nervous arousal disturbing, and will therefore generally produce high N scores. Some evidence exists to show that ectomorphs (see Chapter 1) are more likely than meso-morphs to belong to the latter group.

As to extraversion–introversion, Eysenck suggests that the reti-cular formation area of the brain may be the main physiological source. The reticular formation is the brain area that helps to stimulate and inhibit the cerebral cortex and thus to control a person's state of attention and wakefulness. In Eysenck's submis-sion, the reticular formation of introverts allows them to build up inhibition more slowly than extraverts. They can therefore concen-trate for longer periods on the same repetitive task, and may also remain more sensitive to the constant, subtle signals of their own thoughts and feelings.

Note that the word 'inhibition' in this context has nothing to do with social inhibition. It means that introverts have a lower awareness threshold to the stream of sensory messages coming from the environment. They thus require less external stimulation, and may be more easily satisfied with a good book, or their own company, or with soft music, whereas the extravert is likely to find that these quiet, private pursuits are insufficient to hold the attention for very long.

Eysenck also drew attention to the fact that introverts, again perhaps because their lower inhibition level renders them more sensitive to stimuli, acquire conditioned responses (see Chapter 8) more rapidly than do extraverts. This means that they tend to learn more quickly – not only academic material but also social rules and regulations. Failure to learn the latter may be why there is a significant correlation between extraversion (particularly unstable extraversion) and crime. The extreme extravert may not be as aware of social codes as is the introvert. Or, more particularly, extreme extraverts may not be as aware of the need for these things as are introverts.

A further contributory factor is that, because extreme extraverts may be less sensitive to their own feelings, they may be less able to empathise with the feelings of others, and therefore less able to be sensitive towards others' needs and rights. These physiological factors may also explain why extraverts are generally higher on aggression and leadership qualities than are introverts, and also why at all ages men are more inclined towards extraversion than are women. (Interestingly, extraverts were found in early studies to be generally more mesomorphic than are introverts – another reason, as we saw in Chapter 1, for thinking that heredity could play some part in the matter.) But this evidence in favour of inheritance must not make us lose sight of the fact that Eysenck regarded a very substantial percentage of people's scores on his dimensions to be a result of environment. As he rejected psychodynamic or humanistic explanations for the interaction between heredity and environment, he adopted instead the learning-theory model, which we shall look at in the next chapter.

The psychoticism dimension

The psychoticism dimension has not been used so extensively for research as have Eysenck's other two dimensions, but the evidence suggests a link between high P scores and artistic creativity (Eysenck, 1983). This may be because the personality characteristics that go

---

Personality Change

If a large part of the traits measured by Eysenck's dimensions (and by those proposed by other trait theorists) result from inheritance, to what extent are they susceptible to change? Can the introvert, for example, become more extraverted if he or she chooses, or the extravert more introverted? (The question is particularly important if one end of a dimension is clearly more favourable than the other.)

Carl Jung, whose work we looked at in Chapter 3, took the view that the extreme extravert is in fact repressing the introverted side of his or her nature, just as the extreme introvert is repressing the extraverted side. Thus we all have both ends of any given dimension within us (though birth may have decided which of them is the stronger), and we all therefore have the potential for change. If Jung is correct, we have not so much to learn how to develop the other end of a given dimension (through learning, for example by role play – see page 88 – is helpful) as to identify what it is in us that is preventing its natural expression. Were we over-criticised for showing that side of our personality in childhood? Have we lacked opportunities for its development? Have we felt it is less acceptable to peer groups or to others who have been or who are influential in our lives?

---

with high P scores (independence, solitariness, tough-mindedness, aggression and the like) are aids towards artistic success in Western societies. But, as with most research involving large samples of people and the use of personality questionnaires, a link of this kind does not mean that people with low P scores are excluded from becoming creative artists. The link is a statistical one, and simply indicates that among creative people there are rather more high P scorers than one would expect to find purely on the grounds of chance.

Creativity, by definition, involves an independent and original approach to life, and sometimes creative people have to show a touch of ruthlessness in order to give creative work precedence over the social demands made by others. If we want creativity in friends or colleagues, we have to remember that it may not be without its less comfortable side.

Cattell's Personality Factors

R. B. Cattell has been another major advocate of the trait-based approach. Cattell's research, conducted along similar lines to that of

TABLE 6.2   Cattell's Basic Source Traits (showing popular descriptions for the respective ends of each dimension)

Letter	Cattell's label	Popular description	Popular description
A	Cyclothymia-schizothymia	Outgoing, adventurous, idealistic	Reserved, timid, cynical
B	Intelligence	Intelligent, analytical	Stupid, incoherent
C	Ego strength	Realistic, stable, calm	Unrealistic, changeable, uncontrolled
D	Excitability-insecurity	Self-sufficient, self-effacing, not easily jealous	Demanding, impatient, exhibitionistic
E	Dominance-submissiveness	Self-assertive, confident, willful	Submissive, retiring, meek
F	Surgency-desurgency	Light-hearted	Sombre
G	Superego strength	Conscientious, responsible	Quitting, fickle, neglectful
H	Parmia-threctia	Adventurous, gregarious	Withdrawn, aloof
I	Premsia–harria	Tough-minded, independent	Tender-minded, dependent
J	Coasthenic	Ultra-cooperative, group-orientated, decisive	Obstinate, passive resistance, indecisive
K	Comention-abcultion	Refined	Boorish
L	Protension-haxia	Suspicious	Trusting, cheerful
M	Autia–prexernia	creative, artistic	conventional, practical
N	Shrewdness–naïvete	socially skilled, expedient	socially clumsy, sentimental
O	Guilt proneness–confidence	worrying, suspicious	self-confident, self-sufficient

Eysenck and again using factor analysis, revealed the existence of many more than three dimensions (for example, Cattell, 1980). On the basis of his findings, he constructed a number of personality inventories, namely the Sixteen Personality Factor Questionnaire (16PF), which measures the sixteen traits or dimensions that he claims exist in adults; the High School Personality Questionnaire, which measures those identifiable in children from twelve to eighteen; the Child's Personality Quiz, which is for ages eight to twelve; the Early School Personality Quiz, for children of six to eight years of age; and the Pre-School Personality Quiz for children of four to six years (Cattell and Kline, 1977).

The terms Cattell used for his dimensions (or factors as he preferred to call them) are a little daunting, and were invented in part to emphasise the tentative nature of personality labels. People change, develop, grow, regress, and even when their personality factors are relatively constant, there may be some overlap between them. However, Cattell's terms translate readily enough into layman's language, and the ones that feature in the Personality Factor Questionnaire are given in Table 6.2, together with their lay descriptions. It will be noted that Cattell uses some psychodynamic terms such as ego and super-ego, but he has little else in common with the psychodynamic approach. His differences from Eysenck, on the other hand, are more apparent than real, since he accepted that many of his factors correlate with each other, and can therefore be grouped into a few broad categories, or source traits, which look very much like Eysenck's dimensions of extraversion–introversion,

TABLE 6.3 Factors in Cattell's High School Personality Questionnaire

A	Affectothymia (sociable)—Schizothymia (reserved)
B	High intelligence—low intelligence
C	Ego strength (stability)—low ego strength (instability)
D	Excitability—phlegmatism
E	Dominance (self-assertion)—submissiveness
F	Surgency (exuberance)—desurgency (sobriety)
G	Strong super-ego (conscientiousness)—Weak super-ego
H	Parmia (venturesomeness)—threctia (shyness)
I	Premsia (sensitivity)—harria (toughness)
J	Coasthenia (individuality)—zeppia (group involvement)
O	Guilt proneness—confidence

and neuroticism–stability. The majority of his personality factors can therefore be regarded as being sub-characteristics of Eysenck's dimensions. However, Cattell includes a measure of intelligence as one of his sixteen factors, as this certainly emerges as an important aspect of the way in which we engage with the world.

The factors in Cattell's High School Personality Questionnaire (see Table 6.3) are more readily understandable.

The 'big five' personality factors

In large measure as a consequence of the work of Eysenck and Cattell, there is now general agreement that five personality factors (the 'big five') provide us with most of what can be said about personality (Wiggins, 1996). These factors, together with their descriptions (McCrae and Costa, 1990) are:

Emotional stability	*(calm versus anxious; secure versus insecure; self-satisfied versus self-pitying)*
Extraversion	*(sociable versus retiring; fun-loving versus sober; affectionate versus reserved)*
Openness	*(imaginative versus practical; variety-seeking versus routine-seeking; independent versus conforming)*
Agreeableness	*(soft-hearted versus ruthless; trusting versus suspicious; helpful versus uncooperative)*
Conscientiousness	*(organised versus disorganised; careful versus careless; disciplined versus impulsive)*

The first two of these factors are essentially Eysenck's N and E dimensions, while virtually all Cattell's factors (with the exception of intelligence) come under one or other of these big five. An interesting informal exercise is to rate oneself on a 5-point scale on each of the descriptive dimensions given against these five factors, and then to ask someone who knows you well also to rate you. Self and peer ratings of this kind tend to agree reasonably well (Berkenan and Liebler, 1993), and the closer the agreement, the greater one's self-insight would appear to be. Funder (1995) suggests that if there are high levels of disagreement, the peer report is likely to be the more accurate of the two.

The 'big five' are measured by the Neuroticism, Extraversion and Openness Personality Inventory (or NEO-PI for short – a title chosen before the factors of agreeableness and conscientiousness were added). The NEO-PI (McCrae and Costa, 1990) contains 181 brief items such as 'I really like people well', and there are also items that allow individuals to rate each other.

It is interesting to speculate on which important personality variables, if any, are *not* covered by 'the big five'. For example, perhaps there should be a masculine versus feminine dimension. Self-insight versus self-ignorance, and honesty versus dishonesty might also be relevant. The 'big five' also fail to take into account our openness to Maslow's peak experiences. Perhaps spirituality versus materiality might cover this, and also take into account a number of other variables that have to do with areas of belief and inner experience, all of which can have a profound effect upon person-ality, on philosophy of life, on one's ability to cope with challenge and setbacks, on human relationships, and indeed on a number of aspects of the mature personality (see Chapter 4).

Other personality-measuring devices

The Myers–Briggs Type Indicator classifies people in terms of Jung's personality types (see Chapter 3), and has proved immensely popular, particularly in business and in careers and personal counselling. The Myers–Briggs, as it is commonly known, was originally developed by Briggs and Briggs–Myers and has now gone through many editions (see e.g. Myers 1987). Currently the Myers–Briggs contains 126 questions such as 'Do you usually value sentiment more than logic, or logic more than sentiment?', and while some authorities consider that its wide use has outrun research into its value as a predictor of job performance (Pittenger, 1993), its continuing popularity attests to its accuracy.

Many other personality questionnaires exist, some designed to measure the total personality, and others to measure specific aspects of it. One of the best known examples of the former, from which a number of the latter have been derived, is the Minnesota Multi-phasic Personality Inventory (or MMPI), originally devised in 1943 but revised subsequently (for example, Hathaway, 1972). It now consists of 614 statements, such as 'I brood a great deal' or 'I'm entirely self-confident', to which the subject responds with a simple 'True' or 'False'. The test is derived not from factor analysis but from noting the differences in typical responses of mentally ill and healthy people respectively to an extensive battery of true–false statements such as 'No one seems to understand me'.

In its current revision (the MMPI-2) it contains ten scales indicative of different kinds of mental disorder (for example, depression, paranoia, hysteria) and personality differences (for example, masculinity–femininity and social introversion). There is also a Lie Scale designed to assess faking, and fifteen content scales assessing such things as work attitudes, anger, and family problems. The results provide a 'profile' of the individual's mental health.

The MMPI is used widely in clinical work, but it is also used as part of job selection procedures, and many other tests have been based wholly or in part on questions taken from it. Space allows only two examples; The California Psychological Inventory; and the California F Scale.

The California Psychological Inventory   The original version of this was introduced in 1957 (see Megargee, 1972). Sometimes known as the sane man's MMPI, it contains 480 items designed to measure normal personality, and yields eighteen scales that can be grouped under the four headings of 'interpersonal behaviour and social skills', 'internal control and self-regulation', 'achievement and intellectual efficiency', and 'intellectual and social interests'.

The California F Scale   Devised principally by T. W. Adorno (see for example Adorno *et al.*, 1950), the scale is designed to measure the authoritarian personality which, on the basis of responses to the MMPI and to projective tests such as the TAT (see Chapter 3), appears to be characterised by conformity, submissiveness (to superiors), dominance (to inferiors), aggression, superstition, destructiveness, cynicism, and an exaggerated and repressive concern with sex. Originally containing thirty-nine items, the F Scale has undergone some rather *ad hoc* revisions. It invites a simple 'True'/'False' response to such statements as 'Obedience and the respect for authority are the most important virtues children can learn', and '. . . criminals ought to be publicly whipped or worse'.

The F Scale has generated a great deal of research, and is of particular interest in the workplace as the authoritarian personality is likely to be rigid, stereotyped, unsympathetic in dealings with colleagues and clients, and inflexible in the face of new ideas and practices. Because he or she is unable to tolerate ambiguity (rather like the conformist people in Asch's experiments detailed in Chapter 4), they are reluctant to allow subordinates to find the balance between individuality and conventionality that is often essential for success in business and professional life.

In Freudian theory, such authoritarian behaviour is sometimes seen as evidence of over-controlling ego-defence mechanisms. The individual for one reason or another represses much of his or her own instinctive life, and projects this over-controlling behaviour outwards on to others. Uncertainty, flexibility and ambiguity produce acute discomfort in them, and therefore have to be kept strictly in check. The authoritarian personality is thus seen as suffering from both neurotic and moral anxiety (see Chapter 3).

Support for this psychodynamic view seems to come from the fact that authoritarian parents (and perhaps teachers) tend to produce children who manifest authoritarian symptoms even at a young age (Kelvin, 1970). By their inflexible attitude towards their children, authoritarian people may well awaken in them precisely the kind of over-controlling ego and perhaps super-ego that led to their own problems.

Attitudes

Tests such as the F Scale bring us to an area of personality that has certain similarities to the trait-based approach – namely attitudes. It will be remembered that in the definition of personality adopted in the Introduction, attitudes were mentioned as one of the things that render each personality unique. We may share many of our attitudes with other people – with our family, our colleagues, or our political party – but the exact permutation of attitudes we hold is often distinctive to ourselves.

Attitudes can be defined as the reasonably enduring orientations people develop towards the objects and issues they encounter in life, and which they express verbally in their opinions. Obviously attitudes contain elements of both value and belief, and psychodynamic theorists would argue that we hold both conscious and unconscious ones, and that when we are employing ego-defence mechanisms such as reaction formation, conscious and unconscious attitudes may be at complete variance with each other. Unconsciously, for example, a man may have a hostile attitude towards a brother or sister, but this so outrages the idea of brotherly love that his parents incorporated into his super-ego during his formative years that consciously he adopts a particularly protective and solicitous attitude towards them, while at the same time, almost unwittingly and with great self-justification ('it's for their own good', 'have to be cruel to be kind' and so on), undermining them in various subtle ways.

Attitudes are normally measured either through a 'True'/'False' response to a number of statements of opinion such as those of the F Scale (a variant of the 'True'/'False' response is a five-point scale from 'Strongly agree' down to 'Strongly disagree'), or through non-directional scales such as the Osgood Semantic Differential (see Chapter 4), where individuals choose the adjectives which in their opinion best describe the issue under scrutiny. Obviously, these tests measure conscious rather than unconscious attitudes, though Freudians claim that the latter can often be revealed if the individual is invited to provide free associations to his or her consciously chosen adjectives.

Not surprisingly, in view of his trait-based approach to personality, Eysenck considered that there are a few dimensions which underlie all our conscious attitudes. His Social Attitude Inventory, devised in 1954, measured a conservative–radical dimension and a tough–tender-minded dimension. Judged by their responses to the Inventory back in the 1950s, extreme right-wing politicians appeared to be tough-minded and conservative, and those on the extreme left to be tough-minded and radical. People with extreme liberal tendencies emerged as generally tender-minded and radical.

By means of identification (see Chapter 2), most of our early attitudes are derived from parents, and later ones from teachers and peer groups. They also come from books, television and the media generally, and are subject to quite frequent and sometimes bewildering change. In late adolescence, with the development of a stronger sense of personality, attitudes tend to become more stable, and this process of consolidation generally goes on throughout life, so that many adults, particularly in their later years, prove very resistant to attempts to change their ways of thinking. However, in all of us, attitudes can change quite sharply if we find ourselves having to resist something that threatens our fundamental values and beliefs.

Cognitive dissonance

The readiness with which (and some of the reasons why) we change our attitudes is demonstrated particularly by cognitive dissonance theory, associated initially with the work of Leon Festinger. Cognitive dissonance has to do with the conscious holding by the individual of two attitudes (or ideas or bits of information) which conflict (are in dissonance with) each other, as when, for example, individuals have confidence in their abilities in a certain subject, yet find themselves failing examinations which they believe are a good measure of these abilities, or regard themselves as being talented at their job or profession, yet are consistently unable to produce the results that are a yardstick of success. As cognitive dissonance is difficult to live with, individuals confronted by it usually modify one or other of their dissonant attitudes – typically the one that poses less threat to their self-image (for instance, in our examples above they may say the examiners are unfair, or that their poor career results are caused by the economic climate or employers who fail to provide the right backup).

Festinger calls such modification a dissonance-reducing change. To bring about such a change, people may sometimes greatly distort their true pictures of the outside world. However, factors such as locus of control will also enter the equation. If the locus of control is internal, there is more likelihood that the individual will modify concepts relating to the self rather than those relating to the outer world, and vice versa if the locus of control is external.

Having once made a dissonance-reducing change, we all seek to lower dissonance still further by interpreting all new evidence in terms of this change (for example, the discovery that the examination syllabus is being changed next year would be taken as 'proof' that this year's syllabus was unsatisfactory). Festinger claims that dissonance-reducing changes are particularly likely to happen when people have taken irrevocable decisions. Thus, in an experiment by one of his associates, it was demonstrated that a sample of girls each improved their individual ratings of pop records (which, in fact, they liked only moderately) immediately after they had been manoeuvred into choosing them as free gifts (Festinger, 1962). The girls, it seemed, could not support the dissonance of not liking the records much yet having chosen them as gifts, so they reduced it by convincing themselves that the records were good ones after all. Dissonance-reducing changes are also likely to happen after someone has told a lie. To reduce the gap between public statement and private information, the tendency is to tamper with the latter to bring it in line with the former. Thus one is able to tell oneself that it wasn't really a lie at all. This tendency, it seems, is particularly marked if the lie has brought little significant reward. It is as if our picture of ourselves as basically truthful people can survive more easily if we see ourselves as giving way to strong temptation (as in telling a lie that brings a big reward) rather than as giving way to something much more trifling. Festinger sees the desire to reduce dissonance as a significant motivating-factor in human behaviour. Since dissonance is unpleasant, it sets up tensions that we very much want to reduce.

Numerous studies have supported the existence of cognitive dissonance (for example, Croyle and Ditto, 1990). It may be that future research will show us that the authoritarian personality, who, as we have seen, has a low toleration of ambiguity, takes up his or her dogmatic stance partly because it removes the necessity for choice, and therefore removes the dissonance that is sometimes consequent on choice. It could be that we shall also find that people who consistently avoid making important decisions do so partly because, through insecurity, they have a low tolerance of dissonance (such findings would fit in well with psychodynamic theories). We might also find, in the reverse direction, that people who can tolerate an abnormally high level of dissonance are just as insecure, preferring to be all things to all men rather than to tackle the disagreements with other people (or internal conflicts) that attempts to be consistent sometimes bring (or they may lack moral sense, such as the psychopath we shall be looking at in Chapter 10).

Attitudes and behaviour

There may be much less of a relationship between our attitudes and our behaviour than one might think. Several studies have shown that people often talk and act in quite different ways. Wallace *et al.* (1996) have found that attitudes only appear to be a reliable guide to behaviour if:

(i) Outside influences upon what we say and do are relatively small (social pressures can readily lead to attitude change, as we saw when discussing groups in Chapter 5).

(ii) The attitude is directly relevant to the behaviour. Often attitudes are expressed in very general terms (for example, 'all politicians are dishonest'), and such general expressions are often an unreliable guide to specific behaviour.

(iii)   The attitude is firmly held and based on deep conviction –
        many attitudes are simply habits of thinking that we have
        never looked at very closely.

Personality measurement and career guidance

Most of the measuring devices we have been looking at in this
chapter have been standardised with large samples of people. This
means that norms and standard deviations have been obtained for
them which allow us to say how far the test results of any one
individual differ from those of the average person. If this
standardisation were not done, we would find ourselves asking
what a particular score on, say, the F Scale actually in fact means.
Does it mean that the person is more or less authoritarian than the
average, and if so by how much?

Standardised tests of this kind are of particular use when it comes
to career and vocational guidance. An early example is the Edwards
Personal Preference Schedule, based on fifteen of the 'needs'
suggested by Murray (see Chapter 3 of this volume) such as
achievement, aggression and autonomy. It contains 210 pairs of
statements between which the individual has to choose – for
example: 'I like to be successful in things', 'I like to make new
friends'. Results are then presented in terms of the relative strength
of each of these needs, and the needs themselves can be linked to the
respective rewards offered by different occupations.

One of the most successful of the tests designed specifically for use
in vocational guidance, Rosenberg's Occupations and Values Test
(first introduced in 1957), divides subjects into those orientated
respectively towards people, towards extrinsic rewards (money,
status), and towards intrinsic rewards (creativity, self-expression).
The Rothwell-Miller Interest Blank (first published in 1968) goes
further and divides them into twelve job categories, such as outdoor,
scientific, social service, mechanical, clerical and medical, and then
lists a wide variety of jobs in each of these categories. These jobs
cover various levels of intelligence and attainment. Thus, for
example, people whose interests place them in the 'mechanical'
category would have a choice of jobs ranging from civil engineer
to maintenance worker. The material contained in tests of this kind
is now presented in computer software, thus producing more
flexibility and subject participation.

Recently, interactive computer software has also been developed to help individuals clarify options and interests, which is likely to prove even more helpful. Typically, it invites the client to state, recognise or self-appraise such things as:

- Factors that influence career choice (for example, family and geographical constraints).
- Personal value systems (that is, the levels and forms of satisfaction expected of a career).
- Existing qualifications and readiness to seek further training.
- Interests (including hobbies and leisure interests).
- Previous experience.
- Income and remuneration desired.
- Future ambitions (short-, medium- and long-term).
- Degree of responsibility and autonomy desired.
- Planning and organising ability.
- Personal qualities (including personality variables such as those connected with the 'big five').

The individual interacts with the programme by answering and asking questions, thus indicating such things as the degree of realism, flexibility and adaptability with which he/she approaches career choice; his/her readiness to remedy deficiencies in existing qualifications and experience; and his/her levels of commitment to working life.

Often people find it easier to be open and spontaneous with programmes of this nature than with a careers counsellor, and the speed with which they can access information and see how opportunities are opened up or closed down as a result of their responses and choices proves of particular value in clarifying thinking and determining future action.

Criticisms of the trait approach

Trait theories are of great value when looking at human nature in general, but men and women differ so much in terms of experience and innate potential that general theories of this kind do not always allow us to understand or predict individual behaviour. In addition, the trait-based approach often fails to tease out the complex range of variables that will influence what happens in particular instances. For example, we may find a particular group of workers going against the trend identified by trait research simply because they have a charismatic and very unorthodox manager who still produces excellent results. Or we may find that a sudden change in working practices or conditions produces radical alterations in individual attitudes and outcomes.

Another criticism of the trait approach is that it tells us nothing about the unconscious or about meta needs and long-term goals and aspirations. Trait theorists contend that this is because such things are too vague for precise measurement, but this ignores the fact that in the individual's own life they may be of paramount importance. It is also sometimes argued that trait methods are an oversimplification. As we have seen, Freudian theory divides anxiety into three different kinds, and it could therefore be that a single N score, such as that yielded by Eysenck's questionnaires, is of only limited value.

Similarly, it is argued that research into attitudes gives us only a simplified and superficial picture of people, and that, as we have seen, attitudes and behaviour may often be at marked variance from each other. Thus a person who expresses highly moral attitudes in response to a questionnaire (or even in life generally) may be highly immoral in behaviour. We may know the social desirability of expressing moral views in public, but be quite unable in our private lives to live up to these ideals. Similarly, people may have negative attitudes towards smoking or overeating or laziness or alcohol or smacking their children, yet be quite incapable of giving up these practices themselves. It is also said that the very act of 'measuring' an attitude gives it an appearance of permanence which in fact it may not actually possess.

Finally, it is sometimes argued that human personality is not consistent enough to be assessed in terms of enduring traits. People fluctuate as they move from one environment to another and as the weeks and months go by, and may even hide certain of their traits if circumstances appear to demand it (Buss, 1989). We saw an indication of this more flexible approach to personality when we discussed field and social models in Chapter 5. But as we shall be taking up the issue in depth in Chapter 7 nothing further need be said about it here.

Each of these criticisms of the trait approach has some force behind it. But they do not suggest that the trait approach should be discounted. There is no doubt that we do have personality traits, and that they are socially significant and can influence our job performance and decisions (Hogan *et al.*, 1996).

The appropriate conclusion is that in a complex area such as personality no single approach, whether psychodynamic, humanistic or trait-based, can be allowed to stand on its own. We can learn something of value from them all, and thus be in a position to decide which approach is the most appropriate in any given instance.

Chapter 7

The State-based Approach

The state-based approach to personality differs from the trait-based approach discussed in the last chapter in that it sees personality as being far more fluctuating and context-dependent. This accords well with the humanistic approach discussed in Chapter 4, since humanistic psychologists also see personality as continually changing and developing, but even here there is something of a variation in that state-based theories do not place so much emphasis on models of personality. Instead, they explore men and women as they are from moment to moment, using for the purpose measuring devices that are claimed to be as precise in their own way as those used by trait theorists.

We might suppose that measuring devices are only applicable if we are looking at fixed characteristics such as traits. But this is not so, and an analogy might be helpful, though like all analogies it must not be pushed too far. The measuring devices used by trait theorists are analogous to rulers, enduring units of measurement designed to measure enduring qualities. Those of the state theorists, on the other hand, are analogous to thermometers, designed to measure qualities that fluctuate even in the short term. Of course, since rulers and thermometers are equally useful in their separate ways, this indicates how trait- and state-based approaches can be reconciled. Personality does appear to have enduring traits, as argued by Eysenck and Cattell, but within the context of these traits it has fluctuating qualities, as argued by the state theorists.

Sometimes the trait-based and sometimes the state-based model is found to be more helpful, but many state-based theorists would warn that it can be misleading to regard any aspects of ourselves as being fixed, and that by regarding them in this way we overlook potential for development. As Thomas and Harri-Augstein (1985) put it, we may mistake 'ineffective stabilised states in individuals and groups for permanent features', and thus, in effect, help to perpetuate them. Learning failure, low intelligence and personality traits are therefore seen by many state theorists as being in part the 'creation' of the very tests designed to measure them. By the reckoning of state theorists, human potentialities are largely undiscovered quantities, and by attempting to give them fixed scores we risk imposing limits on them. By labelling individuals, for example as being of low intelligence or unstable, and by then treating them in accordance with these labels, we prompt those concerned to believe in the labels and thus lessen their chances of change and progress.

Certainly, much human behaviour is based on the realisation that everyone possesses relatively enduring factors of personality and ability, and that if this were not so it would be impossible to 'know' someone in any realistic sense. However, we must not confuse 'enduring' with 'fixed'. A quality might have been enduring up to the present, but this does not mean that it cannot change or be helped to change, even in the short term. And its very endurance may be less a feature of the quality itself than of the way in which early labelling has taken place. Thus, while some individuals may be innately more likely than others to experience an emotion such as anxiety, the fact that they have come to see themselves as 'anxious' prevents them from believing in and learning the strategies that would help them to develop beyond their anxiety reactions. State theorists maintain that it is more useful to find out which situations arouse a person's anxiety, and how he or she perceives this anxiety, than simply to assign them a score on an anxiety inventory, and then assume that this tells us something permanent about their nature.

Essentially, state theorists view personality as a process rather than as a static element. We recognise that John is John and Mary is Mary because the processes of change are, in most areas of personality, sufficiently gradual to allow us to see similarities in them as people from day to day – rather in the way in which we identify summer as summer even though some days are cold and wet and there is a perceptible progression towards autumn. This means that state theorists, in addition to placing more emphasis on the possibility of change and development in personality, also take more account of fluctuating emotions, many of which are of great practical relevance in the workplace.

George Kelly

George Kelly (1905–66) remains one of the key figures in the state-based approach. His work has had an important impact on many areas of applied psychology – occupational, clinical and educational. Kelly's starting point (see, for example, Bannister and Fransella, 1980; Webber and Mancusco, 1983) is the premise that behind all our other human needs is the urge to explore the world. We explore it for the basic necessities at the bottom of Maslow's hierarchy of needs (see Chapter 4), and when these needs are satisfied we go on exploring to satisfy the higher social and ego needs, and even for the excitement involved in the very act of exploring. As a species, we are eternally curious. We want to find out about the world and to make sense of what we find. Kelly is thus very much in tune with humanistic psychologists such as Maslow and Rogers (see, for example, Epting and Leitner, 1992), and goes on to claim that we make sense of our phenomenal field, of our own subjective world, by forming what he calls 'personal constructs' about it (hence the term Personal Construct Theory is used to describe his work).

A personal construct is a unit of meaning, a unit that contains all the perceptions, interpretations and evaluations an individual attaches to a particular event, or place, person, or set of people. For example, we all have a construct labelled 'home', which consists of ideas and memories of what home looks like, of the people who live there, of the activities that go on there, of the feelings, attitudes and ideas it arouses in us. Similarly, we have constructs relating to our workplace, our colleagues, our specialist interests, our leisure pursuits and so on.

By virtue of its perceptual content, and because of the personal memories it contains, a construct is more all-embracing than a concept. By means of our constructs, we understand the present and we are able to anticipate or predict the future. Without constructs, we would literally have to start afresh each day, and learn about the world all over again. Because we each inhabit our own subjective world, we build up constructs that are unique to ourselves; no two people ever share an exactly identical construct.

We can see how this works if we go back to the point about sincere witnesses giving conflicting accounts of the same incident. Personal Construct Theory explains that this happens because the witnesses concerned hold differing constructs of the key elements involved, such as the individuals (who may be construed with approval or disapproval), the social codes or laws of the land which may have been broken by the individuals during the incident (which may be construed as just or unjust), and themselves as witnesses (construed in terms of such qualities as helpfulness, truthfulness, reliability, forgetfulness, verbal fluency and so on).

The more experienced we become, the better able we are to sort out which constructs are accurate and relevant to the various people, places and events in our lives. But however appropriate our constructs, there is always an element of subjectivity about them, as inevitably we see the world from our own viewpoint. They are thus not identical with objective truth, and are in consequence always subject to revision or replacement (a state of affairs Kelly called 'constructive alternativism').

Construct theory can also help explain the effectiveness with which we learn and remember. When we tackle an assignment of any kind, we bring to it not only innate ability but also our construct about it, which will include our estimate of the skills required, of the time the task is likely to take, of its importance, of the environment in which we shall have to work while engaged upon it, of the colleagues involved, of the likely reaction of superiors to our results, of the degree of interest and job satisfaction it will involve us in and so on. If the construct is generally favourable, then our motivation to begin the assignment will be high.

Many of the items that go to make up the construct will also be a part of other constructs. If the assignment is likely to earn extra commission or bonuses or marks it will link with constructs surrounding our bank balance, the extra money we need to decorate the house or build an extension or take an exotic holiday, and our standing with our superiors or with teachers. If it might help towards promotions or the approval of others it will link with constructs surrounding career and status, professional or academic self-esteem, and perhaps even consequent improvements in working conditions.

Kelly (1955) identified a number of categories into which constructs can fall, among the most important of which are:

- *Impermeable constructs*, which are relatively resistant to the inclusion of new elements (for example, those formed a long time ago, such as 'my childhood friends'), and *permeable constructs*, which are relatively accommodating of new elements.

- *Broad constructs*, which can be applied widely (for example, 'All pop music is awful').
- *Constricted constructs*, which can only be applied narrowly (for example, 'The only career worth having is one involved with work with animals').
- *Core constructs*, which are central to our existence and help to maintain our identity (for example, 'I'm loyal to my friends', 'I believe in God', 'I enjoy my own company').
- *Tight constructs*, which are likely to collapse altogether if we tinker with them (for example, scientific laws).
- *Loose constructs*, which vary dependent on the situation (for example, summer days can be wet or dry; parties can sometimes be fun).
- *Peripheral constructs*, which refer to information and ideas that are not firmly held and can readily be changed (for example, 'My new neighbours look quite friendly').

Obviously, some constructs can belong to more than one category, as is likely to be the case with many of our core constructs.

Personality problems can arise when an individual's constructs are unrealistic, or too impervious to change (or, conversely, too readily changed), or are inadequate to help him or her predict the consequences of actions, or the behaviour and responses of others. This is one of the main reasons why it is important to treat children, subordinates or those close to us with consistency. If we fail to do so, the constructs they form of us and of working practices and even (particularly in the case of children) of life in general are likely to be confused and contradictory, with consequent loss of comprehension, security and effectiveness. What kinds of constructs of 'desirable behaviour' can children develop if one day they are reprimanded, the next praised, and the next ignored for producing similar performances and in similar circumstances? Life would become as confusing as for example, mealtimes would if one day food satisfied us and the next it made us hungry.

Personal Construct Theory rejects the practice of dividing psychology into separate topics such as 'learning', 'motivation' and 'memory', regarding it as being contrary to the humanistic view that the individual should be treated as a whole person. Mental life is not broken up into these various categories; rather, we function as psychological units. Personal Construct Theory avoids fragmentation by emphasising that behaviour at any given time is largely a

---

Dividing Up Mental Life

If Kelly is correct, and we each function as a psychological unit rather than as a set of separate psychological areas, we may well ask why most psychologists insist on thinking of us in terms of these areas.

The answer is that human psychology is such a vast and complex subject that it becomes convenient to break it down into more manageable sub-categories. And since no single psychologist can be an expert on each sub-category, specialisations inevitably develop. This is no bad, thing provided we are not misled into believing that these sub-categories are in fact independent of each other. In fact, all areas of our psychological lives interact with – and influence – every other area, and changes, developments and problems in one area inevitably influence all the others.

It is therefore particularly valuable to have an approach – such as that of Personal Construct Theory – which allows us to take an overall view, and to remind ourselves that our essential nature is integrated and whole.

---

matter of the constructs we have about the task in hand. Kelly even doubted whether, within education, we have served a useful purpose by taking something we choose to call 'intelligence' and focusing so much attention on it out of the context of the rest of children's behaviour.

As has already been intimated, if someone is labelled 'intelligent', this will inevitably bias the construct we hold of them, and therefore our behaviour towards them. This is the well-known 'halo effect', and it works equally effectively in reverse (the 'demon effect'), as anyone well knows who has tried to live down a bad reputation. For this reason, our constructs of people should be as holistic as possible, which means acquainting ourselves with as wide a range of their behaviour as possible, and trying to learn as much as we can about the constructs they have formed in the course of their life experience. Where these constructs are or have become inappropriate, they can be changed by improving avenues of communication, by providing more information, and by offering the empathic understanding and positive regard advocated by Rogers. Where help of this kind is not forthcoming, the individual will not only continue to use his or her inappropriate constructs, but may form others that are equally inappropriate – for example, by turning existing permeable constructs, which are susceptible to modification and change, into impermeable ones, which are not.

The method developed by Kelly for examining an individual's construct system, which is now widely used in education and the workplace is more time-consuming than Q-sorting or the Semantic Differential (see Chapter 4), but elicits information in a much more structured and more searching way. Basically, it consists of establishing the similarities and dissimilarities that individuals see between the people and things in their lives. Suppose, for example, we want to examine a client's constructs about 'people important to me'. We start by asking him or her to list these people, and we write each name down on a separate card as it is given to us. We then take three of the cards at random – let's say 'partner', 'father' and 'employer' – and ask our client to tell us any way in which two of them are alike and yet different from the third. In response we might be told that partner and father are good listeners, while the employer is not. The words used to describe the way in which the two individuals are alike are termed 'the construct', and those used to describe how the third person is different are called 'the contrast'. Thus, in our example 'good listener' is the construct, and 'bad listener' the contrast. (Construct and contrast are usually logical opposites, as in our example, but they need not be. Thus a construct to emerge might be 'very bright', while the contrast that arises might be 'just average').

We next ask that this construct–contrast variable (good listener versus bad listener) be applied to each of the other people on the list (that is, is person X a good or a bad listener? Is person Y? and so on). Then we return our first three cards to the pile, shuffle it again, and draw another three at random. This time we may be told that two of the people whose cards we have drawn are fun to be with, but that the third person is not. This new construct–contrast variable of 'fun versus not fun' is applied to all the other people on the list, then the cards are again returned to the pile, the pile is reshuffled, and the process repeated once more (note that the same cards can come up – and are therefore used – more than once). In fact, we go on repeating the process until the client has exhausted all the differences and similarities between the important people on the list (experience shows that, whatever the area we are investigating, usually no more than thirty or so of these construct–contrast pairs emerge, and often there are far fewer).

Construct	Partner	Father	Employer	Mother	Best friend	Contrast
Good listener	1	1	2	2	1	Bad listener
Fun	1	2	2	2	1	Not fun
Young	1	2	2	2	1	Not so young
Trustworthy	1	1	2	1	1	Shifty
Responsible	2	2	1	1	2	Feckless

FIGURE 7.1   Repertory grid of 'people important to me'

This method is known as repertory-grid technique because the results are displayed in the form of a grid, with names across the top and variables (that is, the constructs and the contrasts) down the side, and a '1' in each cell of the grid to represent a construct, and a '2' to represent a contrast (see Figure 7.1) – e.g. partner and father would rate '1' on good listening, employer '2'. The finished grid is a representation of the subject's 'people important to me' constructs. Figure 7.1 is a very abbreviated grid. In practice more constructs/contrasts and more important people would be probably be listed, though this depends on the individual.

We can carry out the same exercise with other important areas of a person's life, such as social situations, the workplace, leisure interests and so on. Analysis of the completed grids then shows us the nature and complexity of the person's constructs and therefore of his or her phenomenal field. For example, which kinds of constructs characterise 'important people'? Warm, accepting constructs, perhaps, or cold, rejecting ones? Do these constructs cover a broad range of qualities, such as 'clever', 'interesting', 'sporting', or are they restricted to very few? Do the people concerned seem strong and effective, or weak and negative? And who resembles whom? Do family members, for example, or colleagues, show the kind of divergences from each other likely to lead to conflict and disharmony? Is there a polarisation of qualities between males and females? Between superiors and subordinates? Old and young? Is there evidence of enmity between the subject and those nominally closest to him or her? And so on.

Repertory grids require care in compilation and interpretation, but there are potentially few limits to the kind of information they can provide. Numerous variants of this basic grid have also been devised. Hinkle (1965) has developed the implications grid which compares constructs rather than people or events, and enables us to establish, for example, what the construct 'successful' means to a person (perhaps 'hard working', 'honest', 'like me', or maybe 'lucky', 'stuck up', 'not like me'). Ravenette (1975) has devised a situations grid, of particular value for use with children, which employs pictures rather than words. Grids can now be administered and scored by computer, which speeds up the whole process considerably.

The overriding virtue of the repertory-grid technique is that it directly involves the people who are being scrutinised. They are asked specific questions about the important people and things in their lives, and we give them credit for knowing the answers. In this it differs from so many other psychological techniques (for example, projective techniques, and the behavioural methods we shall be looking at in Chapter 8), which frequently make the assumption that the psychologist knows more about a person than the person knows about him/herself. Repertory grids obey, in fact, what Kelly called his first principle, which is that if you really want to know what is wrong (or right) with people, you should try asking them; 'they might just be able to tell you' (Kelly, 1955).

Using repertory grids

To take an example of how a grid might be used, let us suppose that we are working with a man or boy who has difficulty in learning to read. We decide to compile a grid to establish the construct he has of 'reading' in order to learn more of his motivation in wanting to improve reading efficiency. Typically, we might find that his constructs are very limited, which goes a long way towards explaining why he has so little real incentive to improve. The repertory grid may show that he sees reading as 'boring', as 'unlike my other interests', as a pastime for 'old' and 'dull' people, as identified with 'personal failure' and so on. Once this sorry picture has emerged, it can be discussed with him and its inhibiting nature made apparent. We can then invite him to work through the grid again, this time identifying all the things that would make him take an interest in reading. Reading, it seems, would be worth doing for him if it were 'exciting', if it 'helped with other interests', if it was identified with 'success', if it helped 'get a job' and so on. It would then be the task of the teacher or instructor to demonstrate to him, by suitable choice of reading materials, by setting the right level of difficulty, by relating reading to other hobbies or to career opportunities, that reading can indeed become something interesting and worth doing.

Grids can be used extensively to explore virtually all aspects of the ways we experience ourselves and the world around us. For example, we can construct grids on 'myself', on 'my emotions', on 'how others see me', on 'my goals in life', on 'my work', 'my colleagues' and on anything else we care to mention. Thomas and Harri-Augstein (1985) list over 200 areas of personal experiencing over and above straightforward investigations into personality that they have explored in their research. These range from 'jobs I'd like to do' to 'methods I found successful in breaking habits', from 'families I know' to 'outcomes from listening to a lecture', and from 'responses to personal crises' to 'prayer meetings'. They show how, through the use of the computer, adults and children can work on their own with grid material, exploring their own inner world of fears, enthusiasms, beliefs and feelings, and experimenting with the way in which this inner world might be changed as a consequence of re-sorting the constructs thus revealed.

Work of this kind has implications for all aspects of human learning, and not just for those aspects that have to do with personality. With the universal presence of computers, we now have at our command a powerful medium for helping the personal, academic, therapeutic and vocational/professional development of those with whom we work or whom we teach, and for helping them to take increased responsibility for this development.

Essentially, what the repertory grid helps us to do is to explore the individual's life space in a way that is beyond measuring techniques such as questionnaires. It thus allows us to use what is called the introspective method (inviting people to introspect about their own states of mind), a method which had for long fallen into disrepute in the social sciences because it was held to be too subjective and imprecise. Above all, it allows us to look at the constantly changing state of our mental lives and those of others, to view the fluid nature of personality, and to see where the need and the opportunities for personal change lie.

Two repertory grids referring to the same topic and taken with the same person only days apart can show quite remarkable alterations or developments in the way in which topics are construed. Thus, on the topic of 'self', for example, a student's constructs in the anxious days before a major examination may be markedly different from the constructs that emerge after the exam has been completed successfully, and similar changes may be seen in his or her constructs on a wide range of things that appear to have little to do with the examination itself but which are in fact connected with it, such as constructs of self-image and self-esteem. Discussing the way in which repertory-grid technique has made the inner psychological world accessible, Thomas and Harri-Augstein suggest that it may even mark a 'watershed in social sciences comparable to Copernicus and the telescope in natural science'.

Other state-based theorists

Another valuable approach to the fluctuating nature of personality is that of Michael Apter (1982). Apter differs somewhat from Kelly in that within this fluctuation he identifies certain common dimensions. These are not analogous to the dimensions used in trait theory and upon which the individual has a fixed position, but are dimensions along which the individual moves (or reverses, as Apter puts it) in accordance with the mood or motivational state of the moment. There are a number of these dimensions, but space allows us to look at only the best known, namely the telic–paratelic dimension. When at the telic end of the dimension, the individual tackles life purposefully, producing goal-directed behaviour in which the activities of the moment (the means) are subservient to the ultimate purpose (the ends). In the paratelic mode, by contrast, the activities of the moment are all-important, and the ends, if any, are simply an excuse for engaging in these activities. Thus, to take an example, we might swim to save our lives (in which case our swim would be undertaken very much in the telic mode) or swim for pleasure (in which case it would be undertaken in the paratelic).

Extreme as this example is, it nevertheless illustrates a vitally important point, namely that an activity can be undertaken in either the telic or the paratelic mode. From a behavioural point of view the behaviour looks the same, but from the individual's point of view, there is all the difference in the world.

To take another example, I may walk to the newsagents to buy a morning paper either because I really want a paper, or because I enjoy a brisk morning walk and purchasing the newspaper is simply an excuse for having it. Importantly, intervention by a third party may produce radically different responses from me dependent upon which mode I happen to be in. If I walk to the newsagent because I want my morning paper, and the newsagent offers to deliver it, I will accept the offer and discontinue my morning walk. However, if the newspaper is an excuse for my walk I will refuse the offer and continue as before. A knowledge of the particular mode in which an individual is operating is therefore of great importance to managers, teachers and all those responsible for influencing the behaviour of others.

Some individuals may prefer to be in the telic state for much of the time, while others prefer to be in the paratelic (these preferences can be assessed by a questionnaire known as the Telic Dominance Scale), but most people are able to move between the two states dependent on the context in which they find themselves. The ability to move in this way, appropriately and without inner conflict, seems in fact to be a necessity for the healthy personality. People located rigidly in the telic mode tend to be humourless, sometimes obsessional, over-controlled emotionally, and unable to experience activities for the sheer pleasure of being involved. Individuals rigidly located in the paratelic mode, by contrast, are inclined to be feckless, unable or unwilling to look and plan ahead, and without the necessary self-discipline to apply themselves to a task for the benefits it will ultimately bring.

Compatibility between the preferred modes of people who work together is important. Many misunderstandings and confrontations in the workplace or in the classroom occur when a telic-minded manager or teacher meets paratelic-minded workers or children, with all parties unable to move sufficiently freely between the two states. Failure to recognise the source of the trouble, and to take steps to achieve a practical compromise between the two approaches (or to bring about appropriate movement) may make it very difficult either for useful work to be accomplished, or for harmonious relationships to be established. Currently, Apter is developing measures for assessing the preferred mode of whole institutions, with a view to helping to fit individuals to jobs. For example, a fashion house or an experimental theatre company may function predominantly (and produce best results) in the paratelic mode, whereas a firm of accountants or estate agents may place a decided emphasis on (and function best in) the telic.

Apter's model also stretches to the counselling of people with personality problems. For example, our optimum treatment for a child who steals for telic reasons (that is, to obtain money for a particular purpose) may be different from the way we counsel a child who steals in the paratelic state (that is, simply for excitement). Similarly, a child playing truant because of school phobia (and therefore in the telic state) will require different forms of counselling from the child who plays truant for the sheer fun of it (and who is therefore in the paratelic state), just as the child who bullies others to gain attention (telic state) is a different kind of problem from the child who bullies because he or she enjoys bullying (paratelic state).

A key aspect of reversal theory – and of state-based theories in general – is that they allow for the possibility of producing desirable changes in personality, even in the short term. If personality fluctuates from day to day and even from hour to hour, this gives us the potential to influence such fluctuations. Following suggestions put forward by Bloom (1983), it is therefore important that we examine the various tasks expected of those for whom we are responsible, and determine in advance the *affective* entry behaviours (that is, the personality states) they should be in when they start work. In the case of logical, linear tasks where a definite goal is in mind, a telic mode may be required. By contrast, if the task is more open-ended and freely creative, a paratelic mode may be more appropriate.

One way, proposed by Bloom, of formalising our thinking about affective entry behaviour is that we should study the individual's affect towards, respectively, self; school or workplace; and the subject to be learnt or job undertaken. People may be telic about themselves, with high levels of ambition and purposeful life goals, yet be paratelic about the learning or employment tasks that are given to them, seeing them perhaps solely as opportunities for having a laugh with friends.

Linking reversal theory with other areas of personality, a man may be telic in his attitude towards his job, yet nevertheless lack the ability to remain consistently in the telic state while doing it. Or a woman may be high in telic dominance, yet view the job she has been given as being of low status and therefore likely to lower her self-esteem unless she tackles it in the non-serious paratelic mode.

Similarly, children may be serious and goal-directed about a school subject, yet unable to take seriously the teacher who teaches it. An individual may be concerned with values in his or her personal life, yet uninterested in them in professional life. Thus managers and teachers should identify not only the entry behaviour required of those for whom they are responsible, but also the entry behaviour needed from *themselves* if success is to be achieved.

Emotional states

The discussion of emotions is best carried out within the context of the state-based approach, since the fact that traditionally we use the word 'states' to refer to emotions indicates that we recognise their transitory nature. Pleasant or unpleasant, emotional states come and go, and it is doubtful whether certain high-arousal emotions such as anger, excitement or fear could be sustained by most of us for any length of time. Nevertheless, some people appear much more likely to experience extreme emotions than others, though they may be selective in the emotions they experience. For example, they may frequently experience fear or sorrow, but rarely anger or jealousy; or they may frequently experience joy but rarely sadness.

One of the difficulties psychologists face when exploring emotions is that they are highly subjective states. Both anger and sexual arousal might produce the same physiological symptoms (increased heart rate and blood pressure, rise in body temperature, burn-up of nervous energy, and so on), but it goes without saying that to the person experiencing the emotions they could hardly be more different. Thus simply to take readings of physiological arousal tells us very little about the way a particular emotion feels to the person experiencing it. Indeed, even what seems to be the same emotion (the high arousal associated with risk-taking, for example, or with a horror film) may be experienced quite differently by two individuals: For one person the emotion might be felt as pleasurable and is in consequence sought after, while to the other it is upsetting and becomes something to be avoided. This difficulty in assessing emotions objectively means that we often simply have to rely on what people tell us about themselves, and, as indicated earlier, this kind of introspection is of doubtful value in the eyes of some psychologists on the grounds of its imprecision.

Anxiety as a Motivator

Is anxiety an effective way of motivating people to perform well? Some teachers and managers think so, and may thus be insensitive towards the fears of those for whom they are responsible, or – in extreme cases – may even deliberately play upon these fears in the belief that by doing so they are ensuring that commitment, industry and performance will all improve.

In fact, anxiety, as seen earlier, is only a motivator up to a certain level. Above that level, it may still promote industry, but performance is likely to deteriorate. High anxiety levels lower the individual's self-esteem, inhibit memory, and interfere with clarity of thought and soundness of judgement. In some cases they may even reduce commitment – the individual simply gives up.

A mild degree of anxiety is therefore the most that should be expected of others. Of course, the level at which anxiety remains mild will vary from person to person. High scorers on Eysenck's N dimension will reach this level much more readily than low scorers. Good person- or child-management therefore demands that we know when an individual is likely to be worrying excessively, and take appropriate steps to support and reassure him or her, removing wherever possible some of the anxiety-provoking stimuli.

As was noted in Chapter 6, trait theorists suggest that the best way to conceptualise emotions is to see them as physiological states mediated by the autonomic nervous system (i.e. that part of the nervous system which normally functions independently of our conscious control). That is, to see them as physical experiences set off automatically by the nervous system and perceived by the experiencer as either pleasant or unpleasant. As we go through life we come to learn which environmental stimuli trigger off pleasant states and which trigger unpleasant ones: we generally seek out the former and avoid the latter. Gray (1985) has put forward a model which seeks to show how an emotion such as anxiety can be related directly to changes in brain chemistry associated with autonomic functioning. Some individuals (perhaps innately) are more likely to experience these changes, and therefore to become anxious in the face of threats from the outside world, and could be described in layman's language as 'anxiety-prone', or to have an anxiety trait and therefore to score above average on anxiety measures such as Eysenck's N scale (see Chapter 6).

To the state theorist, however, to say that someone is anxiety-prone is relatively unhelpful. What is of far greater importance is what makes particular people anxious, how they experience anxiety (for example, as something daunting and unpleasant; or as a useful stimulus towards getting work done or problems solved), and what kind of strategies they develop for dealing with or avoiding anxiety. There may be people who rarely experience anxiety because they have learnt how to handle or avoid it. Such people might not score much higher on Eysenck's N dimension than those people who naturally rarely feel anxious about things, yet in a psychological sense they are significantly different, as would become apparent if we asked them to take over the job of teaching other people how to handle their 'nerves'.

The task of the manager or teacher is to observe what causes emotional states in particular individuals and how they try to deal with them, rather than to assign labels such as 'X is timid', 'Y is short-tempered', 'Z is carefree'. In this sense, the state-based approach is likely to be more helpful than the trait-based. The same is true when it comes to 'moods', which we deal with later in the chapter. These are indefinite things but seem to be emotional states persisting over a rather longer period of time, including perhaps the aftermath of an emotional state when we no longer feel the emotion quite so keenly but still allow the memory of it to colour our thinking and our responses to the people and events around us.

In spite of their probable link with inborn temperament (the 'difficult' children we looked at in Chapter 1 in connection with the work of Thomas, Chess and Birch, for example, were noted as having a 'crankiness' of mood from the early weeks of life), there is little doubt that emotions are also very much under an environmental influence. Individuals with a secure background, who have satisfactory levels of self-esteem and who are used to the experience of success, are more likely to be optimistic and happy than are individuals who come from difficult and stressful backgrounds. People who are able to discuss their problems freely and positively with those close to them are less likely to engage in sullen brooding than those who have no one with whom they can communicate effectively. Those with a sensible and humane moral code are less likely to be handicapped by excessive guilt and inadequacy than those who adhere to rigid and perhaps arbitrary standards.

If we take our examples from childhood (though the principles involved apply equally well to adults) we know that those who experience unfairness, frustrations and constant failure are far more likely to be hostile and disruptive than those who experience support, consistency and fairness. Children from schools with meaningless and petty rules, or with timetables that contain little variety or practical work, are more likely to be unruly than children from schools that are more democratic and flexible. Children who have no adults ready to listen to their problems and to provide the right help and guidance are far more likely to take these problems out on others (by attention-seeking behaviour, for example, or by aggression) than children who have someone to turn to in times of difficulty.

These points are particularly true in adolescence, when children are facing the various physical and emotional upheavals of puberty and the transition into adult life. Adults who fail to understand the nature of the search for identity (see Chapter 2) at this stage, and who fail to provide an education which is seen by the children as being relevant to their present and future needs, can hardly expect to encourage the co-operative and positive emotional states needed if educational progress is to be made. But at every stage of development it is vital that teachers monitor these states. Much of this monitoring is straightforward. A class may always be restless when they come from an active lesson such as games or physical education, or when they come from working with a teacher with poor class control, or when the end of the week is near. Similarly, certain individuals may appear to be particularly excitable at certain times (perhaps the lesson before a television programme), or particularly difficult at others. Children from unsatisfactory homes may be extra troublesome on Monday mornings, after spending the weekend in close contact with their families, while children having problems with their schoolwork may be especially disruptive during lessons where they feel their poor progress will be contrasted in public ways with the progress of their more successful classmates.

In all these instances, the teacher can take steps, in consultation where appropriate with colleagues, either to alter the circumstances that lead to problems, or to provide the children concerned with extra support. Sudden changes in children who have hitherto been sunny and co-operative in behaviour should also be identified and watched carefully until the causes (whether at home or school) have been discovered. Children with emotional problems are best helped if they are prompted to understand that we can most effectively gain self-control through the ability to recognise the nature of our emotions, what sparks them off, and what the consequences are for both self and others (see, for example, Fontana, 1985). The more familiar we become with our emotions, the less we feel ourselves to be in their power. The result is that, instead of guilt or self-recrimination when we become involved in undesirable emotions, we experience a sensible and objective appraisal of what is happening to us and why.

With patience and goodwill on the part of both teacher and child, the education of the emotions can become a part of the whole process of school-based learning.

The role of moods

Moods are often related to emotions, and it is important to remember that teachers and managers have moods as well as children and employees, and can affect others just as readily by them. As was indicated in Chapter 7, the best practical advice is to be aware of our own mood changes and of the impact they have on our own behaviour and on the behaviour of others. Children and most adults thrive best on consistent treatment (see Chapter 2), and any teacher or employer whose moods swing wildly or unpredictably from day to day is hardly likely to get the best out of them. Generally, at any age, we respect people with whom we know where we stand, and by remaining conscious of our own moods we lessen the risk of inflicting on groups or individuals negative moods when they are not to blame. The ability to master one's moods usually comes only with practice, but by studying our moods and what lies behind them, we can learn how to express them in non-damaging ways, and to prevent ourselves from being dominated by them.

Apter's work (1982) indicates the extent to which the moods of many people fluctuate during the day. As part of his research, people were assessed at regular intervals during working hours over a period of time, and it was noted not only how rapidly in a majority of instances their moods changed, but also how closely related these mood changes were to external events such as an interview with the boss or a quarrel with a colleague. Such changes in mood coloured attitudes towards events and people in a number of significant ways, suggesting that the manner in which we experience the world, interpret the motives of others, reach decisions, take action and relate to others often depends in some measure upon the mood we are in at the time.

The wider range of stimuli and pressures we experience during the working day, the more our moods are likely to be affected. The lesson to be learnt is that, when we are responsible for others, we should be able to note when our moods are changing particularly rapidly as a consequence of events or of other people's behaviour, and should ponder why we are so much at the mercy of externals. I may very well claim that a particular situation makes me angry, or that a particular colleague makes me impatient or depresses me, but are my claims really accurate? I am not a robot with buttons on my chest labelled 'anger' or 'impatience' or 'depression' which events or individuals or groups can press. In the end, however difficult it may be to appreciate initially, we each of us create our own moods. Certainly these moods may be reactions to outside circumstances, but in the final analysis they are our exclusive creation. We must ask ourselves whether we are really prepared to have our moods dictated to us by what happens around us. If we are not, then we must do some work on ourselves

This is not easy, but the first step has already been indicated: namely, to observe ourselves more closely in order to see what moods we are experiencing, and what external events seem to be associated with them. The next step, if these events cannot be changed in any way, is to see what it is in ourselves that triggers off our emotional reactions to them. What is it in me that prompts anger at the behaviour of a colleague or frustrating circumstances? Is it my sense of professional pride that is being wounded? Or do I have the unrealistic belief that everyone should always behave in ways that best suit me? Or that circumstances should always be as I want them? Whatever factors in me are prompting my reactions, once they are identified I can begin to work on them. I can stop taking things so personally. I can stop seeing the unwanted behaviour of others as a deliberate threat to me as a person. I can see that much disagreement arises through misunderstandings, that the nature of life is to face challenges and frustrations, and that the further I advance professionally, the more the challenges and frustrations are likely to be. This is simply the way life is, and it is going to take much more than me to change it.

Slow-learning children or inefficient colleagues are usually not that way through deliberate choice. Generally, they are that way because the tasks given to them have not been properly explained, or because insufficient attempt has been made to make the tasks rewarding in some appropriate way. The answer lies in altering the manner in which the tasks are presented; in perhaps allowing more time for them to be learnt and tackled; in showing the individuals concerned that we value their contribution – provided it is sincere and well-meant; in offering them opportunities for success at their own level and then building on this success, and in supporting their self-esteem and confidence in their abilities.

Similarly with people whose moods may exasperate or depress one. Such moods are probably not aimed at any individual. In most cases they are an indication of such things as an unhappy home life, or economic problems, or feelings of worthlessness and loneliness. It is in the nature of things for people to have problems, and it is part of the task of the good teacher or manager to recognise these problems and to help where possible by listening to them and contributing to their solutions.

Of course, there are occasions when others, whether children or adults, really *do* want to make someone angry or impatient, perhaps as a way of keeping themselves amused or demonstrating their power over the other person. If this is the case, by reacting with anger or impatience their victim allows them to succeed in their intentions. The victim's reactions will potentially even reinforce the behaviour (see Chapter 8), since the aggressor may enjoy scoring over him or her. Does the victim want the aggressor to have this kind of success? If not, the answer once more is to look at the emotions and ask what it is in one that prompts the unwanted reaction.

We are not going to achieve overnight success with our moods, but by working on them in this way we can begin to see more clearly what is going on in our emotional lives, and through this clarity begin to find ways of bringing these lives more under our own direction. Not only will this make us more effective professionally and personally, it will also cut down on the incidence of stress, which brings me to our next section.

Criticisms of the state-based approach

The state-based approach attracts some of the criticisms also levelled at humanistic psychology (Chapter 4): namely, that it is imprecise and too dependent on the individual's own ability to describe his or her psychological states to us. It is argued that while Kelly's first principle (if you want to know what's wrong with people try asking them: 'they might just be able to tell you') is laudable enough, there may nevertheless be occasions when people might just not be able to tell us what is wrong with them. These criticisms have some justification, but evidence is increasing that the results yielded by repertory grids provide us with information that is impressively accurate. In addition to the successful use of grids in those areas instanced earlier in the chapter, Fransella (1981) reviewed results which show that even with very confused subjects (see Chapter 11) grids can produce information revealing enough to be of great practical benefit in devising and monitoring treatment. Apter has also produced evidence to show how reversal theory can be used to help children in key areas such as learning, counselling and self-development.

Whether the personality is better conceived in terms of a set of persisting traits or in terms of a set of shifting and flowing states, readers must in the end judge from their own experiences. It may be of interest to reflect that in the East, and in the philosophical and psychological systems associated with vast and profound areas of thought such as Hinduism and Buddhism, it has been accepted unquestionably for thousands of years that the state-based explanation is the correct one. Further, it has been accepted that the notion of enduring personality traits is an obstacle on the road to psychological development. There are interesting parallels here with Thomas and Harri-Augstein (1985), whose work within the context of the repertory grid suggests to them that it is the myth of a static mind that is the 'fundamental flaw in any approach to learning', and which underpins 'misguided fixed measures' of personality (and, incidentally, of intelligence and aptitude too).

Trait theorists reply, not surprisingly, that a state-based approach robs us of the chance of seeking common personality principles among the population at large, since of necessity it places the major emphasis on working with individuals. It also robs psychology of the chance of becoming a science, if by 'science' we mean a subject that deals with persistent and consistent data. And there, regrettably, we must leave a debate that is likely to continue to be a major issue in personality studies for some years to come (readers wishing to pursue it further are referred to Fontana, 1983).

Chapter 8
Behaviourism and Personality

We now turn to the contributions that the last of the main forces in psychology, behaviourism, has made to the study of personality. Although behaviourism is no longer the pre-eminent force it once was within psychology, it is still claimed to be – together with its many offshoots and variants – the most objective and scientific approach within the subject, as it concerns itself not with the accounts people give of their own states of mind, but with observations of what they actually do (that is, of their behaviour). It shows little interest in the mechanisms that psychodynamic and humanistic psychology see as underlying personality. The problem with such things, behaviourists have traditionally argued, is that they are based largely on speculation rather than on the structured observation that characterises all good science. It is impossible to observe directly the unconscious processes postulated by Freud and others (or even to test their workings directly, as it is possible to do with qualities such as learning and remembering). Even the concept of personality traits is seen as being of value only if such traits are assessed by questionnaires designed to reveal how people typically behave in various key situations. And as to Kelly's first principle that someone with personality problems might just know what is wrong with him/herself (see Chapter 7), they would answer that we have no way of knowing whether he or she does or not until we have observed his/her behaviour carefully enough.

Behaviourism, which arose from the work of J. B. Watson in the 1920s (for example, Watson 1924), was an enormously important development at a time when psychology was moving away from its parent disciplines of philosophy and theology, and establishing itself as a science. Science deals with public rather than private knowledge, and in place of introspection, which is the largely untestable account by individuals of their own inner life, behaviourism enabled psychology to establish an objective methodology that could be put into operation in the controlled conditions of the laboratory. Instead of being concerned with invisibles such as consciousness, freewill, sensation, attention, will, imagination and even thinking, it set out to study response times to given stimuli together with the physiological changes accompanying such responses (for example, changes to heart rate, blood pressure, skin conductivity and so on), and in particular the effect of rewards, and of success and failure, on the ability to master set learning tasks. Even complex behaviour was analysed into constituent stimulus–response units (conditioned reflexes), and great emphasis placed on work with animals such as rats, in the belief that the basic stimulus–response units apparent in their behaviour underlie all learning, and extrapolations can therefore be made from animals to humans. In the process, behaviourists shifted the determinants of human action from an individual's own free will to the influence exerted upon him/her by the external environment.

Behaviourism has lost its dominant position within psychology because it is acknowledged that there is far more to human beings than bundles of conditioned responses. However, behaviourism, with its insight into the wide range of human functioning that can be explained by such responses, is still an important area, and has particular applications for the workplace. It only led to dissension and division within psychology in the past because of the insistence by some behaviourists that, in order to be a science, psychology must contain nothing but behaviourism.

In its various forms, behaviourism still lays particular emphasis on the importance of the environment (or situation) in human development and action, and on the reciprocal influence of such action upon the situation. In its current form, behaviourism is usually referred to as the social-learning approach (or sometimes the social-cognitive approach), and together with its various subdivisions it is now so extensive that we have space only for those aspects that historically have proved to be the most influential.

Operant conditioning

The central tenet of operant conditioning is the self-evident fact that individuals have an innate tendency to behave in ways likely to produce reward (reinforcement), and to avoid acting in ways that lead to disappointment or punishment. The presence or absence of rewards thus serve to shape behaviour and give rise to learning. Individual differences arise primarily from the variations in the kind of learning experiences people encounter during their lives (and particularly during their early formative years). In addition to direct experience, people also learn by observing the behaviour of others, and noting the rewards or punishments their behaviour brings, a point that will be discussed more fully below.

The principles behind operant conditioning were originally stated by one of the pioneers of behaviourism, the American psychologist E. L. Thorndike (1874–1949) in his 'Law of Effect', but they are now particularly associated with the work of B. F. Skinner (for example, 1974), who maintained that we should abandon the idea that behaviour is prompted by instincts, needs or drives, and should 'shift to the environment a causal role previously assigned to a person's feelings, states of mind, purposes, or other attributes' (Skinner, 1972). Skinner agreed that people differ from each other in their physiological endowments, and therefore must differ from each other in the level of the responses they make to the environment, but argued that our habits, likes and dislikes, beliefs and moral judgements – in sum, our personality – are nothing more than a set of learned responses to the particular environmental circumstances encountered during our life to date. Thus the belief that we have free will, or autonomy, or control over our individual destinies, is an illusion.

In research with animals and humans stretching over nearly five decades, Skinner amassed a great deal of evidence in support of his views. The details of this evidence belong more to a book on learning than to one on personality, but we can see how they can be applied to personality if we take the example of a child who is consistently misbehaving in school. Skinner's argument would be that the child is misbehaving not because of deliberate intention or because he or she 'feels' like it (that is, as the result of a freely taken decision), but because of the experiences that he/she has had in life so far. These experiences have rewarded (reinforced) his/her disruptive behaviour, and have made it a part of his/her personality. He/she may be a child of neglecting parents, who has tended only to receive attention by behaving badly (aggression, temper tantrums, dishonesty and so on).

Good behaviour has been largely ignored and thus produced little in the way of reinforcement. In consequence it has tended to disappear from the behavioural repertoire.

Another possibility is that a boy may be an unpopular child who can only gain peer approval by disruptive classroom behaviour. Or he may be a child who is slow to learn and who is largely ignored by the teacher unless he makes a nuisance of himself. In the case of a child who behaves well, Skinner's argument would be that this good behaviour is also a consequence of the environment – in this instance of the frequent and sympathetic adult attention which has resulted from such behaviour at home and later at school.

If a hitherto well-behaved child becomes difficult after, for example, the birth of a baby sibling, Skinner would deny that this has anything to do with regression (chapter 3), and would insist it is primarily because the mother is now too busy to notice him when he is good, and only turns her attention to him when he behaves badly.

Note that what is being said in these examples is that the very fact of adult attention can be rewarding to a child, even though it be angry attention. This can apply equally to adults. We typically assume that if we speak angrily to someone we are punishing them, whereas in truth the real punishment might be to ignore them altogether. By speaking angrily to them we are at least acknowledging their existence – and perhaps their power to irritate or upset us. This point is returned to later in the chapter, but what it implies is that often we make the behaviour of other people worse by reinforcing it when we imagine ourselves to be doing exactly the opposite.

True to the behaviourist position, Skinner's attitude towards psychoanalysis and humanistic psychology was a dismissive one. In terms of the operant conditioning model, there is no need to postulate the various processes that psychoanalysts and humanistic psychologists advance to account for the existence of neuroses. The operant conditioning explanation is that people become neurotic because their environment makes them so – in particular, through punishing them in confusing and unpredictable ways, or by using harsh and unfair sanctions. In support of this it is argued that laboratory animals can be made to behave in an apparently 'neurotic' way by treatment of this kind, and there is no reason for supposing that laboratory animals possess id, ego and super-ego.

However, operant conditioning is not incompatible with the trait-based approach (Collins and Thompson 1993), or with the attempt by Eysenck and others to relate the personality to such physiological systems as the hypothalamus and the reticular formation areas of the brain. Nor is it incompatible with the view that a large percentage of attributes such as anxiety and introversion may be inherited, if by inherited we mean that some people develop the conditioned responses that are described as 'anxiety' and 'introversion' more readily than do others.

Nevertheless, some behaviourists show themselves to be more in sympathy with the state-based approach, and insist that traits would be more useful if they were redefined in order to make them more specific to situations (Haynes and Uchigakiuchi, 1993). They also make it clear that it is not possible always to point to the precise cause in a person's environment of each item of their present behaviour. The consequences of a particular learning experience, especially in a complex society such as ours, are often long delayed. But, for many behaviourists, the rule remains that behaviour is always caused by circumstances. Thus when we observe an activity that appears to be spontaneous and creative, we are simply witnessing the consequences of experiences that may have taken place much earlier.

'Consequences take over a role previously assigned to an ante-cedent creative mind' (Skinner, 1972). Embedded in this line of reasoning is the emphasis of operant conditioning theorists on performance as well as on learning. We are learning new things all the time, but this learning may not be very apparent in our performance until it is suddenly reinforced by our environment. Thus we may learn early in life to discriminate, for example, between musical notes, but may show little sign of this skill until we are suddenly reinforced by approval when we form a friendship with someone who persuades us to become a member of the local choir.

Operant conditioning theory recognises the existence of both primary and secondary reinforcers. The former (for example, food, warmth, shelter) have intrinsic value; the latter (for example, money, hobbies, interests) do not, but become desirable through their (often indirect) association with the former. A great deal of our behaviour is the result of secondary reinforcement. The educational system operates within a particularly artificial environment, in which children have to learn in a few years information that has come from centuries of research and discovery, therefore it cannot help but rely on secondary reinforcement (such as teacher approval, good grades or, examination success).

Usually these secondary reinforcers are built into 'chains', with each reinforcer being associated with the next and so on back to a primary reinforcer such as parental love and acceptance. Thus a

---

Trial and Error Learning

Operant conditioning is sometimes referred to as trial and error (or, more properly, trial and success) learning. Much of our early learning takes this form. We have no particular clues as to which is the correct response in a given situation, and our previous experience is too limited to offer us any help, so we try first one response and then another until we find one that works. And the next time we meet the same situation, we offer this successful response.

In adult life, our more extensive life experience means that trial and error learning becomes less important. However, there are still occasions when we have no clear guidance as to which is the correct course of action, and we have to fall back on trying a number of different approaches until we meet with success. Clearly, it is important that wherever possible we ensure that those with whom we are working are given sufficient information to make the informed decisions that obviate the necessity for trial and error.

---

student values good grades (secondary reinforcers) because they are associated with parental approval (secondary reinforcer), which is associated in turn with improved emotional and physical rewards (primary reinforcers). Generally, operant conditioning theorists blame the inefficiency of the educational system on a misunderstanding by teachers of the crucial role of reinforcement, and similar claims can be made in relation to other areas of the workplace. We shall be returning shortly to some of the things that Skinner claims can be done to render education and working practices more efficient.

Staats (for example, 1993) takes the idea of chaining even further, and argues that personality consists of a series of behavioural repertoires built up from birth onwards through learning. Each step in each repertoire is a stepping stone for further learning. Staats recognises three of these repertoires, namely language-cognitive (for example, speech, thinking and planning), emotional-motivational (for example, responses to punishment and rewards, enjoyment of work and recreation, and religious and other values), and sensori-motor (for example, feeding, social skills or athletic activities). Behaviour in each of these categories must be learned to provide the basis for later, more complicated, skills, and personality is essentially a learned phenomenon, constructed from the way in which these aspects are put together.

Learning by imitation

Learning by observing the behaviour of others, which was mentioned earlier as an important aspect of behavioural theory, was first emphasised by Albert Bandura (see for example, Bandura, 1973), who recognised that much behaviour takes place in the absence of any kind of obvious reinforcement. Humans, he maintained, have an innate propensity from early childhood to copy the behaviour of others, even when there in no overt reward for doing so. Much learning, therefore, takes place by imitation (or modelling), and this explains broad cultural movements (fashions, fads, mass hysteria and so on) as well as conformity and the socialisation of the individual (Bandura, 1969).

Personality is, therefore, in part an imitation, within the limits laid down by innate differences, of the behaviour of other people. A recognition of the importance of modelling helps to reconcile at least some of the differences between behaviourism and psychodynamics, since the latter also emphasises the individual's acquisition of role behaviour from parents. However, rather than accept the humanistic concept of self-actualisation, social learning theories prefer to see the basic need to imitate as being sufficient explanation of the origin of many of the goals and aims that we develop in life.

Imitation is more likely to take place if the person who is being imitated is seen to be rewarded for their behaviour, and if the imitation itself is then rewarded in turn. The distinction between learning and performance mentioned earlier is also important. An individual need not necessarily immediately perform the actions being imitated. These can be stored mentally and produced at appropriate times later on, as when a person promoted to a position of authority starts to copy the behaviour of a manager he or she served under in the past.

Generally, the more prestigious the model and the less experienced the individual is in the field concerned, the more likely it is that imitation will take place. And as imitation may be learned in the absence of rewards and punishments and not performed until a later date, behaviour may be acquired from a role model without the latter becoming aware of it.

This can be especially true of emotions. Particularly in early life, the individual may have all kinds of emotional behaviour modelled unwittingly for him or her by adults, such as sympathy towards those in trouble, or impatience and anger at their demands. Bandura himself made a special study of aggression (Bandura, 1973), and showed that children at least tend to copy the aggressive behaviour of others, particularly if the latter are significant adults. It is as though aggressive behaviour by important role models sanctions similar behaviour in children. And, of course, if the children find that this aggression pays off in helping them to achieve desirable objectives, then it may become an established part of their behaviour.

Adults are unlikely to be so easily influenced, and even in the case of small children there is often an ability to differentiate between fictional aggression (which they may only act out in play) and realistic aggression, which may be imitated in real life. In addition, innate differences and the individual's previous experiences will obviously affect the extent to which imitation takes place. In an early study, Jakubczak and Walters (1959) showed that dependent children imitate prestige figures more readily than do those who are less dependent, and that timid or anxious children take over fearful responses vicariously more frequently than do secure and confident ones. Children who have learnt to respond warmly to adults in the past will be far readier to take them as models in the present, while someone who has learnt not to value members of the opposite sex will be less likely to copy their behaviour than will someone who has learnt to respect them. Similarly, someone who has been observed behaving ineffectually in the past, or receiving frequent punishment, will be less likely to be accepted as a model than will someone who has been seen behaving with success.

Once again, adults are less likely to be influenced by these variables than children, but a feature of the behavioural approach is that one can extrapolate upwards from simple behavioural systems to more complex ones (for example, from animals to humans; from children to adults; from adults to groups; and from groups to whole societies and cultures), given that the approach considers that the basic building blocks of learnt behaviour are common across these systems. In consequence, modelling is used increasingly as an important part of training programmes in the workplace (Decker and Nathan 1985), and findings indicate that adults are influenced in the same way and by the same variables as children.

The difference is that adults appear to have more ability – based on their greater life experience and their increased capacity to reflect on what is happening to them, to accept or reject role models. Thus modelling becomes more effective for them if it is linked to explanation and debate. For adults, the need to have a measure of control over the experience is also important – for example, the freedom to adapt behaviours to their individual needs, and to build on them through experimentation and innovation.

Classical conditioning

Classical conditioning, first reported by the Russian physiologist Ivan Pavlov (1839–1936), is said to occur when an innate reflex such as fear becomes elicited not just by a natural (or unconditioned stimulus) such as angry shouting or blows, but by the very presence of the person who has been responsible for the shouting and the blows. The person then becomes what is called a conditioned stimulus, as it is now his or her presence even when unaccompanied by verbal or physical violence, that arouses the fear (an emotion which in this case would now be referred to as a conditioned response). In the course of time the fear may even generalise (a process known as stimulus generalisation) to people who resemble the person originally responsible for causing the fear.

Pavlov believed that the whole of the complex activity of human beings is simply a collection of such conditioned responses. The baby's love for its mother, for example, would thus be explained by the fact that the mother is present every time the baby is fed. Over a period of time, the unconditioned pleasure response elicited by being fed becomes associated with the mother, who then begins to elicit pleasure simply by her presence, her touch and the sound of her voice. The feeling of pleasure is thus a conditioned response. By means of stimulus generalisation, this pleasure may in turn be elicited by anyone associated with the mother (such as the father and siblings), or by anyone who physically resembles the mother in some way.

However, the type of learning that takes place through classical conditioning seems to be confined largely to responses occurring in the autonomic nervous system (the system that gives rise to involuntary, as opposed to consciously mediated, responses). In consequence it is thought now to account only for learning that is associated with emotions or affect. For example, when a child is punished for unwanted behaviour of some kind, the punishment arouses the emotions associated with anxiety or guilt. In the future, the behaviour itself, even in the absence of the parent, may come to

---

Classical Conditioning in Daily Life

One of the most ubiquitous examples of classical conditioning in daily life is advertising. Watch television adverts in particular, and note how often the product being sold is paired with images that have nothing intrinsically to do with it. For example, cars are paired with images of attractive women or suave and successful young men; food and household products are paired with happy and competent housewives; perfume is paired with beautiful people enjoying successful love lives; flu remedies with dynamic young executives and so on.

In these and similar instances, the association of the product with something known to arouse a favourable response in viewers ensures that many people will think well of the product. What has happened is that they have been conditioned into thinking highly of it by experiences that have nothing to do with its actual qualities.

Many of our other likes and dislikes, our hopes and our fears, have been conditioned by life experiences. For example, some people are incapable of going to the dentist for a painless check-up – or even of accompanying their children there – through fears conditioned by past experiences. Past experience may also condition us into feeling qualms of fear when facing people in authority, no matter how unthreatening they are in reality. Similarly, certain words – such as holidays, Christmas, parties – spark off pleasant feelings even when we are not thinking of anything specific.

Many people are conditioned into fearing failure whenever faced by challenges, or conditioned into a dislike of people with certain mannerisms or physical characteristics. In all such cases, past experience has associated these variables with the negative responses concerned. Such responses are therefore caused by conditioning rather made by sound judgement.

---

prompt these feelings of anxiety/guilt. Such feelings have become conditioned responses, and the unwanted behaviour itself a conditioned stimulus. For the behaviourist, it is therefore classical conditioning that is responsible for the feelings of anxiety/guilt which Freud and psychoanalysis put down to the operation of a super-ego.

Techniques for modifying behaviour

If, as the behaviourists believe, personality problems such as neuroticism or maladjustment are simply caused by inappropriate conditioning, it follows that, to treat these problems, one must link the situations (that is, the conditioned stimuli) currently prompting anxiety with new and more pleasant associations, thus breaking the bond between situation and anxiety. This is, in fact, the principle behind what is called 'behaviour therapy'.

Behaviour therapy has the advantage of extreme simplicity, and in certain circumstances is highly effective. For example, for a client who has been conditioned to fear public speaking (perhaps as a consequence of derision experienced at the hands of teachers or classmates back in childhood), the therapist might first invite him or her to read a short prepared piece to a sympathetic audience of one or two, followed by the reward of appropriate approval. Next the client is prompted to speak extempore to the same audience, and then to give a presentation in front of progressively larger groups of people. At each stage, the therapist ensures that the client works only at a level that avoids anxiety, and that ample reinforcement in the form of praise and encouragement is given.

The same technique is appropriate in management and sales executive training, with the trainee exposed by easy stages to the work situation in which he or she has difficulty. If the situation involves an audience, as in the above example, and no audience is available during the training process, the experience can be gone through imaginatively. In this approach, the trainee is prompted to visualise the least alarming aspects of the anxiety-provoking situation while remaining relaxed and receiving positive support from the trainer, and then is taken progressively – still in imagination – up through the more intimidating aspects of the situation until the whole scenario can be viewed in a relaxed and confident frame of mind.

The training can in fact, be carried out very successfully alone. When doing so, subjects must try to imagine things in as much detail as possible. For example, if the task for which they are preparing is to present ideas to a meeting of colleagues or superiors, they should build up as clear and accurate a picture as possible of the room in which the presentation is to take place. They should visualise each of the people who is likely to be there, try to imagine the clothes they will be wearing, and look at their body language and the expressions on their faces, even remaining confident and focused when they imagine others looking doubtful about various ideas. Subjects then picture themselves responding to questions and criticisms, remaining always calm and relaxed, seeing themselves avoiding confrontation, listening to and accepting each point of view, yet able to answer openly and effectively any reservations that are expressed. They imagine themselves keeping their temper, protecting the self-esteem of colleagues by giving due weight to their ideas, and remaining good-humoured though clear and incisive throughout.

If at any time during the exercise subjects find themselves becoming nervous or frustrated or experiencing any other negative emotions, all they need to do is to pause, allow themselves to calm down, and then in imagination go back to the last point in the exercise at which they felt at ease, and continue again from there. And as in real life, things should be slowed down if stress levels begin to mount. There is usually a tendency at such times to speed up, often with disastrous results for both fluency and thinking.

Even if at first difficulty is experienced in creating and retaining the required scene in the imagination, practice soon overcomes the problem. I have rarely met anyone who found continuing problems with work of this kind. Imagination is one of our most fundamental human abilities, present from early childhood. With disuse it may become somewhat rusty, but with minimal encouragement will quickly re-establish itself.

In theory, it is possible by methods such as this to desensitise the individual to any anxiety-provoking situation. In effect, one is simply reversing the process which led to the anxiety in the first place.

Similarly, using aversion therapy, it is possible to wean individuals from unwanted behaviour (such as a bad habit, or a destructive or unproductive activity) by associating this behaviour with an unpleasant stimulus. This is the principle behind the deduction of merit marks from students for careless work, or the docking of bonuses from employees for absenteeism. It is also used to help people break unwanted habits such as smoking or binge eating, though it is sometimes difficult to find a stimulus that is sufficiently aversive to outweigh the pleasure gained from the habit.

For example, compulsive gamblers often fail to change their ways even though their gambling typically leads to aversive consequences (financial loss, angry scenes with partners and so on) because the excitement that attends betting outweighs the aversion of losing money or of prompting anger in others. In addition, the occasional win that comes the gambler's way provides what behaviourists describe as intermittent reinforcement, a form of reward that may make a particular kind of behaviour markedly resistant to change.

Nevertheless, desensitisation and aversion therapy and training are extensively used to treat a wide range of anxieties, phobias and undesirable habits. It will be noted that no time is wasted in probing the subject's previous experience to find the exact situation that gave rise to the unwanted behaviour. Nor is this behaviour seen as a symptom of some deeper, unconscious malaise. The symptom and the anxiety or phobia are seen as essentially the same thing, with the curing of the symptom also curing the anxiety or phobia. However, in spite of their short-term effectiveness, desensitisation and aversion procedures may fail to lead to more permanent changes in behaviour unless they are repeated at regular intervals (Wiens and Menustik, 1983). The problem is that in the real world outside the counselling room or the training seminar there may be insufficient rewards and associations to maintain the desired behaviour.

One way of using aversion therapy to help individual personal and professional development is for individuals to penalise themselves each time they identify themselves in a particularly unwanted aspect of their behaviour. For example, each time they catch themselves spending more than a self-allotted period of time over a coffee or a lunch break, they can penalise themselves by missing the next break altogether. Such behaviour sounds extreme, but rapidly proves effective. A natural objection to trying it out is that it pre-supposes strong self-discipline on the individual's part. But strong self-discipline is an important quality in anyone with leadership responsibility for others. If our attempt at aversion therapy exposes us to the fact that we are lacking in that regard, all the more reason to practise it. Self-discipline is largely a learned aspect of personality, and practice, as with so many other desirable areas of learning, is an essential part of the training.

Desensitisation and aversion therapy are based primarily on classical conditioning techniques. The operant conditioning approach to behaviour therapy is somewhat broader. It focuses on consistently reinforcing the wanted behaviour, while at the same time, if possible, withholding reinforcement from that which is unwanted. Thus, to cure an individual of smoking by operant conditioning, the therapist would not rely on the (often impractical) business of associating smoking with something unpleasant, but would concentrate instead on rewarding the smoker for not smoking. As long as the reinforcement of the non-smoking behaviour is consistent and thorough, it is argued that this is a much more effective way of breaking the habit than by treating smoking as a sign of oral fixation (as the Freudian might), or by providing information on the potential hazards of smoking. Where it is felt to be appropriate, the behaviour therapist may also draw the client's attention to role models exemplifying the particular target behaviour at which he or she is aiming.

Behaviour therapy is currently in wide use, especially in the USA, with individuals and within institutions and organisations such as prison, schools and workplaces. A few examples drawn from the school context may be helpful, because they indicate the extent to which, unwittingly, those in authority may be reinforcing (and thus helping to maintain) the very behaviour in others that they wish to discourage.

The first example can be drawn from the case of an isolate child in the early years of schooling who shows great reluctance to mix with other children. The sympathetic teacher frequently spends time approaching the child and trying to draw him/her into group activities, with little or no success. The reason for the teacher's failure, as explained by behaviour therapy, is that she has in fact been reinforcing the child's isolate behaviour by rewarding him or her with attention for refusing to join in. On the few occasions when the teacher has succeeded in integrating him into a group, he has then been 'punished' by the withdrawal of the teacher's attention, thinking it was no longer needed. In order to turn the child's behaviour around, the teacher needs first to turn around her own – that is, to withhold attention from the child each time he behaves as an isolate, and to reward him with attention each time he approaches other children. In this way, he learns that reinforcement comes from approaching others rather than from remaining on his own.

Other examples would be the child who finds difficulty with school work but has discovered that he can get the teacher's attention by disruptive behaviour, or the child who finds he can secure more individual help from a popular teacher by getting his work wrong than by getting it right. In both cases, the logic of the situation remains the same. The children concerned are being rewarded for the very behaviour the teacher wishes to discourage. Behaviour therapists argue that many apparent personality problems are caused by such misapplication of reinforcers, particularly early in life. Apply the reinforcers more appropriately, and the problems, it is claimed, will be ameliorated.The techniques underlying this approach can be summarised in the form of a few simple rules:

(i)   Instances of the behaviour regarded as being a problem are listed in detail (for example, in the case of a child it is insufficient to write down 'rowdiness'; the behaviour must be broken down into such things as 'entering class noisily', 'banging desk lid', 'scraping chair on floor' and so on). These are called target behaviours.

(ii)   Next, against each target behaviour is written the desired behaviour (normally the exact opposite of the former).

(iii) An analysis is carried out of the way in which each of the unwanted target behaviours may have been reinforced by others in the past, and this reinforcement is then withheld.

(iv)   All occurrences of the desired behaviour, even if only minimal, are noted and immediately reinforced.

Application of these rules requires skill and patience. It also requires self-control, as when a teacher deliberately ignores a child's noisy entrances into the class, and greets him pleasantly each time he comes in quietly. The process can be assisted if the teacher models the desired behaviour (for example, by not shouting in class if the teacher is trying to discourage noisy behaviour in others), by drawing favourable attention to children who are modelling the desired behaviour (particularly if they are prestigious role models), and by always stressing in instructions to the class the desired rather than the undesired behaviour (for example, 'Work quietly' rather than 'Keep quiet').

It is also claimed that this approach can be used to encourage less tangible forms of behaviour such as patience, self-control or determination (in fact, the whole range of the things referred to in Chapter 5 as traits). This is done by what is called self-contracting, a kind of course in self-management. In the case of a school, once desirable target behaviours have been identified for individual children, mediators such as parents, local organisations, businesses and tradespeople who can provide the children with suitable rewards are contacted and their help enlisted. Children then contract to produce desired behaviours in return for specified rewards. Each time the target behaviour is produced (for example, truthfulness, co-operation or perseverance) they are awarded notations that can be accumulated and later exchanged for the pre-selected rewards of their choice (for example, extra time watching television, outings, sport and recreational opportunities, invitations to visit interesting workplaces, sponsorships, extra pocket money and so on). As a result of strategies of this kind, children learn, many of them for the first time in their lives, that things such as honesty may in fact pay off.

In the course of this learning, they also acquire a range of other secondary reinforcers as a result of their improved behaviour, such as enhanced school performance, better relationships at home, more teacher approval and more prestige. It is these secondary reinforcers that help to sustain the desired behaviour in the future.

Observations on the social learning approach

One of the most important contributions of the social learning approach is that it draws our attention to the fact that teachers, managers, parents and all those in authority frequently and unintentionally reinforce the very behaviour they wish to discourage in those with whom they are working. The approach also provides specific ways of identifying when this is happening, and of deciding what is needed to put things right. Where institutions or organisations are involved, the relevant techniques work best when practised by all appropriate personnel, who together should work out a common and consistent programme, which should then be applied uniformly.

The learning theory approach is on more controversial ground in maintaining that all personality problems can be tackled by means of its methodology. There is still a suspicion that this methodology tackles the symptoms and not the causes of personality malfunction, and that, in the long run, new sets of symptoms are likely to occur in their place. Behaviour therapists deny that symptom substitution of this kind happens, as long as all the relevant symptoms in a given category of behaviour problems are tackled in the first place. But it may not be possible to do this. In a highly anxious person, for example, particularly one with free-floating anxiety (see Chapter 3), anxiety can be a generalised reaction to virtually every major aspect of life.

Another point of criticism is that much of the initial (although not more recent) research work underpinning the behavioural approach was carried out with animals, and it is unclear how far the results of this work can usefully be applied to humans. An animal can indeed be made to behave apparently neurotically, but this does not demonstrate that anxiety cannot be caused in human through the existence of such a thing as a super-ego, as humans are able to reflect (both realistically and unrealistically) on their experiences. The super-ego is a collection of ideas, values and beliefs acquired and sustained largely through the use of language. Language gives humans a much wider and more complex range of experiences than these enjoyed by animals, and allows people to brood on these experiences, to plan future behaviour, and to suffer guilt.

Language and thinking allow human beings to be aware of the fact that they are being reinforced. If they need the reinforcement, they are likely to produce the appropriate behaviour to obtain it; if not, the behaviour is withheld. Initially, behaviourists denied that humans can choose whether to produce behaviour or to withhold it, since this implies the existence of free will, a point they were not prepared to concede. Here, inevitably, we stray into a field beset with philosophical hazards, where 'proof' is not possible one way or another. Indeed, it is surprising that behaviourists allowed themselves to become involved in a debate of this kind. The salient fact is that men and women think and act as if they have free will. Even the most rigid behaviourists acted as if they had free will in deciding to put across their ideas, and assumed their readers had the free will to accept or reject them. In a deterministic world, devoid of the freedom of choice, one would have to assume that the arguments advanced by behaviourists are also determined, and have no more warrant to be 'preferred' than any other form of argument.

Rejection by extreme behaviourists and social learning theorists of the notion that human behaviour can ever be traced to such things as meta needs raises great problems in the explanation of human motivation and creativity. It is not easy to see how the operant-conditioning model can ever be stretched to explain satisfactorily the work of, say, Beethoven or Shakespeare – still less, perhaps, the pleasure that their work has brought to the rest of mankind. Partly in order to counter points such as this, many theorists now emphasise reciprocal determinism, in which external reinforcers such as reward and punishment, and internal reinforcers such as beliefs, expectations, fears and thoughts are all seen as interacting influences which together determine behaviour (for example, Bandura, 1986). This is a valuable advance, and one which goes much further towards acknowledging the complexity of human personality, and the limited nature of our own knowledge of its development and operation.

Chapter 9

Personality, Intelligence, Creativity and Cognitive Style

Before beginning any discussion of personality and intelligence, we need to dispel a common myth about intelligence itself, that is that it is a 'thing' in the way that the brain is a thing. It is not. Intelligence is simply a socially constructed concept; a term we use for particular kinds of behaviour.

Once we recognise this, we can see that to speak of personality and intelligence as if they are separate 'things' is misleading. They are both simply aspects of the way we think, feel and act in the world. If we look at accepted definitions of intelligence – for example, that it is the ability to recognise relationships between things and to use these relationships to solve problems, or that it is a person's capacity for goal-directed, adaptive behaviour – we realise it is very much a part of the general reaction to life that we call personality. When we speak of people as being bright, or alert, or slow, it is usually this general reaction that we are talking about, not just the fact that they do well or badly in tests of intelligence. The point is well taken by Cattell, who includes intelligence as one of the factors measured by his personality tests (see Chapter 5 of this volume), and by Kelly (see Chapter 7).

We should therefore not discuss whether or not intelligence interacts with personality, but rather *how* this interaction operates. Certainly, intelligence influences some areas of personality more strongly than others. Often there is no straightforward link between intelligence and a person's beliefs and values (though the former will normally affect the manner in which the latter are defended). On the other hand, there is an obvious connection between intelligence and the level of the life-goals that individuals set themselves, and between intelligence and the kind of interpretations that are put on life experiences.

Not surprisingly, as intelligence tests are themselves trait-based devices, most of the research into the relationship between intelligence and other factors of personality has been carried out by trait theorists. With the exception of certain correlations between low intelligence and scores on Eysenck's N dimension (see Chapter 5 of this volume), neither Eysenck nor Cattell has found that intelligence correlates consistently with any of the dimensions or factors of personality measured in their tests (though we saw, again in Chapter 5, some correlation between low intelligence and high L scores).

One very interesting line of research carried out many years ago by the Fels Institute in the USA into samples of children who, between the ages of six and ten, showed either a marked increase or a marked decline in IQ scores (Kagan *et al.*, 1958) found that those in the increased-IQ group were more competitive, and more verbally aggressive than were those in the declined-IQ group. They were also readier to work hard, showed a stronger desire to master intellectual problems, and were less likely to withdraw in the face of challenge.

What this research appears to show is that the possession of certain personality characteristics may help individuals (and probably adults as well as children) to make fuller use of their intellectual potential. If we think back to Chapter 2, it will be remembered that, in higher education, Barron produced similar findings in that he found resourcefulness, energy and adaptability correlated well with satisfactory levels of achievement. In what is still one of the most ambitious studies of its kind ever attempted, Terman and Oden (1947) followed up 750 children with IQs of 140-plus into adult life, and found that those who fulfilled their early potential were more interested in their work, more persevering, more self-confident, and better integrated in their life-goals than those who did not. They were also significantly better adjusted and more socially effective than the average.

Using the terms we have employed in this book so far, we could say that they were higher in achievement motivation, higher in self-esteem, and better adjusted than the average. All these things, of course, correlate strongly with a secure home background, in which the children enjoy the confidence of their parents, and in which they are set definite and consistent standards and encouraged to reach them. However, Roe, in another early study which has not been improved upon (Roe, 1953), showed that many eminent scientists have struggled against early feelings of inferiority, and the same is true of many great men and women, so an unfavourable background by no means ensures that a person will make little of life. Adler (see Chapter 3 of this volume) would have argued that such successful people are struggling extra hard to compensate for their feelings of inferiority. Certainly, whether their backgrounds are favourable or unfavourable, people who achieve eminence frequently seem to have been driven by the need to come up to certain expectations, whether these are formulated by sympathetic but demanding parents, or by the need to prove personal worth in the face of indifference or rejection.

More generally, McCandless, at a time when intelligence testing was even more popular than it is now (McCandless, 1969), found that children with high IQs tended to be taller, better looking, physically stronger and more popular than those at the opposite end of the spectrum. They also emerged as less anxious, perhaps because they found life easier to manage than did less able children. In addition, they seemed to be better judges of other people (particularly strangers) as well as of themselves. Obviously, such high-IQ children found in the main that people reacted favourably towards them, thus helping them to gain a more positive opinion of themselves. In the interaction between heredity and environment, the latter obviously enhances the former, just as the former may help individuals to come to terms with the latter. Sadly, during the childhood years, those who appear less able are likely to be handicapped by lower expectations, by difficulties in achieving competence, and by the low self-esteem that frequently develop in consequence.

Personality and creativity

Systematic psychological research into creativity is of more recent origin than that into intelligence, and suggests that if intelligence is the ability to solve problems convergently (that is, to solve them by identifying specific answers to specific problems), then creativity is the ability to think and behave divergently – that is, to come up with a range of solutions to problems that do not necessarily have single correct answers. Psychological tests to measure creativity are therefore open-ended tests designed to stimulate the mind into producing as many appropriate answers to a given question as possible. Good examples are the 'uses of objects' test (for example, 'How many uses can you think of for a brick?'); the 'meanings of words' test (for example, 'How many different meanings can you think of for the word "bolt"?'); and visual tests such as those that involve converting as many outline drawings of circles as possible into recognisable objects simply by adding details.

It is still not clear whether intelligence tests and divergent-thinking tests are measuring radically different or related human attributes. However, it does seem clear that a certain level of intelligence is needed if an individual is to organise and use creative talent effectively, and research by Canter (1973) suggested that creativity becomes independent of intelligence only at IQ scores of 120 and above (that is, IQ scores above this level make no additional contribution to the ability to make use of creative potential – though an IQ of 120 is quite high, given that the average is 100). It also seems reasonably clear that there is a relationship between high scores on divergent thinking tests and the possession of certain personality characteristics. In a number of studies using Cattell's 16 PF (see Chapter 6 of this volume), it has been shown that creative people in both the sciences and the arts are more independent, more intellectually self-sufficient, and more radical than the average (see, for example, Cattell and Butcher, 1968). Scientists tend to score highly on withdrawal behaviour items, while artists (particularly painters) score on unconventionality and eccentricity (the 'artistic temperament' perhaps).

Taylor and Holland (1964) added to this list of qualities by quoting evidence that shows creative people are more autonomous, self-sufficient, self-assertive and resourceful, while attention has already been drawn (see Chapter 6 of this volume) to the link between creativity and scores on Eysenck's P dimension. Creative people also appear to be more introverted than the norm, more inclined towards so-called feminine interests (such as beautifying the environment), more aware of their impulses, and more open to the irrational in themselves. Barron (1979), in a study of 1500 creative men and women in a wide range of fields, found their life histories included relatively unstable behaviour, such as depression, tension, anxiety, psychosomatic illness, suicide attempts and various criminal offences.

Other investigators have found creative people to have a high tolerance of ambiguity (that is, they function well in unstructured and informal environments where parameters are unclear), and to be capable of a high level of abstract thought. As with intelligence, most studies indicate that people who make effective use of their high levels of creativity are generally strong on achievement motivation. They have a single-mindedness which enables them to work hard in their chosen field and to show a high level of interest and involvement in the things that they do (compare the comments on the mature personality in Chapter 2).

Work by Sternberg and Lubart (1992) and by Amabile and Hennessy (1992) suggests what might be termed the 'big five' components of creativity, namely:

(i)   *Expertise* – an extensive and well-developed base of relevant knowledge upon which to draw;
(ii) *Imaginative thinking* – particularly the ability to see things in new ways and to make connections between them;
(iii) A *venturesome approach* – a readiness to take risks with material and to tolerate ambiguity;
(iv) *Intrinsic motivation* – high levels of personal interest, enjoyment and satisfaction (which count for more than external pressures), together with the ability to work hard and persist after apparent failures; and
(iv) A *creative environment* – colleagues and surroundings which help to stimulate and support creative endeavour.

Like all generalisations, these five components do not hold good in all circumstances. There are unlettered geniuses who have produced major works of art; there are people who triumph in the most unstimulating of circumstances; and there are people who only produce their best work in the face of external pressures such as deadlines and creditors. Nevertheless, these five components give us a good idea at least of the things that work best for most creative people.

As with intelligence, however, it must be stressed that creativity should not be seen as something distinct and separate from personality. Creative people are generally creative in their whole approach to life. Many of the personality characteristics we mentioned above are not just things that the creative person happens to have; they are their creativity in a very real sense. When it comes, therefore, to discussing how best to encourage desirable levels of creativity in the people with whom we work, whether they be children or adults, Rogers (1974) stresses the importance of positive regard, encouragement, and freedom from excessive external evaluation. This means that if we invite creative ideas from others, we may comment on the practicality or otherwise of the results, but we should refrain from passing negative and discouraging judgements on them as, by its very nature, divergent activity contains no immutable rules of correctness.

The important part that teachers in particular can play in developing creativity in others (Jung would say, in freeing them to listen to their unconscious – see Chapter 3) was evidenced by a number of studies (for example, Haddon and Lytton, 1968) which showed that primary school children who were taught by informal methods performed better on divergent-thinking tests than children in more formal schools, and that this enhanced performance persisted when the children transferred to secondary schools, irrespective of the type of secondary school involved (Haddon and Lytton, 1971). Informal teaching methods have now fallen into disfavour in the UK, but what these findings suggest is that if teachers wish to encourage the creative side of children's personalities, the children must not be taught to undervalue this aspect of themselves, or to adopt only a conventional approach to thinking.

Hudson (1966), in a classic early study, found a tendency among boys specialising in science subjects at sixth-form level to think convergently, while those specialising in the arts tended to think divergently, and suggested that this might be because some teachers of science subjects were not prepared to allow as much creative expression in their pupils as were teachers of arts subjects (an unfortunate state of affairs if true, as science, like the arts, stands in need of creativity). Hudson's work also suggested that when pupils who were highly convergent were encouraged to be freer and less self-judgemental in their responses, their ability to think divergently increased significantly.

We still do not possess universally agreed models of the creative act. One of the most useful such models was advanced by Jerome Bruner and his colleagues many years ago (for example, Bruner *et al.*, 1956), and postulated the existence of holistic (creative) thinking and algorithmic (rational) thinking. Bruner considered that the Western educational system encourages the latter at the expense of the former, by laying stress on conformity, on single right answers and right conclusions, on children always using the 'correct' method for solving problems in mathematics and science, on children not guessing solutions (frequently, guessing, Bruner argued, is evidence of creative effort, or of a sudden flash of insight), and on a failure to teach children to tolerate ambiguity (and thus to recognise the fact that uncertainty is an unavoidable aspect of some situations and problems).

It is not that Bruner, or indeed any psychologist, argues against the need for convergent, algorithmic thinking, but simply that this kind of thinking should not be the only form of thought encouraged in children. McKellar (1957) put the case well when he talked of holistic (or, as he chose to call it, 'autistic') thinking as being the author of any worthwhile creative act, while rational thinking is the editor who sifts through the ideas generated by holistic thinking, isolates those that are most relevant, and puts them to use (see also Fontana, 1985b).

In the 1990s there has been little research into creativity *per se* in children, but in the 1960s and 1970s, when such research was popular, there was evidence that teachers generally found it harder to relate to high-creativity children than to those scoring high on intelligence tests. Getzels and Jackson (1962), in another study that has become something of a classic, suggested that the non-conformist and apparently self-sufficient mannerisms apparent in creative children made them less immediately sympathetic to teachers than children with more conformist behaviour.

If Getzels and Jackson were right, teachers may have to take particular care not to allow the independent approach of some creative children to count against them, and this probably holds good for those in authority in the adult world as well. In fact, this caution applies to our relationships with all gifted individuals, whether their giftedness stems from high creativity, high intelligence, or both. It is probably another of the failings of the British educational system – and perhaps also of the business world – that it pays insufficient attention to helping gifted people to live with, and to make good use of, their gifts. Sometimes those who are highly gifted can feel as isolated from others – and as misunderstood and unappreciated – as can those who are disadvantaged in some way. With their high levels of curiosity and activity, and their boredom in the face of unchallenging work, they can sometimes be uncomfortable members of the group, and some of those with, or under whom, they work may feel threatened by their precocious knowledge.

Perhaps because of their very feeling of separateness, there is some evidence that gifted children and adults (particularly, it seems, gifted girls and women) may play down their gifts to avoid unpopularity with others (including those in authority over them). Such self-negation may be as potentially damaging to the personality as are the forms of self-rejection we looked at in Chapters 3 and 4. The

The Creative Act

It may seem strange, but science still has no clear idea of how thoughts arise. They simply emerge into awareness. Where do they come from? What mechanism puts them together?

These questions are particularly pertinent when it comes to creativity. Creative thoughts are, by definition, thoughts that are original as far as the thinker is concerned. How is this originality made possible?

Studies of creative people in many walks of life have not enabled us to answer these questions, but at least they give us some insight into how the creative act appears to operate. Typically, there are four stages involved:

(i)   *Recognition* – we recognise that a creative solution to a problem is required, or that we have a good idea, for example, for a book or a business venture or a lecture;

(ii) *Incubation* – we may work on the problem or the idea for a time, then typically we put it to one side, even if only briefly, allowing it to sink into the unconscious;

(iii) *Illumination* – a creative solution to the problem, or further ideas for the book or the lecture, suddenly emerge into consciousness; and

(iv) *Verification* – we put the solution or ideas to the test.

Thus it would seem that the unconscious plays a major part in the creative act. During the incubation period, the unconscious, below the level of awareness, gets to work on solving the problem or developing our original ideas, and when it arrives at something useful it puts it up into consciousness.

It is unfortunate that examinations rarely allow time for incubation, with the result that many of our best ideas come to us when we have left the examination room. And equally unfortunate that the pressures for instant decisions in the workplace also often leave little space for the unconscious to go about its creative tasks.

cost to the community in terms of lost potential needs no emphasising.

Professional people sometimes query the place of creativity in the workplace, as they tend to associate the word 'creativity' with nonconformity, unreliability and even fecklessness. The caricature of the unkempt, disorganised artist comes all too readily to mind. In fact, creativity is a valuable asset in most contexts. In addition to the originality mentioned earlier, creative people tend to be readier (more fluent) with ideas, and more flexible and adaptable in their thinking. Whether finding ways of beautifying the office environment (and consequently making it a pleasanter place in which to work) or coming up with new initiatives for improving business performance, they can do much to advance the efficiency and effectiveness of an organisation.

Since everyone is creative to some degree, what can be done to encourage individuals to put their talents to good use? Creativity flourishes best in a working environment that gives permission, within clearly defined limits, for original and progressive thinking. The main hindrance to creative expression is the fear that one will get things 'wrong', or have one's efforts compared unfavourably with those of colleagues. In a non-judgmental set-up, where each person is encouraged to put forward ideas, no matter how impractical they might seem at first, creative thinking tends to flourish.

Brainstorming (first developed in the 1960s by Parnes (1967)) is a good example of this non-judgmental set-up. Conducted individually, but more usually in groups, brainstorming focuses creative attention on a relevant and specifically formulated problem (which might be to do, for example, with the need to increase sales penetration in a particularly intractable area, or how to design or re-design a particular product, or how to improve working relationships within the organisation), with each participant invited to contribute whatever responses to the problem come to mid. Usually these responses are taped, and at the end of the session the tape is played back (or transcribed and distributed as hard copy to the participants), and thought is given at follow-up to the usefulness and practicality of the various contributions. During the brainstorming session no restrictions are placed on these contributions, however inappropriate or trivial they may seem. Thus there is no censorship imposed upon one's thinking, either by oneself or others. Ideas are expressed as they come into mind, thus allowing full play to creative freedom, and the ideas of one person frequently spark off those of others.

At follow-up the most improbable ideas yielded by the brainstorming session are sometimes found to contain important new thinking, which can then be developed and extended. Thus brainstorming plays the role of author, and follow-up the role of editor. In consequence, many problems that have proved resistant to solution when tackled by rational, linear thinking, may be resolved by the creative free-for-all opportunities provided by brainstorming.

Creativity also helps the operation of what Edward de Bono (for example 1985 and 1993) has termed *lateral thinking*, a form of thinking that displays both originality and intelligence, allowing the thinker to escape from a line of thought which, although perfectly logical in itself, may have started from false premises, and therefore be incapable of arriving at an appropriate answer. Lateral thinking allows one to move sideways (laterally) as it were, and pick up another line of thought which starts from correct assumptions, and therefore leads to the desired goal. Lateral thinking, rather like a form of brainstorming, allows for the juxtaposition of ideas which at first sight have no apparent logical connection, but which can transform the way in which one views a problem. A good example from car design was the notion of the transverse engine. Previously, car engines had always been mounted front to rear, and this practice had become received wisdom. By questioning this wisdom, and placing the engine across the chassis rather than along it, economies of space were effected, and a whole new era in car design was inaugurated.

Lateral thinking questions existing assumptions and habitual ways of looking at particular problems. Because things have always been done (or organised or stipulated) in a certain way does not mean that this is the only or the best way of doing them. Similarly, because new problems have always been approached using a certain set of strategies does not mean that other and perhaps better sets do not exist. Above all, it recognises that if we start off in the wrong direction, no matter how effectively we travel, we are never going to arrive where we want to be. In all areas of working life, it is of value to remain conscious of the place of lateral thinking. If a current procedure is not producing the desired results, then acceptance that there must be (or at least *might* be) a better way of doing things is essential if progress is to be made.

Cognitive style

Cognitive-style theories link at several points with personality and with both creativity and intelligence. Such theories start from the accepted fact that we are bombarded by so much data from the environment every moment of our lives that we cannot possibly attend to everything without enormous cognitive strain. They then ask how we sort the data out and decide what to attend to and what not. The answer is that we do it by coding – that is, by placing each piece of data into one of a range of categories, to each of which we have assigned a rating of importance. In any situation, things belonging to categories rated relatively high in importance typically gain our attention; while those belonging to categories rated relatively low in importance typically do not.

The way in which we assign things to categories will be determined partly by previous experience, and partly by innate factors, including how we in fact perceive things (for example, some people are innately more sensitive to certain stimuli, such as loud noises, bright colours, or subtle differences in shape, than are others). For example, when we are confronted by a problem to solve, we first study and categorise the information it contains. Next we hunt through the information we already possess until we find data coded into a similar category. Finally, we form a hypothesis and see if it will allow us to reach a workable solution.

Cognitive-style theorists claim that each of us carries out this coding process in our own characteristic and consistent way. We do not change our method drastically from experience to experience, or from problem to problem. They also suggest that as our whole contact with the outside world, including our social interactions, is influenced by the way in which we choose to code things, coding must be seen as an important part of personality.

Cognitive-style theory is not, however, an alternative to the other theories of personality at which we have been looking. It does not concern itself with motivation, or with possible systems within the personality such as the ego and the super-ego. It recognises that neurotic people tend to assign things to categories that have to do with their worries, and then attend to (or alternatively strive to avoid) those they find the most threatening. It accepts that extraverts tend to code in terms of their outer-orientated approach to life, and introverts in terms of their more inner-orientated preferences. And it accepts that coded categories may be built into personal constructs. It is essentially an attempt to explain the mechanisms that the personality uses to interact with and interpret the world, whether the concern is with things, people, ideas or attitudes.

We can illustrate this by looking at the way in which two individuals tackle a given problem. One may characteristically read quickly through the information, gain an overall, and perhaps inaccurate, picture of what the problem is all about, and immediately start trying to solve it. Another may characteristically read the information slowly, and ponder each word and its implications, before starting work. These different methods of tackling the problem are part and parcel of the respective cognitive styles of the individuals concerned. However, such things as the level of enthusiasm they bring to bear towards the task, the degree of importance they assign to its solution, the length of time they are prepared to devote to it, and the amount of interest or anxiety it arouses in them, belong not so much to their cognitive styles as to those areas of personality discussed in earlier chapters.

Obviously, cognitive style has important implications for success and failure in the workplace. We may find ourselves saying that one person tends to rush things, that another always seems to miss the essentials in an argument because they don't listen properly, that another is disorganised in his or her thinking, that another is precise and methodical and so on. And as these characteristics are evidenced in the way people relate to each other as well as to material problems, they have obvious implications for how well people co-operate and work together. They can influence attitudes towards authority, towards members of the opposite sex, towards minority groups, towards people apparently less able than oneself, and can even affect the amount and depth of consideration that is given to the selection of short-term and long-term life goals.

However, terms for these characteristics such as 'disorganised', 'inconsistent', and 'methodical' are somewhat vague and subjective, and psychologists have identified a number of more precise – albeit broad – categories of cognitive style into which people can be divided. As with personality traits, these categories tend to be bipolar dimensions (that is, the ends or poles of each dimension represent the exact opposite of each other). Let us look at some of the most useful of these dimensions.

Field dependence-independence

If you were placed in a mock-up of a room that could be tilted to the left or to the right, and seated in a chair that could be similarly tilted, would you still be able to know whether you were upright or not, no matter what the respective angles of the room and the chair? Strange as it may seem, your ability (or inability) to gauge accurately whether your body was upright or not would give an insight into one important aspect of your cognitive style. Some people are consistently successful in judging their position when taking this Body Adjustment Test, while others consistently lose their sense of the vertical completely as soon as the 'room' starts to tilt; some even claim to be upright when the room and chair are both tilted through an angle of thirty degrees (Witkin, 1959). What seems to be happening is that the first group of subjects is able to sort out the pull of gravity (the relevant stimulus) from the visual experience of the 'room' in front of them (the irrelevant stimulus), while the second group are not. Witkin termed the first group field-independent (FI) and the second group field-dependent (FD).

Further experiments, using both the embedded-figures test (in which the subject first studies a simple black-and-white line pattern and then has to pick it out when it is 'hidden' in a more complex pattern) and the rod-and-frame test (in which the subject sits in a darkened room and attempts to place in the vertical a luminous rod which is surrounded by a tilted luminous frame) confirmed the existence of field-dependence and field-independence as two poles of a dimension, with the majority of the population, as in the dimensions discussed in Chapter 6, located somewhere in the middle but with many individuals at one or other of the two extremes.

Witkin then established that the field-dependent/independent dimension has important applications for the way in which we handle everyday life. For example, FD people seem less able to pick out and remember the details in a given situation than FI people. When presented with a battery of projective techniques (see Chapter 3), they also disclose themselves as being apparently less perceptive in dealing with life, and more subject to outside influences (Witkin *et al.*, 1954). Witkin summed this up by saying that the FD person has a global cognitive style, while the FI has an articulated one (these terms, 'global' and 'articulated', together with the group label 'psychological differentiation', have sometimes been used as alternatives to 'field-dependence/independence').

Some correlations have been found between extraversion and field-dependence (Witkin, 1959), and it is tempting to suggest that the latter is to some extent an expression of the former. Extraverts, with their greater social involvement, greater need for frequent and varied stimuli, and slower rate of conditioning, tend to pay less attention to each unit of experience. Typically, they also give themselves less time in which to identify the most relevant units of experience in any given situation, and would therefore seem, on face validity, to be more likely to be FD than are introverts.

However, though there is a correlation between field-dependence/independence and extraversion/introversion, it is far from a perfect one. Many extraverts are FI; and just as many introverts are FD.

Field independence also seems to go with certain qualities as common in extraverts as in introverts, such as a more developed sense of personal identity (which in Erikson's terms indicates maturity of personality – see Chapter 2), and with higher self-esteem and self-confidence.

Interestingly, it also goes with a particular style of ego-defence mechanism (see Chapter 3). Bertini (1961) demonstrated that when FI people employ repression (for example, blotting out the memories of unpleasant experiences) they seem able to repress selectively, whereas FD people are likely to repress indiscriminately, blotting out large chunks of their past experience in a way which suggests they are much less able, consciously or unconsciously, to single out the precise causes of their anxiety. FD individuals are also better able than FI individuals at keeping their feelings separate from their thoughts and perceptions, which might partially explain why field dependence appears to be more prevalent in women (who are more open to their feelings) than in men.

It is important to stress that while much of what has been said may seem to favour field independence over dependence in many real-life situations, neither of these cognitive styles is invariably 'better' than the other. The FD person may be more sensitive to the needs of others than is the FI, and more gregarious, more socially involved, and perhaps less likely to withdraw socially. It is also likely that extremes at either end of the dimensions are equally adverse, with FD individuals more likely to suffer from identity diffusion and overdependence on others (alcoholics and compulsive overeaters are more often FD), and FI individuals more likely to manifest an over-rigid defence of personal identity which leads them to lay the blame for problems upon others rather than upon themselves.

Field dependence-independence has obvious implications for interpersonal relationships and for problem-solving. Although it throws little light on creativity (different kinds of creativity may possibly demand different styles), it does have a bearing on intelligence. Studies show that, in children, FI goes with better performance on analytical items in IQ tests, though it is no advantage for verbal items. Witkin (1965) argued, somewhat controversially, that many children with learning difficulties also score better on analytical items than they do on verbal, and that in consequence IQ tests should be replaced by those for cognitive style, as the latter can 'recognise the rooting of intellectual functioning in personality'.

Focusing-scanning

A second important dimension of cognitive style, focusing-scanning, is associated particularly with Jerome Bruner. One of Bruner's research tools was to present children with a number of pairs of cards, one pair at a time, each card depicting varying arrangements of squares, circles, lines and colours. The children were then told that one card in each pair was 'correct' and the other 'incorrect', and as more of the pairs were presented they were asked to determine what particular features of the squares, circles, or whatever, denoted 'correctness' or 'incorrectness' (Bruner et al., 1956).

Results indicated that children could be distributed along a dimension which ranged from those who examined the relevant features in each of the pairs until they had amassed enough information to advance a hypothesis (the focusers), to those who formed an hypothesis on the basis of the first pair, stuck to it until enough subsequent pairs had been examined to show it to be untenable, and then had to go back to the beginning and start again (the scanners).

What seemed to be happening was that focusers characteristically delayed hypothesis-making until they had sufficient evidence, while scanners characteristically formed their hypotheses on slimmer evidence, and had no option but to begin afresh if they subsequently found themselves to be wrong. If similar strategies are applied in social situations, we might say that focusers tend to make up their minds about other people only when they have got to know them reasonably well, whereas scanners make up their minds more quickly, but sometimes have to change them subsequently in the light of new evidence about the person concerned.

The importance of the focusing-scanning dimension is considerable within a range of situations. Children and adults who typically scan may have a particular need to be allowed to go back and check earlier clues if their original hypothesis becomes untenable, and therefore may be at a disadvantage in mentally-presented problems. Children and adults who focus, on the other hand, may delay too long over forming their hypothesis, and thus be handicapped in work involving quick responses. And as teachers and managers may also be focusers or scanners, there is the risk that the focuser may be over-cautious in giving praise or good marks, while the scanner may make snap decisions and then have to revise them later (remarks on a child's school report such as 'Has deteriorated this term; must do better next', may sometimes tell us more about the teacher's cognitive style than about the child's progress).

Ideally, individuals should be able to focus or scan, depending on the nature of the problem they are called on to tackle, the amount of time available, and so on. Sometimes a quick hypothesis is called for; sometimes a more cautious one. Extreme focusing can be a sign of insecurity (if you never reach a decision about anything, you can never be proved wrong) and may lead to sitting on the fence at the cost of lost opportunities, while extreme scanning may lead to premature decision-making and consequent difficulties. Good problem-solving demands that one should be a good judge of how long one can delay one's decision while awaiting further evidence.

There are no clear correlations between focusing-scanning and creativity or intelligence. Probably extremes of either are less helpful than a judicious combination of the two. There is also very little of a link between field-dependence/independence and focusing/scanning (it appears that scanners are not, as one might suppose, more inclined to be FD and focusers to be FI).

Reflectivity-impulsivity

A further useful dimension of cognitive style is known as reflectivity-impulsivity. As pointed out earlier, there are typically three stages in problem-solving: first, categorising the given information; second, sifting mentally through one's existing knowledge to find similar categories; and third, forming a hypothesis with which to attempt a solution. Jerome Kagan (Kagan, 1966) suggested that cognitive style particularly influences the first and last of these stages. Some people, he argued, characteristically act reflectively in categorising the information and producing their hypotheses, while others behave impulsively.

Kagan devised a number of tests to explore the reflectivity-impulsivity dimension. In the Delayed Recall of Design Test the subject is presented with a simple black-and-white design for a few seconds, and is then asked to pick it out from a number of similar designs. The test is scored for response time and for accuracy, and, typically, reflective individuals take longer over their responses and make fewer errors than do those who are impulsive.

Apart from highly anxious individuals, who have a long response time and still make many errors, it seems clear that for challenging and difficult problems, reflective people make significantly fewer errors than do impulsive people. They show a strong desire to be right first time, and even in public seem able to tolerate the ambiguity of a long silence while they study the problem. Impulsive individuals, on the other hand, tend to adopt a 'shotgun' approach, and may come up with several quick answers in the hope that one will prove correct. Kagan put it that reflective people have a slow, and impulsive people a fast, conceptual tempo.

Conceptual tempo also seems to be important in serial learning tasks. For example, in research in which children are faced with learning vocabulary lists, impulsive individuals tend to make more errors of commission (that is, including extra words in the recalled list) than do reflective individuals, and the more they are criticised, the more of these errors they tend to make. In the very early years, when learning to read, they are liable to make more orthographic errors, typically by misreading simple three-letter words (for example, 'log' for 'dog'; 'cat' for 'pat'), even when they are perfectly familiar with the individual letters concerned.

Once again, it would be incorrect to suggest that one end of a cognitive style dimension is 'better' than the other, though a reflective style does appear to be associated with maturity in that, as children grow older, their reflectivity scores tend to increase (though the relative differences between impulsive and reflective children may remain the same). Kagan himself suggested that, whereas high reflectivity may be advantageous in highly academic disciplines such as mathematics, it may be a disadvantage in the visual arts and in some areas of the humanities and social sciences. However, he conceded that the highly impulsive child's frequent experience of selecting the wrong hypothesis may be a source of discouragement, and lead to increased anxiety and perhaps even to more impulsive behaviour as he or she tries to correct things.

Authoritarianism

The authoritarian cognitive style is made up of a cluster of traits which together characterise a particular way of behaving, and one that has particular relevance in the workplace. The authoritarian style is marked by rigidity (as evidenced, for example, by the maintenance of beliefs even in the face of direct evidence to the contrary), and by intolerance of ambiguity (for example, a tendency to adopt rapidly one side or other of an argument and to dismiss alternatives, coupled with difficulties in coping with equivocal ideas

---

Authoritative versus Authoritarian

There is a world of difference between being authoritative and being authoritarian. Authoritative behaviour is usually effective and respected by others. It stems from a thorough knowledge of the issues at stake in any decision-making process, from a sufficient wealth of relevant previous experience, from a manner that is decisive yet ready to take other appropriate views into account, and from the self-confidence and courage to back one's own judgement – and to take responsibility for the outcomes.

Whereas authoritarianism stems from the personality problems outlined in the text, the authoritative individual usually possesses personal maturity. He or she acts in response to the needs of the task and of other people, while the authoritarian personality acts more from personal needs, using his or her power over others to counter personal inadequacies.

---

and situations). Research into this dimension has shown that authoritarian individuals tend also to be highly conventional; to be hostile towards non-conformity; to be over-deferential to those in authority; to show antagonism to those who challenge authority; to be tough-minded, bullying, dominating and punitive towards subordinates; to be destructive and cynical towards innovative ideas; to be over-concerned with and hostile towards sexual misdemeanour; and to tend towards superstition and stereotyping.

A useful measure of this constellation of characteristics (the F-scale) was described in Chapter 7, and a later cognitive style, dogmatism, identified by M. Rokeach (1954), appears to be strongly related to these characteristics, and to be typical of people both with extreme right and extreme left-wing political views

Type A and B personalities

Another area sometimes linked in with cognitive style and which has considerable implications for the workplace is that of Type A and Type B personalities. The research that identified these two styles was based on managers and executives working in high-pressure environments (see, for example, Friedman and Ulmer, 1984). One group of personnel (Type A) typically responded to such pressures by intensive activity, becoming highly competitive, rushed and hasty, finding it hard to delegate and driving themselves hard. A contrasting group (Type B) were much more relaxed and ready to delegate, and while equally concerned to overcome problems, tended to see them as obstacles to be overcome rather than as challenges or competitions. Although just as productive as the first group, they experienced less stress, and were less likely to take their worries home with them.

In an eight-year study, (Friedman and Rosenman 1974) found that Type A individuals, as measured by a specially designed questionnaire, were twice as likely to suffer heart attacks as Type B (very high-scoring Type Bs remained completely free from attacks). In addition, they responded differently to situations over which they were unable to gain control. For example, in an experiment in which Type A people were given puzzles which appeared to be solvable but in fact were not, they became much more stressed, and made several attempts before giving up altogether, and proved unable to solve later problems that were similar but solvable. Type B individuals, on the other hand, tackled things more calmly, and continued to try various approaches to the later problems.

Other features of the Type A personality include a tendency to think or do two things at once; to cram more activities into shorter amounts of time; to hurry the speech of others when in conversation; to gesticulate and show physical tension when speaking; to use explosive speech patterns and obscenities; to be obsessively punctual; to become impatient at being kept waiting; to find it hard to relax or to do nothing, or to enjoy beauty and the environment. In addition, they played games to win even against children, and tended to believe that if things are to be done well they must do them themselves. They also tended to smoke more, to sleep less, and to drink more caffeinated drinks, all of which are associated with coronary risks.

Further studies show that it is not just their fast-paced lives that make Type A individuals more likely to suffer to coronary problems. The most important factor appears to be their negative emotions – in particular, their readiness to anger (Williams, 1993). One 25-year study of Duke University law students found that those inclined to be hostile and cynical were five times more likely than their gentler, trusting classmates to die by middle age (Williams, 1989).

However, the Type A personality we have been describing is at the extreme end of the A-B dimension. Most people will show some Type A characteristics, at least on occasion. Nevertheless, the existence of the two very distinct styles at either end of the A–B dimension seems clear. It also seems clear that, in addition to cognitive factors, the style has an emotional component as well, namely the emotional reaction to pressure. This reaction may be linked in turn to self-esteem, with Type A personalities driven by a desire for success in order to prove themselves, and Type B personalities able to take a more objective view of the issues in front of them and of themselves.

Objectivity may also play a part in what can be referred to as people-orientated versus task-orientated approaches to problem-solving. Some individuals tend to be influenced primarily by their feelings for the personnel who are likely to be affected by their decisions, while others focus more on the effect of these decisions on the task itself. The first group may, for example, bend the rules in order to protect people, while the latter may sacrifice people in order to protect the rules. Thus the first may keep on an ineffectual worker knowing that, although this is detrimental to efficiency, redundancy would be tragic for both the worker and his/her family, while the second will dismiss the worker in the interests of business economics and efficiency.

Again, there is an emotional factor at work here, with people-orientated individuals perhaps being better able to empathise with others, or less able to live with a self-image of heartlessness, and task-orientated individuals being better able to identify with the interests of the job. Clearly, the most successful managers are able to balance the interests of both people and task, knowing that the two will frequently influence each other. In other words, they show more of the emotional intelligence that we discussed in Chapter 1. However, when emotions come into the equation, such balance is unlikely to be easy, or may be achieved only at the cost of great managerial heart-searching and even anguish. The first essential, as with so much else to do with psychology in the workplace, is to be clear about what, in fact, is happening – that is, in this case, to recognise when both people and task considerations come into a situation, to note one's own response to them, and to endeavour not to over-personalise the issue by dwelling on one's own feelings rather than on the rights and wrongs of the situation itself.

Proactive-reactive

Proactive-reactive behaviour is yet another style currently attracting some attention, though it is possible that it is less a dimension than a learnt way of coping (and therefore more readily influenced by experience than the various dimensions we have just been discussing). A proactive style suggests the ability to look ahead and make appropriate decisions before being overtaken by events while reactive style suggests a tendency to respond only when events are already upon the individual. For many purposes in the workplace, a proactive style has obvious advantages, although it may become increasingly difficult to be proactive when work or personal pressures are high, and when increasingly the tendency is to seek short-term solutions to most problems. The term 'fire-fighting', which is sometimes used for reactive behaviour, is a revealing one. Individuals with a proactive style can usually identify where the risk of 'fire' exists and take steps to prevent it from breaking out, whereas those with a reactive style tend to rush around with metaphorical buckets of water trying to extinguish conflagrations after – sometimes long after – they have broken out.

A proactive style would appear to have obvious advantages in the workplace, though again we must not come to a hard and fast conclusion. Reactive people can sometimes be enormously resourceful, while rigidly proactive individuals may find it difficult to cope in the face of unexpected emergencies. If they tend to live too much in the future, they can also miss some of the interest and engagement that comes from living in the present. Once again, the ideal managerial style would be to balance the two approaches, recognising the value of proactivity in areas where it appears to be practical, but remaining alert to the need to be reactive in the face of the unpredictable. Professional life, like all aspects of living, can be highly uncertain at times. Good professional training involves helping individuals to learn how to be both proactive and reactive, and to recognise the kinds of situation that call for the respective approaches.

Optimism-pessimism

Although not usually referred to as a cognitive style, this is a convenient point at which to mention optimism-pessimism. The pessimistic person is typically more likely to react with depression and even hopelessness to difficulties, and such people, like those with Type A personalities, appear more likely to coronary ailments (Anda *et al.*, 1993). The cultivation of an optimistic approach to life is obviously important, in both personal and professional life. Such an approach is based essentially on the conviction that if we can change adverse circumstances we should get on and do so without delay, and if we cannot change them we should – and can – learn to live with them.

The more control we feel to have over our lives, the less likely we are to experience pessimism, so another important strategy is to assess how and when we can put ourselves more in charge of what happens to us. In a large organisation we may not be able to change the macro events around us, but there are many micro ones that lie within our power. And often it is the feeling that small things are on top of us that produces much of our pessimism – the sense that life is so difficult we cannot even deal with its minor irritations. Optimistic people approach such irritations with the belief they can do something about them, and usually they are proved right. Positive affirmations – the habit of speaking to ourselves in the language of success rather than of failure – go with optimism, and such affirmations are well within the power of us all.

Further research into cognitive style

It is by no means clear how easy or difficult it is to change one's style on any of the above dimensions. Some research suggests that one's position on each of them seems to remain markedly stable over the years, and Kagan concluded that cognitive style may be a 'basic component of the individual's behavioural organisation' (Kagan, 1966). He considered (Kagan, 1976) that all the various dimensions can perhaps be grouped into three main types. Type I consists of those dimensions that compare the individual's performance against a predetermined standard of correctness (as, for example, in field dependence-independence, where the subject is required to solve problems such as the embedded-figures test). Type II consists of those dimensions where there are no 'right' or 'wrong' answers, but where value judgements can be made as to which end of a dimension is more appropriate in a given situation (for example, proactive-reactive). Type III includes those dimensions where neither performance standards nor value judgements are involved, but which simply indicate variations between peoples' respective views on given issues (for example, A–B personality type). Other investigators have identified as many as nineteen separate types, but the three just mentioned appear to have most practical value.

We still need more research into the relationship between cognitive styles and intelligence and creativity, respectively, and into that between cognitive styles and the causal factors in personality development. As we have seen, a start has been made in relating cognitive style to ego-defence mechanisms, to personal identity, and to particular forms of personality problems. But what part does an individual's sense of security, confidence, self-esteem and so on have to play in his or her style? And is style more a product of, or cause of, these things? And how does cognitive style affect the way in which one forms one's personal constructs, or the freedom with which one moves through one's life space, or the methods one employs to deal with cognitive dissonance? The area is still rich in research possibilities, and it is unfortunate that interest in it has tended to wane among psychologists in recent years.

Chapter 10

Personality in Managers and Teachers

Much of what has been said throughout the book applies not only to those for whom, as teachers or managers, we may be responsible, but equally to ourselves. But there are a number of specific personal points that teachers and managers and other in similar roles should take into account.

What makes a good teacher or manager?

Teaching and managing are such complex multi-faceted tasks that efforts to find a relationship between success and personality have produced somewhat confusing findings. Three of the tests most widely used have been the MMPI, the 16PF and the various Eysenck Personality Inventories (see Chapter 6). Qualities such as Cattell's 'parmia' and 'surgency' have correlated with success in some studies but not in others, as has extraversion on the Eysenck scales. Even significant levels of neuroticism and mental instability (on the MMPI) often fail to predict failure. In the case of teachers, however, those who work with young children have generally emerged as being more understanding, warm, friendly, responsible, systematic, stimulating, imaginative and enthusiastic than their less successful colleagues, while those who work with older children tend to score well on conventionality, non-progressive attitudes, and the ability to put the interests of the school before their own (Cortis, 1985). Less successful teachers tend to be dominant, suspicious and aggressive.

Using student ratings of lecturer effectiveness, research in higher education (for example, Rushton and Murray, 1985) has found that two composite dimensions, which they called *achievement orientation* (composed of traits such as dominance, ambition, leadership, intelligence and endurance) and *interpersonal orientation* (traits such as supportiveness, non-authoritarianism, non-defensiveness

and objectivity) appear to account for the main personality characteristics associated with being a successful lecturer. Also significant were *charisma* (made up of qualities such as expressiveness and
an interest in one's subject) and *organisation* (clear and well-
organised lecture material).

It is unclear whether or not these findings hold good for teachers
at school level, and even less clear whether they apply to those in
authority elsewhere in the workplace. But further research does fail
to back up what we might call the 'common sense' picture of the
successful teacher. Such a picture is of a teacher who is extraverted
with a high level of stability, but not only does research provide little
consistent support for this view, the teaching profession as a whole
comes out as being no more extraverted or stable than the general
population (Eysenck and Eysenck, 1964). Whatever special qualities
of personality teachers possess, it seems clear that they do not show
up readily on trait measures.

State personality theories look at teacher personality from a very
different angle. Bloom (1983) argues that we must jettison the idea of
seeking fixed personality characteristics in successful teachers, and
instead think in terms of affective task entry behaviours, just as we
should with children. Thus before starting a particular teaching task
(whether it be a learning encounter, pastoral counselling, or even an
extra-curricular activity) teachers should determine what particular
affective behaviour is likely to obtain the best results. This sounds
rather like trying to be all things to all people, but in fact it is asking
teachers to exercise a range of professional skills which most of them
will already have at their command. At times, the teacher needs to
behave as the leader, at others to prompt children to take the
initiative for themselves, at others to be decisive and authoritative,
and at others to be flexible and to encourage the democratic process.

On occasion, teachers need to be ready to provide children with
clear answers to their questions; and at others to stimulate children
to find answers for themselves. With some children, the good
teacher is challenging and demanding; with others supportive and
encouraging; with some children trusting; with others more watch-
ful. And so the list goes on. Successful teachers are also able to
recognise when it is appropriate to share jokes with a class and,
when good discipline demands, remain more serious and task-
orientated.

All these qualities are, let us repeat, professional skills rather than
fixed personality characteristics. Some of them are readily culti-

vated; others take a little more time. But no competent teacher will find them beyond reach. Indeed, in some instances it is simply a matter of allowing existing personality states to become more open and apparent. Teachers may, for example, be enthusiastic about teaching and about their specialist subjects, but fail to show this enthusiasm when with the children they teach. Or they may be very sympathetic towards children's personal problems, but fail to indicate a readiness to discuss these problems when the need arises. Or they may be patient with slow learners, but feel that similar levels of patience are unnecessary with those who are more able. In these and similar instances, what is primarily required is simply an enhanced understanding of children as individuals, together with a readiness to communicate this understanding.

Many of these findings generalise to those who are successful in other positions of responsibility. Essentially, such people appear to exercise sound judgement of people and situations, and to be sufficiently flexible to respond to what is needed in work situations. In particular, the quartet of personality qualities identified in the good university lecturer (and to be a good university lecturer involves not just lecturing effectively, but also relating successfully to students in individual tutorials, assessing their abilities accurately, and providing them with the necessary encouragement and guidance to take responsibility, where appropriate, for their own work) – namely *achievement orientation, interpersonal orientation, charisma* and *organizational ability* – would seem to be central to success in any position of leadership.

To these we can add the extensive range of qualities that have emerged from the research findings we have discussed in previous chapters, which can be summarised as follows:

(i)   High achievement motivation, self-esteem and self-expecta-
        tions, the imaginative thinking and venturesome approach that
        go with creativity, flexible and appropriate cognitive styles, a
        tendency towards a Type B personality, proactive thinking
        (Chapter 9);

(ii)   The ability to operate as an effective role model and to give
        appropriate rewards and reinforcements (Chapter 8);

(iii)   The possession of permeable and realistic personal constructs
        and the ability to reverse between telic and paratelic
        behaviours (Chapter 7);

(iv)   High scores on the 'big five' personality factors of agreeable-
       ness, conscientiousness, openness, emotional stability and
       extraversion (Chapter 6);

(v)   The ability to ensure that working systems allow movement
       between the respective organisational areas, the social
       awareness that avoids confronting people with the Type 1, 2
       and 3 conflicts identified by Lewin, a predominantly internal
       locus of control, an active involvement in work and in social
       life, an orientation towards challenge and change, a satisfac-
       tory control over one's own life (Chapter 5);

(vi)   An appropriately developed sense of trust and identity, a high
       level of competence and generativity, a balance between
       thinking, feeling, sensing and intuitive aspects of personality,
       an appropriate value system, the ability to make correct sense
       of the world – for example, not to misunderstand or
       misinterpret the behaviour and motives of others, harmony
       (congruence) between personal and professional needs, a
       genuine, accepting and empathic relationship with others, an
       absence of extreme ego defences and an absence of inferiority
       complexes (Chapter 3); and

(vii) Effective levels of emotional intelligence and emotional
       security, consistency and co-ordination of behaviour, personal
       honesty and self-awareness, and the readiness to change and
       grow with experience (Chapter 2).

Obviously, these various qualities will be more appropriate in
some circumstances than in others, and in any case they suggest a
paragon of virtue and competence that none of us could hope to
equal. However, they certainly point the way towards not only
effectiveness in the workplace, but also effectiveness as a human
being – which includes the ability to enjoy life and to enhance the
lives of others.

Managing stress

Professions such as teaching and managing are potentially highly
stressful, mainly because of the manifold demands involved and the
often less than ideal circumstances in which these demands have to
be met. Stress is an important area of personality study, involving as
it does our emotional lives, our self-concepts, our relationships, and

our ability to make the best use of ourselves. Much has, in fact, been written on the deleterious effect it can have on both psychological and physical well-being.

In personality terms, the stress-prone individual may be less the nervous or neurotic person than the one who is overdedicated to work and who takes things too seriously. Whether we blame others for our professional problems or blame ourselves (external or internal loci of control – see Chapter 5 of this volume), over-dedication and over-seriousness seem to be two of the key factors that leave us open to stress. This is not because over-dedication and over-seriousness in themselves necessarily make us stress-prone, but because they are frequently associated with a hard-driving, determined state of mind which becomes impatient with opposition and frustrated at failure (a syndrome of behaviour associated with the Type A personality – see Chapter 9). This state of mind can lead individuals to push themselves too hard, and to be constantly at war with themselves and with others over the issues that impede what they see as desirable progress. Inevitably, in professional life, where the constraints and obstacles are many, and where the indicators and rewards of success are often less than clear-cut, individuals locked into this state of mind are especially likely to suffer.

This may seem like advising one not to bother very much about work if one wishes to remain stress-proof, but this is not so. The advice is simply that we should be realistic about what can be achieved and what cannot, given the constraints under which we have to work, and that we should be able to laugh a little when things go wrong.

A genuine sense of humour is not only of great value in itself, since the act of laughing helps to reduce tension, but because (see Chapter 2) it appears to be linked to self-insight. A genuine sense of humour (which does not include poking fun at others) is an indication that we can laugh at ourselves and even about the people and things we love without lessening our love. It indicates that we have a sense of proportion, even when it comes to those issues which are most precious to us. A sense of humour shows that we have the insight to recognise that for every one of us there is all too often a gap between aspirations and performance. On occasion, we set out with high intentions, yet find ourselves making a complete mess of things. Humour and self-insight also indicate the ability to realise that the only proper response to this gap is not an orgy of breast-beating and vilification, but amusement, leaving us with the courage and energy to try again.

Stress

As we can see from the text, certain types of personality are more likely to suffer from stress than others, but the symptoms of stress tend to be similar in all cases. Among these are the tendency to:

- Solve problems at an increasingly superficial and short-term level;
- Experience more physical illness and absenteeism;
- Become increasingly emotional – for example, resort to anger or become tearful over relative trifles;
- Suffer from sleep problems;
- Become either sexually promiscuous or lose interest in sex;
- Resort to alcohol or other drugs;
- Show physical dysfunctions, such as excessive fidgeting and other nervy behaviour, and speech defects (for example, staccato word delivery, stammering);
- Show memory deterioration and absent-mindedness.

Symptoms such as these, in oneself or in others, indicate that a thorough assessment of stressors is needed, with a view to removing the most pressing – for example, excessive workload, powerlessness over important decisions, over-demanding colleagues or superiors, inadequate skills for the job, excessive frustrations in completing tasks, or an excess of unpleasant duties (see Fontana, 1989).

Falling short of aspirations, however, is no good or useful reason for thinking the less of ourselves or of others. A tendency to fall short is simply the way things are. Similarly, through self-insight we can accept that we cannot be equally successful at everything, in personal or professional life. We may admire the way a colleague works long hours, and drive ourselves to do even better. We may admire the expertise of other colleagues, their success with difficult problems, the popularity of others, the organising and administrative ability of someone else or their phenomenal powers of memory, but we cannot always hope to emulate them. We simply have to do the best we can, knowing that inevitably we shall often fall short of what we hope for, or of what others seem able to achieve (just as they may feel that they fall short of us in certain respects), and accept once more that this is simply how things are. Certainly, we should try to develop our skills and improve our performance, but we can only do this within a context that is sensible and realistic.

And, in the end, nobody is going to benefit if we drive ourselves into ill health.

Although nervousness and low self-confidence are not linked to a tendency to suffer stress as emphatically as is an over-demanding and over-serious personality, they nevertheless can lead to a number of pressures which are dealt with in this section.

Trait-based theories see anxiety as being a relatively fixed characteristic (see Chapter 6), dependent largely on innate factors. State-based and humanistic theories (and to a certain extent, social and field theories) do not deny that inborn temperament may make some of us more liable than others to suffer anxiety, and this in turn feeds back into our cognitive states and makes us more fearful of facing those events that cause this anxiety. But they nevertheless place more emphasis on anxiety as a transient experience. Even the most anxious among us is unlikely to be anxious *all* the time. So the task becomes to identify what makes us anxious, and how we experience and cope with this anxiety (see Chapter 7 of this volume; and Fontana, 1989).

Psychologists generally agree that anxiety is a response to threat. We feel something or somebody is threatening some aspect of ourselves or of the people or things important to us. In dealing with this anxiety (or fear, if we prefer to call it such), the first step, as with other emotions, is to observe ourselves closely to see when fear arises and what kinds of things appear to prompt it. The next step, again as with other emotions, is to ask what it is in us that feels threatened and why. Are we being physically threatened? Not usually. Is it the small child in us, that part of our psychological life that still reacts with fear when those in authority are at odds with us? Is it a fear of being thought inadequate or incompetent? Is it a fear of *thinking* ourselves inadequate? Once identified, most of these things can be seen to be largely illusory, and capable of being dealt with. Childhood fears are no longer relevant to the daily experiences of adult life. Others may not be thinking we are inadequate, and if they are, this may simply be because we are not doing things their way. In both personal and professional affairs we cannot allow our emotional life to be governed solely by the opinions of others. As for the tendency to think ourselves inadequate, close inspection often shows this to be linked to problems of self-esteem (see Chapter 2), problems which can be countered by taking a more realistic and encouraging view of ourselves, and

---

Meditation

Meditation is the most effective of all methods for mind training. Usually, our minds are full of constant chatter, with one thought leading to another (often sparking off emotions in the process). Meditation helps us to gain a measure of control over this process, and not only to relax more, but also to use our minds more effectively and efficiently.

Methods of meditation differ, but the essentials are the same. The first step is concentration. We choose a point of focus, and keep the mind fixed steadily on it, returning to it each time the thoughts wander away. With practice, this wandering becomes less and less frequent, and the mind enters a tranquil, poised and clear state of being.

Sit comfortably, with the back upright and the feet flat on the floor. Focus the attention on the point just below or just inside the nose where you feel the air cool as you breath in, and warm as you breath out. Pay no attention to the thoughts or emotions that arise from time to time. Allow them to pass out of the mind without judging them, and without allowing them to set off a train of associations. If you find yourself particularly distracted by your thoughts, count each out-breath, going up to ten and then back again to one.

Initially try to meditate for five minutes a day, allowing the time to extend as you become more proficient. If possible, set aside a special time and place for this daily practice, though meditation can be used in addition at any convenient moment, and in particular to calm the mind during a particularly stressful day (see Fontana, 1992).

---

learning not behave like a critic who always stands at our shoulder and finds fault with everything we do.

Physical relaxation techniques, and simple meditation practices in which we train the mind to concentrate calmly and peacefully on the breathing (see Fontana, 1992) are also a great help in allowing us to realise that the mind need not be allowed to brood constantly over fears and problems, and over the emotional reactions that go with them, but can be turned instead to focus on those things that we really want to think about. In meditation it even becomes possible to introduce into our thoughts those experiences that usually cause apprehension (such as potentially contentious meetings), and to contemplate them peacefully without any emotional reaction (Chapter 8). Practice of this kind makes it increasingly easy to face hitherto anxiety-provoking events in daily life, and to see that a fear reaction, far from being inevitable, is simply a product of habit and of the inappropriate use of our own minds. The equanimity with which we can contemplate events during meditation then gradually begins to carry over into real life and into these events themselves.

We all of us remain capable of psychological growth and development throughout life. Difficult as it sometimes is to accept, the fact is that the challenges we face in professional life provide opportunities for this growth and development. Sometimes, by watching our own reactions to them and identifying their cause, we can learn more from those who are difficult and unpleasant to work with than from those who are easy. An essential feature of the ability to deal with stress is the realisation that we are ultimately in control of our own lives, however much our environment may impose constraints upon us.

Chapter 11

Personality Disorders

When discussing Freud's contribution to psychology (see Chapter 3), the point was made that he gave us the notion that normal and neurotic behaviour are simply different points on the same psychological continuum. We all have personality problems of one sort or another, and decisions on when these problems become bad enough to be classified by psychologists and other mental health professionals as *disorders* are to some extent cultural ones. Such decisions differ from society to society, from generation to generation, and from individual to individual. Much of what we can say about personality disorders has therefore already been said in earlier chapters, and it simply remains to build upon this information and to clarify matters of definition and of possible treatment.

There is a suggestion that some severe personality disorders such as schizophrenia and bi-polar disorder may not be on the same continuum as personality problems (for example, Maher, 1970), even though they may be influenced by some of the same causes. This suggestion is supported in part by the fact that personality problems, however distressing, allow individuals to remain in touch with reality and to carry on reasonably normal lives (often with the awareness that they need help and support), while severe personality disorders typically leave people unable to do so, and may require short- or sometimes longer-term hospitalisation. Frequently, individuals experiencing these disorders may be unaware that they are ill, and may in fact regard others as being sick.

It might be argued that personality disorders, of whatever kind, are hardly likely to be encountered in the workplace. Sadly, this is not the case. In Britain, 10 per cent of people will need psychiatric in-patient care at some point in their lives for extreme disorders, and a further 16 per cent will need outpatient treatment for somewhat lesser conditions (these percentages do not include the large numbers who seek medical help for milder personality problems). The figures for the USA are very similar (Robins and Reiger, 1991), and according to the World Health Organisation, some 400 million people worldwide suffer from severe disorders of one kind or another (Sartorius, 1994). All those in positions of responsibility in the workplace therefore need to have at least some understanding of these disorders, as they are virtually certain to encounter them in the course of their professional duties.

In an important work some years ago, Ryle (1969) showed that the problem is not uncommon even among students in higher education. In fact, studies have shown that schizophrenia, the most troublesome of the disorders, sometimes manifests its presence as early as the adolescent years. The treatment of this and other disorders is a matter for psychologists, psychiatrists and other medical professionals, but all those with responsibilities in the workplace should be alert for the symptoms of these conditions, and recognise when people are under the kind of stress likely to make matters worse and thus be in need of particular support and understanding.

Definition of personality disorders

Mental health professionals generally consider that personality disorders are apparent when the individual's behaviour is judged to be atypical (abnormal), maladaptive, disturbing or unjustifiable. The American Psychiatric Association's *Diagnostic and Statistical Manual of Mental Disorders* (the fourth and most recent edition, published in 1994, and generally known as DSM–IV) records no fewer than seventeen major categories of such disorders, but for our purposes it is convenient to think of them under two main headings, namely disorders of thinking and learning (*disorders of cognition*), and disorders of feelings and emotions (*disorders of affect*). We will look at these two headings (and some of the categories that can be listed under each of them) separately, but the distinction between them is not a hard and fast one. They can influence and overlap with each other at a number of points. However, before attending to them, something should be said of the factors that appear to influence their development.

Some general causes of personality disorders

Many of these disorders may have their origin in part in the factors, discussed in earlier chapters, that lead to personality problems – for example, in faulty relationships with care-givers during childhood and adolescence, in low self-esteem and high levels of guilt, in reinforcement incorrectly applied, in constant demands of parents and teachers for appropriate behaviour, in the absence of love and of emotional security, in a lack of sympathy and understanding, and in physical or sexual abuse. Psychologists may disagree about the actual mechanisms involved, but there is a general consensus that many disorders may have their genesis less in the child's own nature than in the treatment he or she receives from adults (who may themselves be psychologically disordered). Children who are the victims of wildly inconsistent behaviour among their care-givers, who are not allowed to recognise and express their own feelings, who live with fear and with a sense of rejection, who are forced to experience undue inner conflict, who are constantly accused of inadequacies, or who have to witness violent or dysfunctional relationships among those around them, are, not surprisingly, unlikely to learn to relate to the world or to themselves in positive and satisfying ways.

Of course, since heredity and environment interact throughout psychological life, genetic and temperamental factors play a part in how individuals react to these and other adverse environmental circumstances. Some people come through apparently unscathed, often showing enormous strength of character which reveals itself in such things as a determination to make a success of life, or to help the underprivileged, or as a philosophical equanimity that rides out every challenge, while others are more obviously damaged.

One way of thinking about some of the consequences of adverse environmental circumstances is to see them as arousing two powerful emotions, anger and fear (the so-called fight or flight emotions), either of which can be turned inwards against oneself or outwards against others. Anger turned inwards can contribute to feelings of depression, guilt and self-rejection. Fear turned inwards can lead to a dread of one's own emotions (Freud's neurotic anxiety) Either way, the individual victimises him or herself, just as they are victimised or have been victimised by others. Consciously or unconsciously, they blame themselves for their troubles, or see themselves as being worthless – much as they believe the world sees them.

Turned outwards, anger and fear result in aggressive and often disruptive and destructive behaviour. This time it is others who, often indiscriminately, are held to blame for everything that goes wrong. Obviously, in whichever way the emotions are turned, an essential aspect of treatment is to offer acceptance in the place of rejection, sympathy in the place of indifference, consistency in the place of inconsistency, encouragement in the place of censure, and harmony in the place of conflict. Unfortunately, we are frequently unable to alter the behaviour of parents and care-givers who relate badly to children, and in adult life we cannot turn back the clock and create happy childhoods for ourselves. But a recognition of the causes of personality problems is nevertheless an important step forward for all concerned.

Cognitive disorders

Cognitive disorders, which, as already made clear, are concerned with disorders of thinking, can take a number of different forms. Space allows us to look at only two of them.

Attention deficit disorder   At one time known as hyperactivity, attention deficit disorder (ADD) is a term used to cover a range of restless and uncontrolled behaviours in the young, with inattention, low impulse control and non-compliance among the most important (Barkley, 1983), and with poor social relationships and learning disabilities being a typical consequence. ADD can manifest itself as early as the first year of life, and may persist through into adolescence. Symptoms of it may even remain into adult life, though here it must not be confused with the workaholic behaviour shown by some adults. The distinguishing feature of ADD is that much of the overactive behaviour concerned appears to be random and unfocused, with the individual turning from one thing to another without apparent purpose beyond the need for activity itself. The behaviour is inconsistent, unfocused, unproductive, and typically the attention remains on any one thing only very briefly.

The cause of ADD may be some chromosomal abnormality, and it is known that the condition can sometimes be controlled medically with amphetamines, which act indirectly on the hypothalamus (one of the areas of the brain that, as we saw in Chapter 5, may be involved in some way in personality). Marston and Scott (1970), who called the condition 'Inconsequentiality' (or 'Q'), suggested that it is also related to high impulsivity scores on Kagan's reflectivity–impulsivity dimension (see Chapter 9).

The ADD child can place a great strain on the patience of teachers and parents. In addition to the other characteristics mentioned above, Barkley also found that ADD children have problems relating to peers, are immature and generally below average in intelligence, are easily frustrated and low in self-esteem, and tend to suffer from a range of physical allergies. Approximately 4 per cent of children fall into the category, with boys outnumbering girls by six to one. In dealing with such children it is vital to remember that they may have little conscious control over their behaviour. Thus it is useless to insist on more than momentary quiescence. Often it is the very frustrations and checkings they receive from adults that exacerbate their behaviour.

Ideally, ADD children should be given scope by adults for their constant need for activity. As such children are usually extraverted, it is wrong to deny them group work in spite of the attendant problems (though sometimes they respond well to opportunities for group leadership). There is some evidence that praising them for periods of concentration and co-operation, and for the initiative and inventiveness they often show, is of value in helping them learn to self-control (see Fontana, 1994). ADD is not a recognised condition among adults, and most sufferers tend to show less extreme symptoms as they grow older. However, adults vary greatly in their ability to show sustained concentration, and good leadership involves the ability to recognise when this is the case, and to suit the task to the person. Meditation techniques that involve focusing the attention on a single stimulus such as the breath help to develop concentration, but many people are reluctant to put in the sustained practice that such techniques demand.

Schizophrenia In many ways the most extreme personality disorder, schizophrenia has historically accounted for the largest single group of patients receiving in-patient treatment in psychiatric units. Modern treatments have in most cases ended the long-stay residential care that the condition once required, but it still typically necessitates long-term medication. Without treatment, individuals may variously:

- Lose all sense of personal identity;
- Suffer from auditory and visual hallucinations – for example, hearing disturbing voices and seeing visions (*paranoid schizophrenia*);

- Show deviant motor behaviour – for example, remaining in a statuesque position for long periods, or carrying out rocking or repetitive actions (*catatonic schizophrenia*);
- Perceptual abnormalities (colours and sounds may be experienced with heightened intensity, everyday objects may appear to be unfamiliar or menacing, and all sense of body image may be lost).

Most striking of all, they may show cognitive disorders that prevent logical thought and communication. Their thinking becomes fragmented, bizarre and distorted by delusions (sometimes of grandeur, supposing themselves to be royalty, or film or sports stars). Sometimes there is parrot-like repetition of another's speech or movements. The sufferers may use what are called 'word salads' – incongruous mixtures of words which make little or no sense to the listener, and which may indicate an inability to remain concentrated on a single one line of thought. Some authorities take the view that this disorganised thinking (extreme cases are labelled *disorganised schizophrenia*) stems from a breakdown in selective attention. We are continually bombarded by perceptions, sensations and ideas, yet normally we have a remarkable capacity to select and focus on only a small part of it, and filter out the rest as being irrelevant. In schizophrenia, this capacity appears to break down (Gjerde, 1983).

In the course of these various symptoms, the individual may withdraw altogether from normal social contact, and inhabit a private world dominated by illogical ideas and unreal images. In addition, he or she frequently shows an incompatibility between the ideas being expressed and the emotions that accompany them – hence the term schizophrenia, which literally means 'split mind' or 'split personality' (terms that were once used to describe the condition). For example, sufferers may talk of sad things with apparent levity or even joy, and of happy things with sorrow and tearfulness or lapse into what is called 'flat affect', a state of apparent total apathy in which there is no emotional arousal of any kind. The former state, which is more responsive to treatment (Fenton and McGlashan, 1994), is usually described as 'schizophrenia with positive symptoms', and the latter as 'schizophrenia with negative symptoms'. Some sufferers remain predominantly in either the positive or the negative state, prompting the suggestion that there may be two (and perhaps more) different kinds of schizophrenia.

Much is still uncertain about the specific causes of schizophrenia. Sometimes the condition develops gradually (*process* schizophrenia); while at others it comes on suddenly, sometimes in response to particular stress (*reactive* schizophrenia) – the latter condition being more readily treatable (Fowles, 1992). There is strong evidence that genetic factors play a part (Plomin *et al.*, 1997), and also that maternal viral infections during pregnancy may be involved (Waddington, 1993). Either way, various brain abnormalities are evident in most schizophrenics (Andreason, 1994), though whether these are a cause or a result of the disorder is open to debate.

Genetic and other physiological factors may predispose some people to schizophrenia, but they do not themselves cause it. Nor, on their own, do psychological factors. A combination of the two is required. The psychological factors concerned may vary depending on the type of schizophrenia involved, but in addition to the general psychological issues summarised earlier in the chapter and discussed throughout the book, a number of others have been suggested from time to time. One theory that attracted a great deal of attention from the 1960s until relatively recently was that psychological pressures that may be responsible, and which begin in early childhood, may include what Bateson and his colleagues (Bateson *et al.*, 1956) called the *double bind* situation. This situation is a form of inconsistency, particularly within the mother–child relationship, in which children habitually have certain kinds of behaviour demanded of them and are then criticised for producing this very behaviour (as, for example, when the mother tells the child not to pester her with chatter, and then accuses him or her of sulking when he/she tries to be quiet). The double bind punishes children emotionally whatever they do, and they have no chance to acquire the capacity to distinguish logic in human behaviour. Not surprisingly, they withdraw increasingly from close relationships with others.

Bannister (1960) suggested that, in terms of Kelly's personal construct theory (see Chapter 7), the double bind means that the child's personal constructs are constantly being invalidated. Laing and Esterson (1964) presented several case studies illustrating the double bind in action, as well as some of the other emotional pressures that a schizophrenic person can come under from his/her family, and in particular from a mother who is often dominating and restrictive, and who consistently interprets her child's behaviour in terms of the effect it has on her own feelings and on her personal well-being, health, outlook on life, and so on.

More recently (for example, Olin and Mednick, 1996) a number of other possible factors in early relationships have emerged as being of significance. For example, a mother who herself has a long-standing history of schizophrenia (this may point also to the importance of genetic factors); birth complications and low birth weight; separation from parents; and poor peer relationships. Attention has also been focused on early variables in child development which may indicate a higher than average risk of subsequent schizophrenic behaviour; these include a short attention span and poor muscle co-ordination, disruptive or withdrawn behaviour, and emotional unpredictability.

The early symptoms of the disorder itself, some or all of which may become apparent in adolescence and early adulthood, include increasingly withdrawn behaviour; an inability to relate satisfactorily to others, and sudden and apparently groundless suspicion and hostility towards them; a marked deterioration in standards of personal appearance and in study and work habits; and a general inability to organise personal and professional life. Subsequently, these symptoms may become further complicated by irrational and bizarre thought patterns, and an inability to follow a consecutive or logical argument or to manifest the kind of emotions that others feel are appropriate. If paranoia is present, delusions of self-importance or persecution by others also become apparent.

The treatment of schizophrenia – now much more effective than in previous generations – involves appropriate medication backed up by psychological counselling, and, as stressed earlier, is very much the concern of medicine rather than of the workplace. However, alertness to early symptoms is clearly of great importance, as is the ability, especially during the recovery phase, to listen carefully to what sufferers have to say about themselves. Often they have a clear need to talk about the experiences encountered during the acute phase of the disorder, and it is important to recognise that, however bizarre these may seem, they were real enough to sufferers at the time, and should never be dismissed or belittled. To do so only adds to their feelings of being different or odd in some way, and hinders their return to normal, active and productive life.

Affective disorders

There is less of a dichotomy between problems and disorders in the affective area than there is in the cognitive (in fact, it is to the

Attitudes to Personality Disorders

At one time, a great deal of stigma was attached to extreme personality disorders (under such names as mental illness, insanity, madness, lunacy). Mistaken notions were widespread, such as the belief that these disorders were inescapable in certain families, and that, once afflicted, sufferers had little chance of a cure. Not surprisingly, there was a great fear of mental illness, exacerbated by the fact that many people associated it with violent and dangerous behaviour. At one time, to have had even a minor incidence of mental illness caused one to be seen as something of a social outcast and even as unemployable.

Attitudes have undergone a radical change in recent years, partly as a result of the effectiveness of modern treatments, partly as a result of the realisation that the link between mental illness and heredity is a relatively weak one, and partly as a result of the recognition of just how prevalent personality disorders are in modern society. Our understanding of these disorders has also greatly improved, as has our knowledge of the causes. Mental illness is no more the fault of the individual than is physical illness, and the prognosis is very much better than it is with many physical illnesses. In the vast majority of cases the individual is able to return to work and to a perfectly normal life.

It is also worth saying that we have learned to listen to what people tell us about their illnesses. In many cases, people report profound, mystical experiences which leave them with a deeper understanding of themselves. Sometimes they will emphasise that the period of their illness was the most significant experience of their lives. Viewed in this way, the illness can be seen as an important learning opportunity, and one that should be regarded with compassion and respect by the rest of society. Furthermore, as we shall see later in the chapter, there is evidence that highly creative people may be more likely to suffer certain personality disorders than the rest of the population. This perhaps supports the idea that in extreme disorders the conscious mind is flooded by uncontrolled material from the unconscious – an unconscious that is also the wellspring of our creativity.

affective area that Freud's continuum between normal and abnormal personality particularly applies). Much that has been said about the causes and treatment of personality problems throughout this book (and particularly in Chapters 2 to 5) therefore applies equally to affective disorders, and need not be repeated.

Currently, affective disorders are divided into *anxiety disorders* (with several subdivisions, which will be looked at separately); and *depression* (which also can take different forms).

Generalised anxiety disorders Grouped in this category are such things as persistent feelings of tension, apprehension and nervous arousal. Sometimes there is no obvious cause for these feelings (a condition traditionally referred to as *free-floating anxiety),* while others sufferers may be conscious that they are worrying over unnecessary trivia or imagined disasters, but feel relatively powerless to halt the process. Often generalised anxiety is linked to feelings of personal inadequacy, with depleted physical energy and zest for living. In children, disorders of affect typically take the form of this generalised anxiety, with such symptoms as withdrawn and isolate behaviour on the one hand, and aggressive, violent and disruptive behaviour on the other. Generalised anxiety is best regarded as a deep-seated aspect of personality (a high N score on Eysenck's dimension) which requires treatment through the psychodynamic or humanistic therapies covered in Chapter 3 to 5.

Phobias Phobias are persistent irrational fears, usually coupled with excessive and sometimes bizarre attempts to avoid the objects or situations concerned. Phobias often appear to be conditioned fears (the object or situation, although harmless in itself, became associated in the past with a real anxiety-provoking experience, with the result that the fear that properly belonged to the latter is now also aroused by the former), though some may point to deeper issues. Freud, for example, considered that some phobias symbolise repressed fears and insecurities (for example a phobia of spiders may represent a fear of the mother, or a phobia of snakes a fear of sex).

Phobias are relatively common and often appear by the early teens or even earlier (Burke *et al.*, 1990). Many people are able to live with them without too much difficulty, but phobias can become very troublesome when they are connected with social situations such as eating out, or speaking or even appearing in public, or of open spaces (agoraphobia) or enclosed places (claustrophobia), or of real or imagined dirt or infections.

A phobia about heights – which at its worst may prevent the sufferer from even standing on a chair – is one of the most common (shared by some 18 per cent of people), with phobias about flying (around 12 per cent), and of insects and mice close behind (see, for example, Myers, 1998). With the possible exception of flying, it is certainly tempting to see each of these as representing unacknowledged insecurities and fears. The theory that phobias are linked to objects and situations with intrinsic symbolic meaning is further strengthened by the fact that people rarely develop phobias about other stimuli that are associated with far more realistic dangers. For example, even after experiences of air raids, few phobias develop about aeroplanes (Mineka and Zinbarg, 1996); few people have phobias about crossing the road or about car travel, even though they may have had some narrow escapes from danger; few people develop phobias about cycling in spite of many falls in childhood; and few people have ever developed phobias about books, in spite of having frightening stories read to them in childhood. The subject is, to say the least, an intriguing one.

However, although phobias, like generalised anxiety, may have their origins in the early years and are more likely to be associated with things that have symbolic value, behavioural methods (see Chapter 8) prove particularly effective in their treatment. Without probing into these origins, the behaviour therapist concentrates on pairing, in small and easy stages, the feared object or situation with pleasurable, comforting and supportive stimuli. Little by little the individual learns to replace earlier negative associations with positive (or at least more bearable) ones.

Obsessive-compulsive disorders   These involve unwanted repetitive thoughts and/or actions. To some extent, most of us are aware of these in ourselves from time to time. We may sometimes find ourselves going over and over an embarrassing, though minor, incident without being able to shake off the thought; or we may check home security more often than is necessary; or be ultra fussy over small things; or be excessively tidy – in each case we feel decidedly uncomfortable if we do not repeat these actions. Sometimes such obsessions may be a source of pride, as in the excessively houseproud individual or in the excessively meticulous desk clerk, in which case it is reasonable to regard this as a personality trait.

However, exaggerated obsessive-compulsive behaviour can become highly disabling, as when the individual has such a fear of dirt that he or she showers forty or fifty times a day and insists that family members have a complete change of clothes each time they enter the house. This example shows the connection that can exist between phobias and compulsions – the phobia of dirt is controlled only by compulsive washing, which suggests that phobias and obsessive-compulsive disorders may have similar origins, and that some obsessions, like some phobias, may have symbolic undertones. Nevertheless there may also be a physiological explanation. Individuals with extreme obsessive-compulsive disorders show high activity levels in certain areas of the brain (Rauch and Jenike, 1993), though whether this activity is cause or effect is a moot point. Either way, anti-depressant drugs, which dampen the activity concerned, can be helpful in treating the disorder.

There is some suggestion that bulimia (binge eating) and anorexia (self-starvation) belong under the heading of obsessive-compulsive disorders. Certainly they show many of the same characteristics as these disorders, and while genetic factors may once again play a part, environmental circumstances seem to be equally important. Both conditions accompany low self-esteem, and the families of bulimia sufferers have an above-average incidence of alcoholism, depression and obesity, while anorexics tend to come from competitive, high-achieving and protective families who set high standards and are concerned about appearances (Yates, 1989; Heatherton and Baumeister, 1991). Social pressures also play a part, as bulimics are usually women in their late teens and early twenties, while anorexics are generally women in their late teens – ages at which body consciousness and the desire to conform to an unrealistic cultural norm are at their height. Both conditions have increased dramatically in Western countries since the 1950s as the fashion industry and the media have publicised slimness as a norm, yet the conditions remain virtually unknown in other cultures where the norms are different (Dolan, 1991).

Depression Like many other conditions, depression is something that most of us experience from time to time, usually in response to difficult life circumstances. When the circumstances change (or we learn to adapt to them) the depression lifts, even though it may do so only gradually. However, without any clear reason, some people experience consistently depressed moods over many years. Rarely disabling, such depression is nevertheless associated with low self-esteem, low energy, sleep problems and poor concentration. When depression takes this form, it is referred to as *dysthymic disorder*, and can make its appearance as early as adolescence or sometimes even in childhood (children certainly can be depressed, though grown-ups often fail to take them seriously when they are).

Depression (which is reported by twice as many women as men) is the most common reason for seeking medical or psychological help, but usually, even with dysthymic disorder, people's spirits do gradually pick up over time, or sufferers may find ways out of the condition for themselves (for example, by becoming aware of those brief moments when they are not conscious of their depression, and praising themselves warmly for having achieved these moments of respite – a powerful strategy for helping the mind to stop dwelling on its depression and gain confidence in its ability to come out of the darkness).

However, sometimes there is a powerful rebound from depression which tips the individual into its opposite state, that of mania. This condition, once referred to as manic depressive psychosis, but now more usually referred to as bi-polar disorder, warrants a section to itself.

Bi-polar disorder   Together with schizophrenia, bi-polar disorder is the main condition necessitating in-patient treatment. As the name suggests, bi-polar disorder involves swings from the deepest depression, in which everything seems pointless and purposeless, to high levels of excitability and manic energy, frequently associated with grandiose optimism, exaggerated self-esteem, poor judgement, reckless spending, and various other unbalanced behaviour.

In both depression and mania, sufferers often retain some hold on reality. Their thought processes, although confused and disturbed, do not show the bizarre patterns of the schizophrenic, and work and study habits and thought patterns are initially less likely to suffer in the way that they do in schizophrenia. Far from withdrawing, an individual in the manic phase may show increased involvement with everything and everybody. Typically, however, sufferers end up exhausting family and friends either by the depths of their apathy and despair, or by their hyperactive energy. Sometimes the swings are brought about by environmental factors, but more often they are spontaneous, and attempts to reason with the sufferer when in extremes of either state usually meet with failure.

There is some evidence to link bi-polar disorder with extraversion (Eysenck and Eysenck, 1969), which suggests that, once again, there may be a constitutional factor at work. There is also a tendency for the condition to run in families (Pauls *et al.*, 1992). But there is little doubt that environmental circumstances are also involved, and in developed countries at least these circumstances seem to be very much on the increase, as the twentieth century has seen a sixfold growth in depressive disorders in general (though this may be partly accounted for by a greater readiness to seek help).

Freud considered that depression was largely a consequence of a traumatic experience of loss in childhood, but other psychological variables have also been identified. Self-defeating attributions (see Chapter 6) at any time in life seem to play a part (Endler, 1982), as do an external locus of control and the feeling of powerlessness that goes with it; low self-esteem (see Chapter 2); stressful life experiences; the tendency to brood rather than to act (Seligman, 1994); and a hopeless, pessimistic attitude to life (Seligman, 1995) .

Bi-polar disorder typically responds more rapidly to treatment than does schizophrenia, though sufferers may need to remain on medication in order to stay well. Interestingly, some sufferers report highly positive and creative experiences while in the manic phase, and may even describe the experience as being one of the most profound of their lives. As with studies of schizophrenia, there is a great deal we can learn about personality by listening to the experiences of those who have suffered a bi-polar disorder. There is even evidence that highly successful creative people – particularly poets, novelists, artists and those who rely on emotional expression and vivid imagery – may experience bi-polar disorder more frequently than the general population (Ludwig, 1995).

Anti-social personality disorder   Originally known as psychopathy or sociopathy, APD is characterised by an apparent lack of social conscience (Freudians would say of super-ego), and is often correlated with delinquent and anti-social activity. The person concerned (typically a male) first manifests symptoms before the age of 15 and sometimes as young as the age of 3 (Caspi *et al.*, 1996), and appears to be unable to experience the emotions normally present in interpersonal behaviour. He or she seems incapable of affection, sympathy or remorse, and is likely to be selfish, superficial, impulsive, uninhibited, low in anxiety, and indifferent both to the feelings of others and to fear or punishment. In addition, APDs demand instant impulse gratification regardless of the long-term consequences to themselves or others, typically have an extreme disregard for the truth, and are distinguished from other neurotic or emotionally disturbed individuals by their complete absence of guilt.

Around 50 per cent of APD children become anti-social adults, unable to keep a job, irresponsible as parents and as partners, and

---

Stress and Personality Disorders

Reference has been made several times to the possible connection between stress and personality disorders. It is important to make clear, however, that while the stress encountered at work or in personal life may contribute to the appearance of personality disorders in individuals who are vulnerable to them – for psychological or physical reasons – it does not by itself *cause* personality disorders. Nevertheless, as we have seen, excessive amounts of stress can have a deleterious effect on efficiency and effectiveness, on mood, on physical wellbeing, on cognitive functions, and on relationships.

Stress is an inescapable part of living – and particularly of modern living. At the right levels, it can be of great value, offering us challenges, prompting us to get things done, to complete undertakings, to meet deadlines, and to make better use of our abilities and our potential. It only becomes a problem when it consistently makes more demands on us than we can meet. People differ greatly in the levels of stress that they are able to handle. One person's welcome challenge is another person's nemesis.

The causes and treatment of stress are dealt with fully in Fontana (1989), and have also been referred to elsewhere in the present volume, but among the most important in the workplace are:

- Powerlessness over one's own workload and working conditions;
- An excess of tasks over the time available for their completion;
- An excess of boring or repetitive tasks, or tasks contrary to one's beliefs and value systems.
- Constant frustration of one's creative or other relevant abilities;
- Colleagues who are excessively authoritarian, unpredictable or critical, and who fail to accord value to others or to recognise their achievements; and
- An environment of constant conflict and confrontation, with relatively minor matters turned into major issues.

Extraverts may handle stress by enjoying the flow of adrenalin, introverts by detaching themselves and allowing it all to flow past them. Either way, it is important to develop coping methods that suit one's personality and allow one to keep everything in perspective.

---

inclined towards violent crime (Farrington, 1991). APDs are generally of normal intelligence, and can learn things unconnected with emotional responses readily enough, which often means they quickly find out how to manipulate others. Thus, instead of their usual callous aggressiveness, they may adopt a guise of charming plausibility and become excessively manipulative, superficially charming, and adept at conning others in order to achieve extrinsic goals or simply for the intrinsic pleasure it appears to give them. Alternatively, they may become parasitic, relying on their apparent helplessness and repeated, insincere promises of remorse and of atonement to get their own way.

Psychoanalytical theory has it that APDs have failed to develop both a super-ego and a sufficiently reality-orientated ego. The reasons for this failure seem to be both psycho-social and physiological (Raine *et al*, 1996). Psycho-socially the condition is associated with early experiences of broken and loveless homes, and with fathers who are alcoholic or themselves APD. Physiologically it may be related to brain immaturity, as even in adult life APDs show an excessive amount of the slow brain-waves usually found in children (Hare, 1975).

Of relevance in the light of our discussion in Chapter 6 about the physiology of extraversion–introversion and neuroticism–stability, APDs seem to have a low level of arousal in the autonomic nervous system, which may mean that they need an excessive amount of stimulation in order to achieve the 'kicks' that arousal of this system brings. Eysenck, whose P dimension measures some of the factors associated with APD, suggests that the condition may be linked to a degree of unstable extraversion so extreme that it is far beyond the range measured by the dimension.

Our knowledge of the appropriate treatment for APD is less clear than our knowledge of the causes. The callous and sadistic behaviour and frequent betrayal of trust shown by most APDs tends to alienate family and friends. Their lack of remorse means that moral lectures and appeals to their better nature usually have little effect. Sometimes they settle into more reasonable social behaviour in adult life, but in many cases treatment may have to rely on psychopharmacology (mood-changing drugs), or on long-term monitoring and guidance by psychiatrists, psychologists and social workers, with consistent reinforcement being offered for appropriate and socially aware behaviour.

Conclusion

I have ended this book with a chapter on personality problems, and psychologists are commonly accused of looking too frequently on the negative side of human personality rather than on the positive. This is partly, of course, because so much of their work has been with people who have problems. Like the medical doctor, the psychologist often tends not to see so much of people when they are well. Many of our insights into personality come, therefore, from the clinical work of people such as Freud, Rogers or Kelly, and even personality tests for general use often have their origin in tests designed for use with the mentally ill.

But, this being said, I hope I have stressed strongly enough that few psychologists now see the normal and the abnormal personality as two quite separate things. Whether it be Freud talking about normal and abnormal behaviour as being on a continuum, or Eysenck measuring neuroticism by a single dimension somewhere on which we all find our place, psychologists stress that through the study of even the most unfortunate and disturbed of our fellow men and women we gain insights into what it means, essentially, to be human.

Perhaps we can leave this point by saying that humanistic psychologists in particular, but probably all psychologists in their heart of hearts, see the human race as characterised by joy as well as by suffering, by hope as well as by despair. Teachers in particular see all these various aspects of personality, and see them, moreover, as they develop from the experimental world of childhood to the more formed and self-assured one of late adolescence and early adulthood. But all those in the workplace who are responsible for the performance and wellbeing of others are familiar with the great variations in personality not only between individuals but within individuals themselves. Ultimately, this is one of the things that gives life its texture and richness, in spite of the difficulties it sometimes causes.

The other thing I hope I have stressed sufficiently is that, although psychologists' ideas about personality seem to cover such a disparate range, there is a consistent pattern among these ideas – not always a very finished one, but a pattern nevertheless. Although psycho-analysts may differ from behaviourists, and behaviourists from humanistic psychologists, men and women who operate in the workplace can take something of value from all of the approaches covered in the previous chapters. Psychologists, at times, make too much of their differences, and not enough of their similarities.

Finally, I hope the book makes it clear that although each individual personality is unique, men and women, children and adolescents, share the same basic psychological and social needs, even though the emphasis they place upon each of these needs may differ. This is why, although there are no glib formulas that work for everybody in every case, we can understand something of the dynamics that go to make people what they are, and thus identify the kind of approach that gets the best out of each of them, and helps them not only to function effectively and confidently but to find fulfilment in the tasks which make up their working lives.

Bibliography

Adorno, T. W., Frenkel-Brunswick, E., Levinson, D. J. and Sanford, R. N. (1950) *The Authoritarian Personality*. New York: Harper

Allport, G. W. (1961) *Pattern and Growth in Personality*. London: Holt, Rinehart & Winston.

Amabile, T. M. and Hennessy, B. A. (1992) 'The motivation for creativity in children', in A. K. Boggiano and T. S. Pittmen (eds), *Achievement and Motivation: A Social Developmental Perspective*. New York: Cambridge University Press.

Anda, R., Williamson, D., Jones, D., Macera, E., Eaker, E., Glassman, A. and Marks, J. (1993) 'Depressed affect, hopelessness, and the risk of ischemic heart disease in a cohort of US adults', *Epidemiology*, 4: 285–94.

Andreason, N. C. (1994) 'Thalmic abnormalities in schizophrenia visualised through magnetic resonance image averaging', *Science 266*, 294–8.

Apter, M. J. (1982) *The Experience of Motivation*. London: Academic Press.

Asch, S. E. (1955) 'Opinions and social pressure', *Scientific American*, November, 91–115.

Bandura, A. (1969) *Principles of Behaviour Modification*. New York: Holt, Rinehart & Winston.

Bandura, A. (1973) *Aggression: A social learning analysis*. Englewood Cliffs NJ: Prentice Hall.

Bandura, A. (1986) *Social Foundations of Thought and Action: A social-cognitive theory*. Englewood Cliffs NJ: Prentice Hall.

Bannister, D. (1960) 'Conceptual structure in thought disordered schizophrenics', *Journal of Mental Science* 106.

Bannister, D. and Fransella, F. (1980) *Inquiring Man*. Harmondsworth: Penguin.

Barkley, R. A. (1983) 'Hyperactivity', in R. J. Morris and T. R. Kratochwill, *The Practice of Child Therapy*. New York and Oxford: Pergamon Press.

Baron, R. A. (1990) 'Environmentally induced positive affect: its impact on self-efficacy, task performance, negotiation and conflict', *Journal of Applied Social Psychology*, 20: 368–84.

Barron, F. (1979) *The Shaping of Personality*. New York: Harper & Row.

Bateson, G., Jackson, D., Haley, J. and Weakland, J. (1956) 'Towards a theory of schizophrenia', *Behavioural Science* 1.

Baumgardner, A. H. (1990). 'To know oneself is to like oneself: self-certainty and self-effect', *Journal of Personality and Social Psychology*, 58: 1062–72.

Baumrind, D. (1991) 'Parenting styles and adolescent development', in J. Brooks-Gunn, R. Lerner and A. C. Petersen (eds), *The Encyclopedia of Adolescence*. New York: Garland.

Benson, P. L., Sharma, A. R. and Roehikepartain, E. C. (1994) *Growing up Adopted: A Portrait of Adolescents and their Families*. Minneapolis: Search Institute.

Berkenan, P. and Liebler, A. (1993) 'Convergence of stranger ratings of personality and intelligence with self-ratings, partner ratings, and measured intelligence', *Journal of Personality and Social Psychology*, 65: 546–53.

Bertini, M. (1961) 'Il tratto dell'isolamento nella sua determinazione dinamica e strutturale', *Contributi dell'Instituto di Psicologica* 25.

Block, J. (1981) 'Some enduring and consequential structures of personality', in A. I. Rabin (ed.) *Further Explorations in Personality*. New York: Riley.

Bloom, B. S. (1983) *Human Characteristics and School Learning*. New York: McGraw-Hill.

Bloom, B. S. (ed.) (1985) *Developing Talent in Young People*. New York: John Wiley.

Bouchard, T. J., Lykken, D. T., McGue, M., Segal, N. L. and Tellegen, A. (1990) 'Sources of human psychological differences: the Minnesota study of twins reared apart', *Science*, 250: 223–8.

Brody, L. R. and Hall, J. A. (1993) 'Gender and emotion', in M. Lewis and J. Haviland, *Handbook of Emotions*. New York: Guilford Press.

Brown, J. A. C. (1964) *Freud and the Post Freudians*. Harmondsworth: Pelican.

Bruner, J., Goodnow, J., and Austin, G. (1956) *A Study of Thinking*. New York: Wiley.

Burger (1987) 'Increased performance with increased personal control: a self-presentation interpretation', *Journal of Experimental Social Psychology*, 23: 350–360.

Buri, J. R., Louisell, P. A. Misukansis, T. M. and Mueller, R. A. (1988) 'Effects of parental authoritarianism and authoritativeness on self-esteem', *Personality and Social Psychology Bulletin*, 14: 271–82.

Burke, K. C., Burke, J. D., Regier, D. A. and Rai, D. S. (1990) 'Age at onset of selected mental disorders in five community populations', *Archives of General Psychiatry*, 4: 511–18.

Buss, D. M. (1989) 'Personality as traits', *American Psychologist*, 44: 1378–88.

Canter, S. (1973) 'Some aspects of cognitive function in twins', in G. S. Claridge, P. Canter and W. I. Hume (eds), *Personality Differences and Biological Variations: a study of twins*. Oxford: Pergamon.

Caspi, A., Moffitt, T. E., Newman, D. L. and Silva, P. A. (1996) 'Behavioural observations at age 3 years predict adult psychiatric disorders: longitudinal evidence from a birth cohort', *Archives of General Psychiatry*, **53**: 1033–9.

Cattell, R. B. (1980) *Personality and Learning Theory*. New York: Springer.

Cattell, R. B. and Butcher, H. J. (1968) *The Prediction of Achievement and Creativity*. New York: Bobbs-Merrill.

Cattell, R. B. and Kline, P. (1977) *The Scientific Analysis of Personality and Motivation*. London: Academic Press.

Chess, S. and Thomas, A. (1987) *Know Your Child: An Authoritative Guide for Today's Parents*. New York: Basic Books.

Christianson, S. A. (1992) 'Emotional stress and eyewitness memory: a critical review', *Psychological Bulletin*, **112**: 284–309.

Cohen, S. and Edwards, J. R. (1989) 'Personality characteristics as moderators of the relationship between stress and disorder', in R. J. Neufeld (ed.), *Advances in the Investigation of Psychological Stress*. New York: Wiley.

Collins, F. L. and Thompson, J. K. (1993) 'The integration of empirically derived personality assessment data into a behavioural conceptualisation and treatment plan: rationale, guidelines and caveats', *Behaviour Modification*, **17**: 58–71.

Coopersmith, S. (1968) 'Studies in self-esteem', *Scientific American*, February.

Cortis, G. A. (1985) 'Eighteen years on: how far can you go?', *Educational Review* 37, 1.

Costa, P. T. and McCrae, R. B. (1993) ' "Set like plaster"? Evidence for the stability of adult personality', in T. Heatherton and J. Weinberger (eds), *Can Personality Change?* Washington DC: American Psychological Association.

Croyle, R. T. and Ditto, P. H. (1990) 'Illness, cognition and behaviour: an experimental approach', *Journal of Behavioural Medicine*, **13**: 31–52.

Crutchfield, R. S. (1955) 'Conformity and character', *American Psychologist* 10.

Davie, R., Butler, N., and Goldstein, H. (1972) *From Birth to Seven*. London: Longman.

de Bono, E. (1985) 'The CORT Thinking Programme', in J. W. Segal, P. F. Chipman and R. Glaser (eds), *Thinking and Learning Skills, Vol. I, Relating Instruction to Research*. Hillsdale, NJ: Erlbaum.

de Bono, E. (1993) *Water Logic*. Harmondsworth: Penguin.

Decker, P. J. and Nathan, B. N. (1985) *Behavioural Modelling Training: Principles and Applications*. New York: Praeger.

Dolan, B. (1991) 'Cross-cultural aspects of anorexia nervosa and bulimia: a review', *International Journal of Eating Disorders*, **10**: 67–78.

Dweck, C. S. and Elliott, E. S. (1983) 'Achievement motivation', in P. Mussen and E. M. Hetherington (eds), *Handbook of Child Psychology* (Vol. IV). New York: John Wiley.

Eagly, A. H. and Johnson, B. T. (1990) 'Gender and leadership style: a meta-analysis', *Psychological Bulletin*, **108**: 233–56.

Endler, N. S. (1982) *Holiday of Darkness: A Psychologists's Personal Journey Out of His Depression*. New York: John Wiley.

Epting, F. R. and Leitner, L. M. (1992) 'Humanistic psychology and personal construct theory', *The Humanistic Psychologist*, **20**: 243–59.

Erikson, E. (1987) *A Way of Looking at Things: Selected Papers from 1930 to 1980*. New York: Norton.

Evans, R. I. (1975) *Carl Rogers: The Man and His Ideas*. New York: Du Hon.

Eysenck, H. J. (1983) 'Human learning and individual differences', *Educational Psychology* **3**: 3–4.

Eysenck, H. J. (1985) *The Rise and Fall of the Freudian Empire*. Harmondsworth: Penguin.

Eysenck, H. J. (1990) 'An improvement on personality inventory', *Current Contents: Social and Behavioural Sciences*, **22**(18): 2.

Eysenck, H. J. (1992) 'Four ways five factors are *not* basic', *Personality and Individual Differences*, **13**: 667–73.

Eysenck, H. J., and Eysenck, S. B. G. (1964) *Manual of the Eysenck Personality Inventory*. London: University of London Press.

Eysenck, H. J., and Eysenck, S. B. G. (1969) *Personality Structure and Measurement*. London: Routledge & Kegan Paul.

Eysenck, H. J., and Eysenck, S. B. G. (1976) *Psychoticism as a Dimension of Personality*. London: Hodder & Stoughton.

Eysenck, H. J., Arnold, W. J. and Meili, R. (1975) *Encyclopedia of Psychology*, vol. 2. London: Fontana/Collins.

Fadiman, J. and Frager, R. (1994) *Personality and Personal Growth* (3rd edn). New York: HarperCollins.

Falbo, T. and Poston, D. L. (1993) 'The academic, personality and physical outcomes of only children in China', *Child Development*, **64**: 18–35.

Farrington, D. P. (1991) 'Antisocial personality from childhood to adulthood', *The Psychologist*, **4**: 389–94.

Fenton, W. S. and McGlashan, T. H. (1994) 'Antecedents, symptom progression and long-term outcome of the deficit syndrome in schizophrenia', *American Journal of Psychiatry*, **151**: 351–56.

Festinger, L. (1962) 'Cognitive dissonance', *Scientific American*, October.

Fincham, F. D. and Bradbury, T. M. (1993) 'Marital satisfaction, depression, and attributions: a longitudinal analysis', *Journal of Personality and Social Psychology*, **64**: 442–52.

Fincham, R. I. and Rhodes, P. (1992) *The Individual: Work and Organization*. London: Weidenfeld & Nicolson.

Fisher, S., and Greenberg, R. P. (1985) *The Scientific Credibility of Freud's Theories and Therapy*. New York: Columbia University Press.

Fonagy, P. (1981) 'Research on psychoanalytic concepts', in F. Fransella (ed.), *Personality: theory, measurement and research*. London: Methuen.

Fontana, D. (1983) 'Individual differences in personality: state-based versus trait based approaches', *Educational Psychology*, 3: 3–4.

Fontana, D. (1985a) *Classroom control: understanding and guiding classroom behaviour*. London: British Psychological Society/Methuen.

Fontana, D. (1985b) 'Creativity in the educational context', in M. J. Apter, D. Fontana, and S. Murgatroyd (eds), *Reversal Theory: current trends and developments*. Cardiff: University College Cardiff Press.

Fontana, D. (1989) *Managing Stress*. London BPS Books.

Fontana, D. (1992) *The Meditator's Handbook*. Shaftesbury: Element Books.

Fontana, D. (1994) *Managing Classroom Behaviour* (2nd edn). London: BPS Books.

Fowles, D. C. (1992) 'Schizophrenia: diathesis-stress revisited', *Annual Review of Psychology*, 43: 303–36.

Fransella, F. (1972) *Personal Change and Reconstruction*. New York: Academic Press.

Friedman, M. and Rosenman, R. H. (1974) *Type A Behaviour*. New York: Knopf.

Friedman, M. and Ulmer, D. (1984) *Treating Type A Behaviour – and Your Heart*. New York: Knopf.

Funder, D. C. (1995) 'On the accuracy of personality judgement: a realistic approach', *Psychological Review*, 102: 652–70.

Garry, M., Loftus, E. R.,and Brown, S. W. (1994) 'Memory: a river runs through it', *Consciousness and Cognition*, 3: 438–51.

Gay, P. (1988) *Freud: A Life for Our Time*. New York: W. W. Norton.

Geen, R. G. (1984) 'Human motivation: new perspectives on old problems', in A. M. Rogers and C. J. Scheirer (eds), *The G. Stanley Hall Lecture Series (Vol. 4)*. Washington DC: American Psychological Association.

Getzels. J. W. and Jackson, P. W. (1962) *Creativity and Intelligence*. New York: Wiley.

Gilligan, C., Lyons, N. P. and Hanmer, T. J. (eds) (1990) *Making Connections: The Relational Worlds of Adolescent Girls at Emma Willard School*. Cambridge, Mass.: Harvard University Press.

Gjerde, P. E. (1983) 'Attentional capacity dysfunction and arousal in schizophrenia', *Psychological Bulletin*, 93: 57–72.

Glueck, S. and Glueck, E. (1956) *Physique and Delinquency*. New York: Harper & Row.

Goldfarb, W. (1955) 'Emotional and intellectual consequences of psychological deprivation in infancy; a re-evaluation', in P. Hoch and J. Zubin, (eds), *Psychopathology of Childhood*. New York: Grune.

Goleman, D. (1980) '1,528 Little Geniuses and How They Grew', *Psychology Today*, February, 28–53.

Goleman, D. (1995) *Emotional Intelligence*. New York: Bantam.

Gray, J. A. (1985) 'A whole and its parts: behaviour, the brain, cognition and emotion', *Bulletin of the British Psychological Society* 38, April.

Grossman, M. and Wood, W. (1993) 'Sex differences in intensity of emotional experience: a social role interpretation', *Journal of Personality and Social Psychology*, **65**: 1010–22.

Haddon, F. H. and Lytton, H. (1968) 'Teaching approach and the development of divergent thinking abilities in primary school children', *British Journal of Educational Psychology* 38: 2.

Haddon, F. H. and Lytton, H. (1971) 'Primary education and divergent thinking abilities – four years on', *British Journal of Educational Psychology* **41**: 2.

Hare, R. D. (1975) 'Psychophysiological studies of psychopathy', in D. C. Fowleds (ed), *Clinical Applications of Psychophysiology*. New York: Columbia University Press.

Harlow, H. E., Harlow, M. K., and Suomi, S. J. (1971) 'From thought to therapy: lessons from a primate laboratory', *American Scientist*, **59**: 538–49.

Hart, D. (1988) 'The development of personal identity in adolescence: a philosophical dilemma approach', *Merrill-Palmer Quarterly*, **34**: 105–14.

Hartshorne, H. and May, M. (1928) *Studies in the Nature of Character*. New York: Macmillan.

Hathaway, S. R. (1972) *An MMPI Handbook*. Minneapolis: University of Minnesota Press (revised edn.).

Haynes, S. N. and Uchigakiuchi, P. (1993) 'Incorporating personality trait measures in behavioural assessment: nuts in a fruitcake or raisins in a mai tai?', *Behaviour Modification*, **17**: 72–92.

Heatherton, T. F. and Baumeister, R. F. (1991) 'Binge eating as escape from self-awareness', *Psychological Bulletin*, **110**: 86–108.

Hinkle, D. (1965) 'The Change of Personal Constructs from the Viewpoint of a Theory of Implications' (unpublished PhD thesis, Ohio State University).

Hogan, R., Hogan, J. and Roberts, B. W. (1996) 'Personality measurement and employment decisions', *American Psychologist*, **51**: 469–77.

Hudson, L. (1966) *Contrary Imaginations*. Harmondsworth: Pelican.

Jakubczak, F. and Walters, R. (1959) 'Suggestibility as dependency behaviour', *Journal of Abnormal Social Psychology* 59.

Jung, C. G. (1933) *Modern Man in Search of a Soul*. London: Routledge.

Kagan, J. (1966) 'Developmental studies in reflection and analysis', in A. Kidd and J. Rivoire (eds), *Perceptual Development in Children*. London: University of London Press.

Kagan, J. (1976) 'Emergent themes in human development', *American Scientist*, **64**: 186–96

Kagan, J. (1995) 'On attachment', *Harvard Review of Psychiatry*, **3**: 104–6.

Kagan, J., Sontag, L., Baker, C. and Nelson, U. (1958) 'Personality and IQ change', *Journal of Abstract Social Psychology*, 56.

Kelly, G. (1955) *The Psychology of Personal Constructs*, 2 vols. New York: Norton.

Kelvin, P. (1970) *The Bases of Social Behaviour*. London: Holt, Rinehart & Winston.

Kline, P. (1983) *Personality: measurement and theory*. London: Hutchinson.

Kobasa, S. C., Maddi, S. R. and Kahn, S. (1982) 'Hardiness and health: a prospective study', *Journal of Personality and Social Psychology*, 42: 168–77.

Kohlberg, L. and Candee, D. (1984) 'The relationship of moral judgement to moral action', in W. M. Kurtiner and J. L. Gewirtz (eds), *Morality, Moral Behaviour, and Moral Development*. New York: John Wiley.

Laing, R. D. and Esterson, A. (1964) *Sanity, Madness and the Family*. London: Tavistock.

Lewin, K. (1935) *A Dynamic Theory of Personality*. New York: McGraw-Hill.

Lewis, M. (1972) 'State as an infant–environment interaction: an analysis of mother–infant behaviour as a function of sex', *Merrill-Palmer Quarterly in Behavioural Development* 18.

Ludwig, A. M. (1995) *The Price of Greatness: Resolving the Creativity and Madness Controversy*. New York: Guilford Press.

Lykken, D. T., McGue, M., Tellegen, A., and Couchard, T. J. (1992) 'Emergenesis: genetic traits that may not run in families', *American Psychologist*, 47: 1565–77.

Lytton, H. and Romney, D. M. (1991) 'Parents' differential socialization of boys and girls: a meta-analysis', *Psychological Bulletin*, 109: 267–96.

Maccoby, E. E. (1990) 'Divorce and custody: the rights, needs and obligations of mothers, fathers, and children', *Nebrask a Symposium on Motivation*, 42: 135–72.

Maehr, M. L. and Braskamp, L. A. (1986) *The Motivation Factor: A Theory of Personal Investment*. Lexington, Mass.: Lexington Books.

Maher, B. A. (1970) *Principles of Pschopathology*. New York: McGraw-Hill.

Malinosky-Rummell, R. and Hansen, D. J. (1993). 'Long-term consequences of childhood physical abuse', *Psychological Bulletin*, 114: 68–79.

Manaster, G. J. and Corsini, R. J. (1982) *Individual Psychology*. Itasca, IL: F. E. Peacock.

Marston, N. and Scott, D. (1970) 'Inconsequence as a primary type of behaviour disturbance in children', *British Journal of Educational Psychology* 40: 1.

Maslow, A. H. (1970) *Motivation and Personality*. New York: Harper & Row.

Maslow, A. H. (1976) *The Further Reaches of Human Nature*. Harmondsworth: Penguin.

Maslow, A. H. (1987) *Motivation and Personality* (3rd edn). New York: Harper & Row.

McCall, R. B. (1994) 'Academic underachievers', *Current Directions in Psychological Science*, 3: 15–19.

McCandless, B. (1969) *Children: behaviour and development*. London: Holt, Rinehart & Winston.

McCrae, R. B. and Costa, P. T. (1990) *Personality in Adulthood*. New York: Guilford.

McGregor, D. (1960) *The Human Side of Enterprise*. New York: McGraw-Hill.

McKellar, P. (1957) *Imagination and Thinking*. London: Cohen & West.

McLelland, D. C. (1961) *The Achieving Society*. Princeton: Van Nostrand.

McLynn, F. (1997) *Carl Gustav Jung*. London: Black Swan Books.

Megargee, E. I. (1972) *The California Psychological Inventory Handbook*. San Francisco: Jossey-Bass.

Mehrabian, A. (1969) 'Measures of achieving tendency', *Educational Psychological Measurement* 29.

Milgram, S. (1974) *Obedience to Authority*. New York: Harper & Row.

Mineka, S. and Zinbarg, R. (1996) 'Conditioning and ethological models of anxiety disorders: stress-in-dynamic-context anxiety models', in D. Hope (ed.), *Perspective on Anxiety, Panic, and Fear. Nebraska Symposium on Motivation*. Lincoln, Neb.: University of Nebraska Press.

Morelli, G. A., Rogoff, B., Oppenheim, D. and Goldsmith, D. (1992) 'Cultural variation in infants' sleeping arrangements: questions of independence', *Developmental Psychology*, 26: 604–13.

Mussen, P. H., Conger, J. J., Kagan, J. and Huston, A. C. (1984) *Child Development and Personality*. New York: Harper & Row (6th edn.).

Myers, D. G. (1998) *Psychology* (5th edn). New York: Worth.

Myers, I. B. (1987) *Introduction to Type: a description of the theory and applications of the Myers-Briggs Type Indicator*. Palo Alto: Consulting Psychologists Press.

Newman, D. L., Caspi, A., Moffit, T. E. and Silva, P. A. (1997). 'Antecedents of adult interpersonal functioning: effects of individual differences in age-3 temperament', *Developmental Psychology*, 33: 206–17.

Olin, S. S. and Mednick, S. A. (1996) 'Risk factors of psychosis: identifying risk factors premorbidly', *Schizophrenia Bulletin*, 22: 223–40.

Osgood, C. E., Suci, G., and Tannenbaum, P. (1957) *The Measurement of Meaning*. Urbana: University of Illinois Press.

Parnell, R. W. (1958) *Behaviour and Physique*. London: Edward Arnold.

Parnes, S. (1967) *Creative Behaviour Guidebook*. New York: Scribners.

Pauls, D. L., Morton, L. A., and Egeland, J. A. (1992) 'Risks of affective illness among first-degree relatives of bipolar old-order Amish probands', *Archives of General Psychiatry*, 49: 703–8.

Peterson, C., Seligman, M. and Vaillant, G. (1988) 'Pessimistic explanatory style as a risk factor for physical illness: a thirty-five year longitudinal study', *Journal of Personality and Social Psychology*, 55: 23–7.

Piotrowski, C. and Keller, J. W. (1989) 'Psychological testing in outpatient mental health facilities: a national study', *Professional Psychology: Research and Practice*, 20: 423–5.

Pittenger, D. J. (1993) 'The utility of the Myers-Briggs Type Indicator', *Review of Educational Research*, 63: 467–88.

Plomin, R., DeFries, J. C., McClearn, G. E. and Rutter, M. (1997) *Behavioural Genetics*. New York: Freeman.

Presson, P. K. and Benassi, V. A. (1996) 'Locus of control orientation and depressive symptomatology: a meta-analysis', *Journal of Social Behaviour and Personality*, 11: 201–12.

Raine, A., Brennan, P., Mednick, P. and Mednick, S. A. (1996) 'High rates of violence, crime, academic problems and behaviour problems in males with both early neuronmotor deficits and unstable family environment', *Archives of General Psychiatry*, 53: 544–9.

Rauch, S. L. and Jenike, M. A. (1993) 'Neurobiological models of obsessive-compulsive disorder', *Psychomatics*, 34: 20–32.

Ravenette, A. (1975) 'Grid techniques for children', *Journal of Child Psychology and Psychiatry* 16.

Reason, R. (1987) 'The Chernobyl errors', *Bulletin of the British Psychological Society*, 40: 201–6.

Robins, L. and Reiger, D. (eds) (1991) *Psychiatric Disorders in America*. New York: Free Press.

Roe, A. (1953) 'A psychological study of eminent psychologists and anthropologists, and a comparison with biological and physical scientists', *Psychological Monograms* 67: 2.

Rogers, C. R. (1957) 'The necessary and sufficient conditions of therapeutic personality change', *Journal of Consulting Psychology* 21.

Rogers, C. R. (1974) 'In retrospect: forty-six years', *American Psychologist* 29.

Rogers, C. R. (1980) *A Way of Being*. Boston, Mass.: Houghton Mifflin.

Rohner, R. P. (1994) 'Patterns of parenting: the warmth dimension in worldwide perspective', in W. J. Lorimer and R. Malpass (eds), *Psychology and Culture*. Boston Mass.: Allyn & Bacon.

Rokeach, M. (1954) 'The nature and meaning of dogmatism', *Psychological Review*, 61: 194–204.

Rorschach, H. (1942) *Psychodiagnostics: A Diagnostic Test Based on Perception*. Bern: Huber (2nd edn).

Rosen, B. C. and d'Andrade, R. G. (1959) 'The psychosocial origin of achievement motivation', *Sociometry* 22.

Rotter, J. B. (1966) 'Generalised expectancies for internal versus external control of reinforcement', *Psychological Monographs* 80.

Rushton, J. P. and Murray, H. G. (1985) 'On the assessment of teaching effectiveness in British universities', *Bulletin of the British Psychological Society* 38, November.

Rutter, M. (1972) *Maternal Deprivation Reassessed*. Harmondsworth: Penguin.

Rutter, M. (1975) *Helping Troubled Children*. Harmondsworth: Penguin.

Ryle, A. (1969) *Student Casualties*. Harmondsworth: Allen Lane.

Sartorius, N. R. (1994) 'Description of WHO's mental health programme', in W. J. Lorimer and R. Malpass (eds), *Psychology and Culture*: Boston, Mass: Allyn & Bacon.

Satir, V. (1972) *Peoplemaking*. Palo Alto, California: Science and Behavior Books.

Scheinfeld, A. (1973) *Twins and Supertwins*. Harmondsworth: Penguin.

Seligman, M. E. P. (1994) *What You Can Change and What You Can't*. New York: Knopf.

Seligman, M. E. P. (1995) 'The effectiveness of psychotherapy: *The Consumer Reports* study', *American Psychologist*, 50: 965–74.

Seligman, M. E. P. and Schulman, P. (1986) 'Explanatory style as a predictor of productivity and quitting among life insurance sales agents', *Journal of Personality and Social Psychology*, 50: 832–8.

Semeonoff, B. (1976) *Projective Techniques*. New York: Wiley.

Semeonoff, B. (1981) 'Projective techniques', in F. Fransella (ed), *Personality: theory measurement and research*. London: Methuen.

Shadish, W. R., Montgomery, L. M., Wilson, P., Wilson, M. R., Bright, I. and Okwumabua, T. (1993) 'Effects of family and marital psychotherapies: a meta-analysis', *Journal of Consulting and Clinical Psychology*, 61: 992–1002.

Shaver, P. R. and Hazan, C. (1993) 'Adult romantic attachment: theory and evidence', in D. Periman and W. Jones (eds), *Advances in Personal Relationships* (Vol. IV). Greenwich, Conn.: JAI.

Sheldon, W. H. (1954) *Atlas of Men*. New York: Harper & Row.

Sheldon, W. H., Lewis, N., and Tenney, A. (1969) 'Psychotic patterns and physical constitution', in D. Sankar (ed.), *Schizophrenia, Current Concepts and Research*. New York: PJD Publications.

Shields, J. (1962) *Monozygotic Twins*. London: Oxford University Press.

Simonton, D. K. (1994) *Greatness: Who Makes History and Why*. New York: Guilford Press.

Skinner, B. F. (1972) *Beyond Freedom and Dignity*. London: Jonathan Cape.

Skinner, B. F. (1974) *About Behaviourism*. New York: Knopf.

Smith, P. B. (1981). 'Research into humanistic personality theories', in F. Fransella (ed.), *Personality: theory measurement and research.* London: Methuen.

Smith, P. K. (1974) 'Ethological methods', in B. Foss (ed.), *New Perspectives in Child Development.* Harmondsworth: Penguin.

Sroufe, L. A., Fox, N. E. and Pancake, V. R. (1983) 'Attachment and dependency in developmental perspective', *Child Development,* **54:** 1615–27.

Staats, A. W. (1993) *Psychology and the World of Work.* London: Macmillan.

Stanovich, K. (1996) *How to Think Straight About Psychology.* New York: HarperCollins.

Sternberg, R. J. and Lubart, T. I. (1992) 'Buy low and sell high: an investment approach to creativity', *Psychological Science,* **1:** 1–5.

Suomi, S. J. (1987) 'Genetic and maternal contributions to individual differences in rhesus monkey biobehavioural development', in N. A. Krasnegor *et al.* (eds), *Perinatal Development: A Psychobiological Perspective.* Orlando, Fl.: Academic Press.

Tannen, D. (1990) *You Just Don't Understand: Women and Men in Conversation.* New York: Morrow.

Taylor, C. and Holland, J. (1964) 'Predictors of creative performance', in C. Taylor (ed.), *Creativity, Progress and Potential.* New York: McGraw-Hill.

Terman, L. and Oden, M. (1947) *Genetic Studies of Genius IV.* Stanford: California University Press.

Teyler, T. J. (1975) *A Primer of Psychobiology.* San Francisco: Freeman.

Thomas, A., Chess, S., and Birch, H. (1970) 'The origin of personality', *Scientific American,* August.

Thomas, L. and Harri-Augstein, S. (1985) *Self-Organised Learning.* London: Routledge & Kegan Paul.

Triandis, H. C. (1994) *Culture and Social Behaviour.* New York: McGraw Hill.

Vernon, P. E. (1975) 'Personality', in H. J. Eysenck, W. Arnold and R. Meili (eds), *Encyclopedia of Psychology,* vol. 2. London: Collins/Fontana.

Waddington, J. L. (1993) 'Neurodynamics of abnormalities, cerebral metabolism and structure in schizophrenia', *Schizophrenia Bulletin,* **19:** 55–69.

Wallace, D. S., Lord, C. G. and Bond, C. F. (1996) *Which Behaviours do Attitudes Predict? Review and meta-analysis of 60 years research.* Unpublished manuscript, University of Ohio.

Wankowski, J. (1970) *Personality Dimensions of Students and Some Educational Implications of Eysenck's Theory of Extraversion and Neuroticism.* Birmingham: University of Birmingham Research Report.

Waterman, A. S. (1988). 'Identity status theory and Erikson's theory: commonalities and differences', *Developmental Review*, **8**: 185–208.

Watson, J. B. (1924) *Behaviourism*. New York: Peoples' Institute Publishing Co.

Webber, R. and Mancusco, J. C. (eds) (1983) 'Humanistic theory and personal construct theory', *The Humanistic Psychologist*, **20**: 243–59.

Weiner, B. (1979) 'A theory of motivation for some classroom experience', *Journal of Educational Psychology* 71.

Wells, B. W. P. (1983) *Body and Personality*. London: Longman.

Werker, J. F. (1989) 'Becoming a native listener', *American Scientists*, **77**: 55–9.

White, P. H., Kjelgaard, M. M. and Harkins, S. G. (1995) 'Testing the contribution of self-evaluation to goal-setting effects', *Journal of Personality and Social Psychology*, **69**: 69–79.

Wiens, A. N., and Menustik, C. E. (1983) 'Treatment outcome and patient characteristics in an aversion therapy program for alcoholism', *American Psychologist*, **38**: 1089–96.

Wiggins, J. S. (ed.) (1996) *The Five-Factor Model of Personality: Theoretical Perspectives*. New York: Guilford

Williams, R. (1989). *The Trusting Heart: Great news about Type A Behaviour*. New York: Random House.

Williams, R. (1993) *Anger Kills*. New York: Times Books.

Witkin, H. A. (1959) 'The perception of the upright', *Scientific American*, February.

Witkin, H. A. (1965) 'Psychological differentiation and forms of pathology', *Journal of Abstract Psychology* 70.

Witkin, H. A., Lewis, H., Hertzman, M., Machover, K., Meissner, P. and Wapner, S. (1954) *Personality through Perception*. New York: Harper & Row.

Wood, J. M., Nezworski, M. T. and Stejskal, W. J. (1996) 'The comprehensive system for the Rorschach: a critical examination', *Psychological Science*, **7**: 3–10.

Yates, A. (1989) 'Current perspectives on the eating disorders: I. History, psychological and biological aspects', *Journal of the American Academy of Child and Adolescent Psychiatry*, **28**: 813–28.

Zimbardo, P. G. (1970) 'The human choice: individuation, reason, and order versus deindividuation, impulse, and chaos', in W. J. Arnold and D. Levine (eds), *Nebraska Symposium on Motivation, 1969*. Lincoln, Neb.: University of Nebraska Press.

Zimbardo, P. G., Banks, W. C., Haney, C. and Jaffe, D. (1973) 'The mind is a formidable jailer: a Pirandellian prison', *New York Times*, 8 April, 38–60.

Name Index

Subject Index